A Is for Abductive

You may contact Jerry Haselmayer at Leadership Pathways in Cincinnati, Ohio:

www.leadershippathways.com
jhaselmayer@leadershippathways.com
(513) 366-3697

A Is for Abductive

The Language of the Emerging Church

Leonard Sweet

• • •

Brian D. McLaren

• • •

Jerry Haselmayer

ZONDERVAN™

GRAND RAPIDS, MICHIGAN 49530 USA

ZONDERVAN™

A Is for Abductive
Copyright © 2003 by Leonard I. Sweet, Brian D. McLaren, and Jerry Haselmayer

Requests for information should be addressed to:

Zondervan, *Grand Rapids, Michigan 49530*

Library of Congress Cataloging-in-Publication Data

Sweet, Leonard I.
   "A" is for abductive : the language of the emerging church / Leonard I.
   Sweet, Brian D. McLaren, and Jerry Haselmayer.
   p. cm.
   ISBN 0-310-24356-4
   1. Pastoral theology. 2. Postmodernism — Religious aspects — Christianity.
I. McLaren, Brian D., 1956– II. Haselmayer, Jerry. III. Title.
BV4011.300 S84 2002
253 — dc21   2002007549

Interior design by Todd Sprague

Printed in the United States of America

---

02 03 04 05 06 07 08 /❖ DC/ 10 9 8 7 6 5 4 3 2 1

This book is dedicated to the next generation of church planters, pastors, thinkers, artists, and leaders ... dynamic young women and men like Karen Ward, Tony Jones, Doug Pagitt, Pam Fickensher, Chris Seay, Jonathan Lee, Chris Backert, Kyle Lake, David Hopkins, Jason Clark, Rogier Bos, Lammert Vreiling, Jordan Fowler, Daniel Hill, Eric Cage, Jarrod Hunt, Stephen DeFur, Rob Wegner, Melvin Freeman Jr., Gordon Wohlers, Peter Barnes, Becky Chin, Jordan Cooper, Karen Gygax Rodriguez, Peter Ho, Jeff Shinabarger, Rodolpho Carrasco, Derek Weber, Dottie Escobeno-Frank, Younglae Kim, Rob Seewald, David Wahlstedt, and Cary Dunlap.

Contents

Preface by Leonard Sweet

YOU CAUSED THIS BOOK.

"Isn't there one book that could explain all this to me?"

"Can you recommend a one-stop introduction to postmodern ministry?"

"Where can I find a bibliography about all this stuff you're talking about?"

When I compared notes with Brian McLaren about what he was hearing after his presentations, we could reach only one conclusion: People like you were insisting on a beginner's guide on the pathway of postmodern ministry.

We looked at each other and said, "So which one of us is going to do it?" Then we had a better idea: "Why not tailgate?" And since we are only beginners ourselves, "Let's invite others to tailgate along with us." We made a pitch to the editors at Zondervan, who were enthusiastic about the proposal.

We have made this resource as comprehensive in scope in as limited a space as we could. We designed it to be a nonlinear experience, so we hope you don't start at the beginning, or even start at the end, but work on all the letters according to your curiosity or need. Consider even making it a horizontal experience. Robert Louis Stevenson, Mark Twain, and Truman Capote (for starters) lay down when they wrote. (Next to being strapped into an airplane seat, it's my favorite writing position.)

Capote called himself "a completely horizontal writer." Why not try horizontal reading? It's the test of how well we did. Let us know if we made you saw logs or see stars.

We also packed it full of the literature that has shaped our perceptions. We hope you will find the footnotes a gold mine of resources on various aspects of postmodern ministry. As a living body of mentalities and activities, postmodernity resists being laid out on a slab for spiritual or historical dissection. We don't agree with all of these resources, nor do we three authors always agree with each other. I for one don't even agree with some of my own assessments of a couple years ago. But turnovers are to be expected in anything that isn't stagnant.

The EPICtivities Jerry Haselmayer worked up for your pleasure are intended to jump-start some tailgate parties you can host wherever and whenever your friends gather. Michel Foucault called "modernity" an attitude of mind. We have analyzed postmodernity as an attitude of the mind, body, and soul. We hope these EPICtivities will help you bring mind, body, and spirit together.

This book would not have been possible without a deep compatibility of perspectives between Brian and me. For both of us, the originating doctrine of Christian faith is the Incarnation. Another pastor-friend, Tim Wright, summarizes God's strategy for reaching the world this way:

> God, in the person of Jesus, decided to become like
> culture. He became like the people he wants to find—so
> that he can put his arms around them, affirm them,
> welcome them, and ultimately lead them.[1]

From the moment I first heard Brian speak, and then rushed to read his *Reinventing Your Church*[2] (even though I didn't

---

1. Tim Wright, *The Prodigal Hugging Church: A Scandalous Approach to Mission for the 21st Century* (Minneapolis: Joy Resources, 2001), 17.

like the title and abhorred the book's cover), I knew that I had found a kindred incarnationist. We both allow (as God demands) a role for culture that leaves it in vibrant creative relationship with the church. Too much of the church sees the culture through the gun-slits of its ecclesiastical bunkers.

But we also are convinced that when faith isn't positioned to code cultural resistance, there is a high price to pay. This is the obverse, "not-of" side of the incarnational "in/not-of/but-not-out-of-the-world" strategy for reaching every culture. For example, it is one thing to use the "committee" metaphor to reach an industrialized, modern world, as revealed in this marvelous letter from missionary C. T. Studd to a "Dr. Wilkinson":

> The Committee I work under is a conveniently small Committee, a very wealthy Committee, a wonderfully generous Committee, and is always sitting in session—the Committee of the Father, the Son and the Holy Ghost.
>
> We have a multi-millionaire to back us up, out and away the wealthiest person in the world. I have an interview with Him. He gave me a cheque-book free and urged me to draw upon Him. He assured me His Firm clothes the grass of the field, preserves the sparrows, counts the hairs of the children's heads. He said the Head of the Firm promised to supply all our need, and, to make sure, One of the Partners, or rather Two, were to go along with each member of our parties, and would never leave us or fail us. He even showed me some testimonials from former clients. A tough old chap with a long beard and hard-bitten face said that on one occasion supplies had arrived and been delivered by black ravens, and on another, by a white-winged angel. Another little old man who seemed scarred and marked all over like a walnut shell said he had been saved from death

2. Brian D. McLaren, *Reinventing Your Church* (Grand Rapids: Zondervan, 1998). The book was reissued in 2000 with a different cover and a different title: *The Church on the Other Side*.

times untold, for he had determined to put to proof the assurance that he who would lose his life for the Firm's sake should find it. He told stories more wonderful than novels and Arabian Nights, of escapes and hardships, travels and dungeons, and with such a fire in his eye and laugh in his voice, added, "But out of all them the Partner delivered me."[3]

But it is quite another thing to make committees definitive of what it means to be a church, and to so identify an incarnational method with the message itself that the method morphs into the message. When that happens, people start thinking that a church with no committees is a church without Christ[4] or that Gothic cathedrals were put together by committees. Altogether too much modern fat (like committees and so much more) has accumulated on the body of Christ. Therefore, a recurring theme in this primer is the need for a serious diet and exercise program as we enter this postmodern culture.

As we eye the future and call the church to have an eye to the future, we are excited and at the same time of heavy hearts. We know only too well how Jeremiah could in one breath say, "Your words became to me a joy and the delight of my heart" (15:16 NRSV) . . . and the next moment, "My heart is crushed within me, all my bones shake" (23:9 NRSV).

Easter is all about dying into the new. This new world rings with biblical resonance; postmodern culture thrums with possibility. But only if we do more than dip a toe into the mystery of God's continuing incarnation story.

3. As quoted in Norman P. Grubb, *C. T. Studd: Cricketer and Pioneer* (Atlantic City: World-Wide Revival Prayer Movement, 1943), 146–47.

4. God didn't send a committee—for a reason. According to "comitology" (the science of committees) and comitologists (scientists of committees), there are three classic definitions of a committee: "(1) A collection of the unfit chosen from the unwilling by the incompetent to do the unnecessary; (2) A group of people who, individually, can do nothing, but collectively can meet and decide that nothing can be done; (3) A group which succeeds in getting something done when, and only when, it consists of three members, one of whom happens to be sick and another absent." For more such wisdom see Thomas L. Martin Jr., *Malice in Blunderland* (New York: McGraw-Hill, 1973), 79.

Preface by Brian McLaren

IT WAS A GREAT honor to be invited to coauthor this book with Len Sweet. In the mid-90s, when my own theology reached a kind of crisis that I later diagnosed as a postmodern "re-booting" of my spiritual computer, I made a list of people I hoped to meet. I felt that I had started asking questions that my modern mentors (who had meant so much to me to that point, and still do) could not answer (because they were not yet asking them). I needed to seek out some new mentors, and Len was the first on my list. I had enjoyed and benefited from Len's writings, so when I had the chance to hear him and meet him at a conference, I introduced myself and expressed my hope that we could get together sometime. He graciously opened up a lunch meeting, and I drove up to Drew University a while later. He took me to a wonderful Indian restaurant, and the conversation we enjoyed was even more tasty, spicy, and delightful than the curries and chutneys of our meal.

Len and I, in our previous and separate writings, have shared a desire to move beyond a critique of modern ministry (a hobby that can be dangerously preoccupying). Instead, we have tried to be more constructive, sketching out some preliminary lines along which postmodern ministry can develop and in fact is beginning to develop. This book gives us a chance to lodge in key words some of our best thinking so far in this regard, to help our friends and colleagues in ministry on our shared pilgrimage from our old modern homeland to our new postmodern matrix of ministry.

We are also grateful to Jerry Haselmayer for his collaboration on this project. Len and I both believe that, while books and public speaking open up important new territory for people, the kind of radical transformation needed in our churches and Christian organizations will require more direct, sustained, and personal intervention. Jerry is helping us envision and develop an expanding network of consultants who, we hope, will be available as guides for churches who set out on the journey toward meaningful and effective ministry "on the other side."

We are keenly aware that this project is a long, long way from being the last word on anything. That's why we consider this book a primer. Primers are for beginners—such we are, and such we invite you to be, in these exciting times.

• • •

P.S. For readers who are sick to death of hearing the word *postmodern* and all its derivatives, we offer this hope: Someday, when enough of us have gotten through to the other side of this transition, we can use *ministry* and *gospel* and *neighbors* and *grace* and other words we love, never needing to use "the p-word" again. Our hope is that through this book we are accelerating the arrival of that day when books on *postmodern* ministry are no longer necessary.

Preface by
Jerry Haselmayer

HAVING BEEN GREATLY INFLUENCED by Len and Brian's writings over the past several years, it is a privilege to collaborate on this book. My role was to create experiential team activities at the end of each chapter that we are calling "EPICtivities." The hope is that leaders will have a menu to select from that will help their team rise together to new levels of experience and understanding. I believe what people hear can easily be forgotten, but what people experience is hard to forget. We also know there are new EPICtivities to be created, and we hope you, our fellow traveler, will contribute your ideas as well!

I believe our paths have crossed for God's purposes, in part by the writing of this book and in part for what will yet unfold in the future. My soul is touched by the Scriptures when they say, "One lonely strand by itself can easily be broken, put together two strands and look how much it can withstand. . . . Oh but see the strength and magic when three are in community!" (THE MESSAGE). This passage in Ecclesiastes has been my experience working with Len and Brian. Guys, thanks.

Yes, it is difficult to let go of the familiar and change is often painful—painful for all of us! The opposite is true as well. These are exciting times to be disciples! Think: For a moment, we get to be in the middle of a new thing God is doing. We get to experience in real time God's unfolding Story.

Acknowledgments

"Certain authors, speaking of their works, say 'my book,' 'my commentary,'" Pascal once wrote. "They would do better to say 'our book,' 'our commentary,' because there is in them usually more of other people's than their own."

This primer on ministry in the emerging culture is not only "our book" in the literal sense, but also "our book" in that its ideas have been drawn from or tested out on multiple sources. Some doctor of ministry students at Drew University first downloaded the entries for the book as "lectures" in an online course (Fred Allen, Lisa Bandel-Sparks, James Beebe, James Biedenharn, Donna Ciangio, Cathy Cook, Rhonda Cushman, Louis DelTufo, Chris Hammon, Vicki Hollon, Chris Hughes, James McClain, Richard Mitchell, Grant Nicholls, Randall Rogers, and Charlie Weir). Leaders and congregations from various denominations and non-denominations helped us understand the shape of the emerging church in their own colors and configurations.

A special thanks to Carl Savage, whose investment in this project led to some advice we didn't take but sometimes wish we had. Why not order the letters of the alphabet, he suggested, by their frequency of usage (which would mean starting with "e") or anything but the ordinary "a-b-c-d-e-f-g"? We're sorry we didn't listen to you, Carl.

It is nice being able to outsource your worries ... and references and quotes and footnotes. Betty O'Brien's contributions to the bottom of the page rival anything at the top.

William Wordsworth's sonnet "A Parsonage in Oxfordshire" celebrates a clergyman's garden where "no distinguishable line" divides garden from graveyard: the lands of living and dead, "friends and neighbors" in both categories, "confound/Their several features." While we have dedicated this book to those tending the gardens of the living, we honor those who for 2,000 years have prepared the garden and passed it on for us to tend and till. We begin by referencing our reverence and respect for them and their living example of the truth behind this book: If we will do what we're called to do, God will do what God has promised to do.

Introduction

THIS IS A PRIMER WITH A MISSION.

There is the story of a motorist who asked a West Virginia farmer for directions to a certain place. After musing for a few moments, the farmer replied: "If I was wanting to get there, I sure wouldn't start from here."

None of us get to choose our starting place. So we have to start where we are, even committed Christians like us.

God doesn't seem to give his people special exemptions from history or shortcuts in the spiritual journey. The church may think that time can stand still for it the way the sun stood still for Joshua in the Old Testament story (Josh. 10). But even Joshua only got a delay, a short reprieve from the inexorable inrush of the future. Soon enough the sun started moving (or the earth started turning) once again.

True, more than a few Christians have hit the Pause button in the 1950s or 1970s or 1990s, and some of them seem to be doing just fine. But it is inevitable: The sun will start moving for them soon enough, and they will have to wake up and see where they are and realize it is not where they want to be. And their journey will begin.

That is where this primer fits in. Primers are beginning books: ABC's. They are for kids, beginners, stuttering strugglers trying to learn the first syllables of a new language. And that's us—a few of us, only a few so far. But more and more of us are realizing that the world has changed, a new language has emerged, and if we want to communicate, we need to speak it. So we have to start where we are, with what we know, embarking on the journey before us.

So we open our hearts to where we are.

Transitioning

Let's talk about the starting place God has put us in.

We are living literally "on the edge," or in ecological terms (terms that are particularly useful in these times), in an "ecotone" between Past and Future, between Modern and PostPostmodern. Ecotones are places where two or more ecosystems come together, a transition between two entities that blend into one another where they meet. San Francisco Bay, the largest estuary in the western U.S., for example, is an ecotone: a place where fresh water from the Sacramento and San Joaquin Rivers meets the salt water of the Pacific Ocean. Wetlands are ecotones: transitions between dry land and deep water. Hydrothermal vents at the ocean floor are ecotones: transitions where sea water meets the earth's interior.

You can't get from one place to another without going through a transition. Transitions imply endings and beginnings— some things come to an end, some things begin. Transitions are times of great creativity and change. Transitions are renewing. Transitions are gone through at different speeds by different organisms. Most of us run a transition deficit most of the time— that is, we lag behind the learning/practice/reality curve of most situations.

The dawning of Millennium Three is such a transition: an ecotone between the modern era and a time we cannot yet define. So we paradoxically inaugurate this new era by identifying it by what it isn't: postmodern.[1]

1. Daniel Bell first pointed out the paradox of our naming in *The Coming of the Post-Industrial Society* (New York: Basic Books, 1973).

Introduction

It would be nicer if we could call our times pre-something, but alas, maybe our great-grandchildren can look back and do that. Not us. Not here. Not yet. We're stuck with "the posties." Other "post" candidates include post-capitalist (Ralf Dahrendorf), post-bourgeois (George Lichtheim), post-civilized (Kenneth Boulding), post-collectivist politics (Samuel Beer), post-industrial (Daniel Bell), post-ideological (Lewis Feuer), post-literate (Marshall McLuhan and John Leonard), post-Puritan, post-Protestant, post-Christian (Martin Marty, Winthrop Hudson), post-Constantine (Jim Wallis), and post-foundationalist (Stanley Grenz). Zygmunt Bauman, who has written extensively on postmodernism, says he now prefers the phrase "liquid modernity" to describe what has happened over the past 20–50 years.[3]

There are both problems and possibilities to ecotones. Whether in biology or history, edges support great diversity, facilitate movement and energy, and are highly fertile. Some life thrives on the edges where conditions are most volatile. Fishermen, for example, discover that the best fishing is at the edges—edges of drop-offs, edges of aquatic vegetation. "Fishers of men," as Jesus called his followers, similarly can discover that there is no better time to be in ministry than now.

But life on the edge increases predation, parasitism, and fragility. Many species don't survive on the edge. And ecotones are easily damaged: The San Francisco Bay has lost 60% of its

---

2. John Scotus Erigena, *Periphyseon,* or *The Division of Nature* (Washington, DC: Dumbarton Oaks, 1987), 700.

3. Zygmunt Bauman, *Liquid Modernity* (Malden, MA: Blackwell, 2000). See also Leonard Sweet, *AquaChurch: Essential Leadership Arts for Piloting Your Church in Today's Fluid Culture* (Loveland, CO: Group Publishing, 2000). Ron Martoia in *Morph!* (Loveland, CO.: Group Publishing, 2002) calls this the "Aesthetic Age."

water area to land reclamation over the past 140 years. So there is some truth to what many of us say on our worst days: There is no worse time to be in ministry than now.

We are living on the edge, in an ecotonic interregnum unique to the millennia of emerging human civilization. Of course, we are not telling you anything you don't already know. We've said it before: The world has come to an end. The world you and I were prepared to lead and minister in is over. We now function in worlds that are either defunct, in ruins, gasping their last breath,[4] or not yet built.[5] We stumble constantly over the disintegrating elements of a worn-out paradigm.

The social, economic, political, and ideological world we once knew has been done in by new turns in sign theory (including mathematics, color theory, music theory), physics, metaphysics, cosmology, biology, and philosophy. In philosophy, the foundations have been spirited away by postfoundationalism. While much of the church is trapped in foundationalist thinking, where truth is "out there" to be hauled in by objective methods, the foundationalist model cannot hold up under either postmodern or biblical hermeneutics.

It is hard to find scholarship that is not destabilizing assumptions about rationality and challenging intellectual categories

4. Gilbert Adair, in *The Postmodernist Always Rings Twice: Reflections on Culture in the 90s* (London: Fourth Estate, 1992), 15, calls this transitional period "the last gasp of the past."

5. Thomas Hohstadt, *Dying to Live: The 21st Century Church* (Odessa, TX: Damah Media, 1999); Leonard Sweet, *SoulTsunami: Sink or Swim in New Millennium Culture* (Grand Rapids: Zondervan, 1999); Brian D. McLaren, *The Church on the Other Side: Doing Ministry in the Postmodern Matrix* (Grand Rapids: Zondervan, 2000); Alan Roxburgh with Mike Regele, *Crossing the Bridge: Church Leadership in a Time of Change* (Rancho Santa Margarita, CA: Percept Group, 2000); Chuck Smith Jr., *The End of the World—As We Know It: Clear Direction for Bold and Innovative Ministry in a Postmodern World* (Colorado Springs: WaterBrook Press, 2001); Harry Lee Poe, *Christian Witness in a Postmodern World* (Nashville: Abingdon, 2001); Erwin McManus, *An Unstoppable Force: Daring to Become the Church God Had in Mind* (Loveland, CO: Group Publishing, 2001); Michael Slaughter, *The unLearning Church* (Loveland, CO: Group Publishing, 2001).

inherited from the Enlightenment.[6] Nearly every field is being redefined. An old Oxford Dictionary defines a community as "a body of people living in one place, district, or country." As outmoded as that definition of community is our understanding of how to do ministry in this new world.

So how can this be such a palmy day for ministry, you counter, when we who minister are the products of a dying social and intellectual order, when almost everything we thought we knew now seems wrong? The school of declinology has some powerful statistics on its side. Ninety-eight percent of U.S. churches have less than 300 in attendance on any Sunday morning; 85% of these experience a net loss or no net gain in membership each year; 2000 new churches are started each year; 6000 are closed permanently. On any given Sunday, more people in London visit Ikea than all the churches of London combined. Once the heart of Lutheranism, Leipzig is now nearly 90% atheist or agnostic.[7]

Yet living in the "last gasp" of anything means living in the first breath of something new (especially for believers in resurrection). It is the first breath of a new paradigm (Thomas Kuhn), a quantum leap (Neils Bohr), a form of punctuated equilibrium (Stephen Jay Gould and Niles Eldredge), a new dawn (Sweet)—a leap of knowledge, we believe, that is most comparable to the Athenian classicism of the sixth to fourth centuries B.C. or the Renaissance and Reformation. God will not be without a witness in this future. The question is whether the church as it is will be willing to unlearn what it knows so it can learn to become the church it must become . . . so as to be God's witness in this future. Part of living on the edge today is learning to function on the edge of ignorance.

6. For more, see Walter Truett Anderson, *Reality Isn't What It Used to Be: Theatrical Politics, Ready-to-Wear Religion, Global Myths, Primitive Chic, and Other Wonders of the Postmodern World* (San Francisco: HarperCollins, 1990).

7. Uwe Siemon-Netto, "Minefield to Mission Field," *World* 15 (14 October 2000), 25–27.

We count ourselves among a growing cadre of Christian leaders who are enormously enthusiastic about this future, but our intent is not to take the edge off living on the edge. The heroine in Margaret Drabble's A Natural Curiosity says, "England's not a bad country. It's just a mean, cold, ugly, divided, tired, clapped-out, post-imperial, post-industrial slag heap covered in polystyrene hamburger cartons."[8]

The same basic adjectives can be applied to our postmodern landscape.[9] We identify with that commencement speaker who began his speech to the graduating class with these words: "My advice to you young people who are going out into the world today . . . don't go."

Living on the edge is like living on the ledge, which means one can easily topple off into the abyss. Living on the ledge means one lives at knife-edge where one can easily be torn to shreds. Living at the precise point where two things come into contact and don't overlap means one has to go one way or the other. Scissors are useful, but we can't recommend living in between the blades.

Yet, saying all this, we say it again: There is no more exciting time to be in ministry than now when the entire planet seems poised at the edge of a profound transformation. The rest of the quote from Margaret Drabble conveys our sentiments exactly: "It's not a bad country at all. I love it." Or to paraphrase 2 Corinthians 6:2: Now Is the Time (literally, "now is the acceptable time; now is the day of salvation"). Now . . . today . . . this moment . . . is the time of salvation. This is our moment—to live momentarily in eternity—to live eternity in our moment.

It's as simple as that.

It's as exciting as that.

8. Alix Bowen, as quoted in Margaret Drabble, A Natural Curiosity (New York: Viking, 1989), 308.
9. Steven Connor, Postmodernist Culture: An Introduction to Theories of the Contemporary (Oxford: Blackwell, 1989).

Better Days Ahead

We believe that the postmodern condition, rather than being a threat to Christian theology, can actually return us to the roots of our faith and reinforce many of Christianity's primary concerns. It is not just that a theistic worldview continues to make sense in a postmodern world. A biblical worldview seems almost tailor-made for the emerging culture.

We believe that there are better days ahead for the church of Jesus Christ in all its forms . . . if we are willing to adapt our forms to seize the opportunities these new conditions present to us. If, however, we are prone to rigidly and unthinkingly defend old forms, we will sadly discover, as Jesus indicated, that we have three options:

1. We may reject the new wine of the gospel and stay with an old wine of modern religion that is easily contained by our cherished, inflexible forms.
2. We may try to contain the new wine of the gospel in old familiar forms—and as a result lose both.
3. We may trade in our old forms for new forms—and see better days.

Cautious critics will counter that there are huge risks associated with engaging postmodern culture. To mention but one: There is the danger of syncretism—mixing, adulterating, or diluting the gospel with foreign elements that weaken, damage, or distort its integrity.

Of course, the critics are right—this is a great danger. But then again, one might respond, Are these critics equally vigilant regarding the ways in which they themselves may have already accommodated to *modern* culture? And if they have themselves fallen prey to an unconscious modern syncretism, how do the postmodern pioneers know which of their warnings and concerns deal with departures from the gospel and which with departures from modernity? Could some of the very splinters in the eyes of postmodern pioneers also be planks in the eyes of their modern critics?

Make no mistake: Those who do engage the emerging culture risk being attacked as dumbed-down theologians or wild-eyed mavericks. We shouldn't be surprised at these attacks. Our history tells us that pioneers can expect chiding . . . and arrows in the back. For example, in 1792 William Carey preached a sermon from Isaiah 54:2: "Enlarge the place of thy tent, and let them stretch forth the curtain of thine habitations: spare not, lengthen thy cords, and strengthen thy stakes" (KJV). The result of this sermon was the creation of the Baptist Missionary Society, and a new era in missions was born.

Was Carey, "the father of modern mission," lauded for his courage in 1792? Not at first! "When they came to deliberate, the old feeling of doubt and hesitation predominated."[10]

Similarly, was Peter lauded for bringing the gospel to Cornelius, as related in Acts 10? Not at first!

Was Hudson Taylor lauded for his identification with the Chinese people? Not at first.

More recently, was Chuck Smith Sr. lauded for welcoming in hippies and the Jesus People? Or Bill Hybels and Rick Warren for being gentle and respectful toward "seekers"? Not at first.

Eventually the church comes around. But at first, a lot of arguments and arrows are slung about the legitimacy of exploring new territory.

Remember the situation in Acts 15 when the early apostles argued over whether Gentiles who were coming to the faith had to be circumcised first? That was an argument worth having, an argument that needed to happen.

10. As quoted in S. Pearce Carey, *William Carey: D.D., Fellow of Linnaean Society* (London: Hodder & Stoughton, 1923), 84. For an account of the sermon and its aftermath, see 80–85.

Introduction

Did the early church fathers welcome Gentiles as partners in Christ? Not at first.

Yet the book of Acts gives us the eventual outcome of this first major church battle: Christ, the Jewish Messiah, has come as Savior of the world to enter every culture as it is in order to help it become what it can and should become. Gentiles do not need to be culturally circumcised or Judaized to follow Jesus.

If Luke were writing a new volume of Acts today, maybe he would record the corresponding argument: Does a postmodern first have to become modern in order to become Christian?

We believe the answer will emerge along the lines of this paragraph by emerging postmodern theologian Jonathan Stuart Campbell:

> The postmodern crisis calls for nothing less than a complete repentance (metanoia)—a transformation of the mind and a thorough change of heart. The church must come to the harsh realization that in many ways the church has been influenced more by modernity than by the life of Jesus and patterns of the early church. Therefore, renewal is not enough. Nothing less than a radical reorientation is needed for the church to break free from the modern influences. Just as Gentiles can now receive salvation as Gentiles, so postmoderns have a right to be followers of Jesus, without having to become modernists or to become institutionalized.[11]

It is time for the church to hear that Carey sermon again. Scholars are now beginning to see what William Carey saw more than 200 years ago: Putting faith and culture together is a missiological problem.[12] Will our missiological future fall to the level of this sad prediction articulated by Ronald Cole-Turner?

11. Jonathan Stuart Campbell, "The Translatability of Christian Community: An Ecclesiology for Postmodern Cultures and Beyond," (Ph.D. diss., Fuller Theological Seminary School of World Mission, 1999), 100–101.

12. Alan Roxburgh, *The Missionary Congregation, Leadership, and Liminality* (Harrisburg, PA: Trinity Press International, 1997).

It is altogether too likely that the church will marginalize itself
in the role of chaplain, picking up the pieces, caring for the
bruised, mopping up the damage, but never engaging the
engines of transformation themselves, steering, persuading,
and transforming the transformers.[13]

This is not the first missiological crisis the church has
faced, and it may not be the last. But it is proving to be a very
difficult one for church establishments. Consider the 100 Asian
bishops summoned to the Vatican in 1998 to explain why Christianity was making such little headway in Asian cultures. In
their response, the Asian bishops admitted to chafing under
the bit of "Roman imperialism." Some of the first to speak were
the Vietnamese bishops:

Western, and especially scholastic, theology is not adapted
to the religions of Asia because it is too rational. For the
Asians, one cannot analyse the truth nor explain the mystery. And there is a preference for silence over words and
not getting entangled in quarrels over words.[14]

The Franciscan Bishop of Naha, Bernard Toshio Oshikawa,
spoke for the majority of the bishops when he called for a
"radical decentralisation of the Latin rite" ("bishops are not
branch secretaries waiting for instructions from headquarters")
and for greater cultural indigenization: "The language of our
theology, the rhythm and structure of our liturgies, the pro-
gramme of our catechesis fail to touch the hearts of those who
come searching."[15]

The bishops' warnings and forewarnings are similar to what
you will read in this book. Religious leaders (i.e., Roman

13. Ronald Cole-Turner, "Science, Technology, and the Mission of Theology" in *God
and Globalization: The Spirit and the Modern Authorities*, ed. Max L. Stackhouse with
Don S. Browning (Harrisburg, PA: Trinity Press International, 2001), 2:143.
14. "Look at It Our Way: Asian Bishops Respond to Rome," *The Tablet* (2 May
1998), 571.
15. As quoted in *The Tablet* (2 May 1998), 565.

authorities) "often don't know the language and the culture of [our] country."[16] In the words of the Philippines bishops, the "Christian life" must become "'at home' in Asia." In many ways we are but stating the obvious: The Christian life must become "at home" in the emerging culture. But the obvious has not been integrated into our systems, thinking, and strategies.

We are still in the earliest stages of this unfolding conversation. No one has The Program or The Five Easy Steps for doing postmodern ministry. And no one ever will, because those formulaic approaches are themselves part of the fading world. That is why our format is a kind of trick. This book is organized around the ABC's, and ABC's sound simple, but really they aren't. True, we learn our ABC's as children, but we all spend our whole lives learning to *use* them, combining them into words and sentences, books and poems, queries and statements of infinite variety.

First Words, Not Last Words

This format makes sense for our subject, in this liminal time when we have glimpses and fragments, not programs or five easy steps.[17] We are uttering first words, not last words; garnering first images, not lasting impressions. We hope the insights you gain here can be combined into meaningful and practical ideas for ministry where you live. If you have ideas to add, or maybe new entries for the primer, or maybe even "yes-but-this-is-also-true" paradoxes to offer, we hope you will contribute them via a website for emerging culture citizens (*emergentvillage.com*). We invite your insights, push-backs, and perspectives, because, again, we don't believe these ABC's are the last word on emerging ministries.

16. Ibid.
17. We have been inspired by Stanley J. Grenz's excellent aid to understanding the intellectual and philosophical world of postmodernism in his work *A Primer on Postmodernism* (Grand Rapids: Eerdmans, 1996) and by "The ABCs of Ministry in the 21st Century" by David Hopkins (College Class of 2000), found in the online magazine *Next-Wave, www.next-wave.org* (January 2000).

> *Die Grenzen meiner Sprache bedeuten*
> *die Grenzen meiner Welt.*
> The limits of my language mean the limits of my world.
>
> —LUDWIG WITTGENSTEIN (1922)[18]

This primer was created in partnership. Len Sweet offered a first draft, and Brian McLaren added elements, especially focusing on how Len's insights translate into church- and street-level ministries.

We think this primer can also best be used in partnership. That is why we include with many of the entries an EPICtivity compiled by Jerry Haselmayer for study groups, leadership retreats, and staff meetings so groups can experience the kind of partnership and synergy in studying this book that the authors did in producing it.

Perceptive readers will notice that there are apparent contradictions within these pages. Be assured that most, at least, are not accidental. Where such plural versions of postmodernity are found,[19] the reader is invited to ponder the mystery (or laugh) rather than resolve the tension. We are emboldened to attempt a pen-flashed spiritual geography of postmodernity in the spirit in which Dr. Johnson defended dictionaries: "Dictionaries are like watches," he wrote. "The worst is better than none, and the best cannot be expected to go quite true."

---

18. Ludwig Wittgenstein, *Tractatus Logico-Philosophicus* [5.2], 2d ed. (London: Routledge & Kegan Paul, 1933), 149.

19. This is precisely why some refuse to use the word *postmodern*. William J. Abraham refuses to speak of contemporary culture as "postmodern" because it "posits a monolithic generalization which is deeply distorting.... If we look at our culture as a whole, we are confronted by a *discord* of voices, of worldviews, of moral traditions, of lifestyles, and of inner informal logics which cannot be flattened out into a comprehensive theoretic analysis—whether intellectual, economic, or sociological." See William J. Abraham, "C. S. Lewis and the Conversion of the West," in *Permanent Things: Toward the Recovery of a More Human Scale at the End of the Twentieth Century*, ed. Andrew A. Tadie and Michael H. Macdonald (Grand Rapids: Eerdmans, 1995), 271.

Introduction

We hope you will go through this text at your own pace, starting where you need to, ending where you want to. We hope you will read it any way except from A to Z. (Consider reading it in the order of the most-used letters to the least-used, demonstrating a nonlinear linearity: ETAIONSHRDLUCMF-GYPWBVKXJQZ.) We hope to open a passageway between modernity and postmodernity, to offer a tour of this ecotone.

We are making every effort to be among the postmoderns. We never want to be postmodern*ists*. Our aim is biblical integrity and cultural indigeneity: Not a first-century church reproduced in the 21st century, but a 21st-century church incarnating Jesus' presence and biblical values, leaning forward into God's gift of the future.[20]

We want to do for our day what our ancestors did for their day. Rather than despair and curse the darkness, they released the Christ within them (Col. 1:26), who then changed the world.

20. Del Birkey, *The House Church: A Model for Renewing the Church* (Scottdale, PA: Herald Press, 1988), 28.

A is for Abductive Method

Deductive method: Start with abstract principles and build toward concrete reality. (Preachers use this method when they begin with doctrine and move to application.)

Inductive method: Start with concrete reality and build toward abstract principles. (Preachers use "biblical induction" when they observe Scripture, then articulate doctrines or principles based on their observations. Induction is what a doctor does with your body to determine what's wrong with you).

Abductive method: Seize people by the imagination and transport them from their current world to another world, where they gain a new perspective. (Preachers use this method when they speak in parables. These sermons are so different from either inductive or deductive that some practitioners are calling them, not sermons, but "phd's," or "post-homiletical discourses."[1]

Abductive reasoning (a seismic little phrase coined by the philosopher Charles Sanders Peirce)[2] has powerful implications for preaching—and all communication, really. To go abductive, get rid of your inductive/deductive outlines and points and make your sermons pointless! In other words, don't build your messages around analysis (the A-word of modernity), but instead, build them around an abductive experience, one that takes people out of their current world of assumptions and issues, of boredom and anxiety. Instead of asking yourself before creating a sermon [note: we didn't say

1. This is a phrase coined by Episcopal priest Jim Beebe of Akron, Ohio.

2. K. T. Fann, *Peirce's Theory of Abduction* (The Hague: Martinus Nijhoff, 1970). Compare Peirce's abduction with philosopher/psychoanalyst Julia Kristeva's concept of abjection; see Julia Kristeva, *Powers of Horror: An Essay on Abjection,* trans. Leon S. Roudiez (New York: Columbia University Press, 1982).

"writing a sermon"], "What's my point?" ask yourself, "What's my image?" or in more musical terms, "What experience do I want to compose?"

Rather than leading your hearers along in an orderly, step-by-step, predictable, reasoned argument, like a lawyer before a jury—proving and moving on, proving and moving on—seize them by their lapels, like a friend in a crisis. Grab them by the scruff of the neck (their imagination) and throw them into something they never expected.

Surprise and unpredictability are the key elements to the abductive method. You can't abduct someone if they're expecting it. This unpredictability is the opposite of modern approaches to preaching, where you set up something very predictable, such as "I'm going to define the problem, analyze the causes of the problem, and offer the steps to solving the problem" or "I'm going to name the topic and then break the topic down into subtopics and illustrate and apply each sub-point." These approaches are clear, useful, good—but predictable and of limited effectiveness in the emerging culture.

> I've learned that if you're really wanting to get a message across, it has to go down with a sweetening dollop of comedy. You've got to keep reminding yourself that your point has to be a pill in the dog's food.
>
> —COMEDIAN/TV HOST BILL MAHER[3]

Disorientation, astonishment, amazement, surprise—all these things stimulate the abductive process. You abduct your hearers with a metaphor, a problem, a shocking or poignant story, a question or puzzle or paradox, and you beam them up into the spaceship of an unexpected experience. The experience

3. Bill Maher, as quoted in an article by Larry Platt in the magazine *George* (December/January 2001), 98.

may come in the form of a thought-game or search (great abductive activities), like these:

- What would you do if you were given five years off work and unlimited funds and this assignment: Be as happy as you can?
- Why do many Christians feel bored with the Bible?
- Why do you think more about sex or chocolate than sharing your faith with friends?

Or it may come in the form of a story: There once was a man who had two sons . . . a sower went out into his field to sow . . . I was stuck in traffic the other day, when suddenly a large black bird landed on my hood. . . .

Then the abductive message unfolds. Rather than following analytical points, it goes through turns, switchbacks, leaps, rests, sidetracks—the way a conversation does—until you are "abducted" into an experience that takes you outside yourself. (If you need examples, try Garrison Keillor's Lake Wobegon monologues.)

By the way, Peirce argued that the first person in history who fully developed and deployed this "abductive method" was Jesus of Nazareth. "Without a parable he told them nothing" (Matt. 13:34).

(So after you try a Lake Wobegon monologue, try a parable of Jesus.)

A is for Attention

● Becoming the scarcest resource in the emerging culture. Therefore the most coveted and costly.

Why did Procter & Gamble give $5 billion in cash to drugmaker Bristol-Myers Squibb in early summer 2001? To buy Clairol, primarily for their hair dye products. Hair colors now change with each season. Why? To be noticed. To gain attention.[4] Postmod-erns pay big money to force new kinds of attention.

Big money is spent on attention management—getting you *to* and protecting yourself *from* these two words: "Pay Attention." Look for the replacement of the "experience economy" with what architect William J. Mitchell calls "an economy of pres-ence,"[5] in which the variety of ways of "being present" is only matched by the variety of means of "attendance." In the emerg-ing culture, to "pay attention" is almost a kind of offering—a sacramental gesture of self and sacrifice. The cumulative effect of attention avalanches will be able to change the world.

Attention is the critical resource for postmodern evangel-ists. Modern evangelists needed a loud voice, a forceful close, an amplifier, a microphone, an organ to play "Just As I Am"— and maybe a couple of clean jokes and clear diagrams. In con-trast, postmodern hearers generally won't pay attention to you until you shut up, turn off the amplifier, and "pay" them in the priceless currency of respectful attention, compassionate lis-tening. Then, try whispering.

A is for Augmentation

All areas of life are being "supersized," "powerized," and "mega-fied"—an enhancement phenomenon called augmentation. It's not as if this hasn't happened before. In the modern era, human intelligence was augmented through notes, reminders, paper, watches, alarm clocks, calculators, computers. Our brains are being augmented today by the silicon/software partnership.

4. To those skeptics who say that the global market for hair colorants, the fastest-growing segment of the $37 billion hair-care industry, reflects an aging boomer popula-tion, Clairol reports that their fastest growth is coming from the 14-to-24 age group, "where the prime objective is to be noticed." See "Fast-growing Business," *The Economist* (26 May 2001), 68.

5. William J. Mitchell, *E-topia: "Urban Life, Jim—But Not as We Know It"* (Cambridge, MA: MIT Press, 1999), 129–44.

But augmented reality is now taking unprecedented and unpredictable forms through the merging of genetic and digital technologies and computer-brain interfaces. Need an improved heart? Implant a pacemaker or defibrillator. Need an improved chest? Implant some silicon. Need improved computer skills? Try some software agents or avatars (digital butlers) that act on your behalf and simplify every area of your life. Need improved memory? Implant. . . .

Enhancement technologies are not just rewriting the laws of Mother Nature. They are renegotiating our understandings of self, society, community, even soul. Where does the "true self" end and the "augmentation" begin? Is the augmentation now a part of the self? If so, what of words like *identity* and *integrity*, not to mention *soul*? This blurring of boundaries between the natural self and augmented self is revolutionary enough. But we have only just started down the trans (transnational, transcultural, transethnic, transgenic, transhuman) track.[6]

Every augmentation is an amputation. The adoption of pocket calculators diminished our mental skills at mathematics. The typewriter and computer diminished our capacity for beautiful calligraphy.

There are two immediate implications of augmentation for emerging ministry. First, we need to acknowledge the tradeoffs of our augmentation-induced amputations. For example, we have augmented our ability to travel by cars and airplanes, but have amputated our ability to be rooted anywhere in particular for very long. We have augmented our voices through amplifiers and speakers, but have amputated our ability to listen and be silent. We have augmented our ability to stay in touch with one another through email and cell phones, but have amputated our ability to be alone. We have augmented our ability to be amused and occupied by video games and 67 channels of cable

6. Yet we are a lot farther down the road than most people realize. USAmerica has already grown some 3.5 trillion genetically modified plants since 1994.

TV or 128 channels of satellite TV, but have amputated our ability to ... to ... to do whatever creative things that people did before these augmentations came along. (What *did* they do, anyway?)

We have augmented our ability to feed people with pizza and subs and take-out Chinese or Thai food in those little white cardboard cartons with wire handles. But have we lost something precious in amputating potlucks and the home-baking of bread in old-fashioned hospitality? Emerging leaders need to ask these kinds of questions, because when augmentations increase, so do amputations.

Second, we need to move beyond a naive modern optimism regarding new augmentations. Not all enhancements are enchantments. We need to anticipate the costs of benefits.

For example, back in the 1960s one particular Mennonite church augmented its communication system by handcrafting (as you'd expect) beautiful pigeon-hole-style wooden mailboxes, one for each member. Whenever anyone had a message for a fellow church member, he or she would simply slip it into the appropriate box, a clear benefit to communication. But at what cost? The church's current pastor hates those mailboxes. Why? Because every newcomer to the church is unintentionally excluded from the communication system. The system was designed for a nongrowing church; it was not expandable, so it reinforced a static mindset in the members. The cost of the benefit has been high. The pastor now wishes the church would amputate the outmoded augmentation and reach for a new one. (Maybe an email list? But email brings its own amputations, right?)

Consider this: A time is coming (and now is) when you can take a pill to reduce your sex drive and then take another to "turn it on" again. Would taking self-control augmentations make you a better Christian, or a worse one? Would taking medications (or so-called "natural supplements") that elevate your mood augment your "love, joy, peace" quotient, thus making you more Christlike? What would be the cost of the benefit? You can already pay $3000 and get the sex of a child you want.[7] Would this build a better Christian family?

The ethics of augmentation will open a bigger and bigger barrel of monkeys, and it won't all be fun. Using technology to augment relationships or to repair something to normal is not an issue. There are reproductive technologies, such as *in vitro fertilization* (IVF). But there are also genetic technologies, which actually alter the shape of future organisms.

Whether or not to "repair" to supernormal and transnormal (making people "better than well"[8]—more musical, more intelligent, more athletic) will be one of the key ethical issues for our 22nd-century kids. Princeton biologist Lee Silver envisions a two-class system: the genetically enhanced "GenRich" existing alongside and lording it over poorer "Naturals."[9]

What do you see? Which would you be—a "GenRich" or a "Natural"?

EPICtivity A: Augmentation

The early design of tractor trailers—semis—had a very flat front, and for many years different designs were unheard of.

A new design with a more rounded front end was developed but was shunned by many truck drivers as a fad. Resistance dissipated when it was later proven that the design change significantly increased performance and miles per gallon. The change

---

7. This is offered by a process called "Microsort" available from the Genetics and IVF Institute in Fairfax, Virginia, which separates male from female sperm. For more on this, see "The Politics of Genes: America's Next Ethical War," *The Economist* 14 (April 2001), 21–23, esp. 22.

8. The phrase is that of Peter D. Kramer in *Listening to Prozac* (New York: Viking, 1993), 41.

9. Lee Silver, *Remaking Eden: Cloning and Beyond in a Brave New World* (New York: Avon, 1997), 4–7.

represented only about a 10% difference to the design. For a small change the outcome was huge!

Discuss the following questions in your group:

- What do you think caused the most emotional resistance (not air!) when the new model was first introduced?
- What would the impact have been if the changes were never initiated?
- How does this EPICtivity relate to your church?
- What 10% change can you make in a current project you are working on?
- What will the augmentation potentially amputate? Can you live with this? Why? Why not?

B is for Beauty

Beauty: A vibration or resonance between novelty and order that transports us to heights and depths outside ourselves not otherwise reached. In the presence of beauty we become transformed into artists of creation engaged in being. The postmodern church will reconceive itself as a community of artists—the church as an art colony, if you will.

Beauty myth: The adoration of things that are more real than reality itself—"hyper-realities," they're called—created by technology and causing the disappearance of true reality right before our eyes. French social theorist Jean Baudrillard has a name for this theft of reality: "This pure, absolute reality, this unconditional realization of the world—this is what I call the Perfect Crime."[1] It is the one crime that would leave no evidence of itself behind.

Beauty truth: Another name for the revelation of God. Handel's oratorio *Messiah* is, for postmoderns, "evidence that demands a verdict."

Maybe you studied the Romantic poets in college. They are of special interest to people doing postmodern ministry because romanticism was a recurring protest movement in the modern era representing a dissatisfaction with modern rationalism. In some ways romanticism anticipated postmodernism. John Keats, one of the great Romantic poets of the early 19th century, said, "Beauty is truth, truth beauty,—that is all / Ye know on earth, and all ye need to know."[2] In those memorable words Keats struck a chord with which postmodern hearts

---

1. Jean Baudrillard, *The Vital Illusion,* ed. Julia Witwer (New York: Columbia University Press, 2000), 67.
2. Concluding lines of "Ode on a Grecian Urn."

resonate, although "beauty" has been the favorite category for God among many theologians throughout history (Jonathan Edwards, for example).

Perhaps, then, the most effective apologetic for today is beauty,[3] and not just beauty in the arts, but also beauty in open-book relationships. Along with the Gospels according to Matthew, Mark, Luke, and John in the NT (New Testament), postmodern seekers want to see the beauty of the Gospel According to You (the Gospels' continuing story in you) in the YT (Your Testament—a life well-lived) and the YG (Your Gospel), the Fifth Gospel.

> Beauty is an epistemological necessity; it is the way in which the gods touch our senses, reach the heart and attract us into life.
>
> —PSYCHOANALYST JAMES HILLMAN

If modernity was the age of the engineer (formulas, blueprints, measurements) and the lawyer (cases, evidence, proof, argument), the postmodern world will be the age of the artist.[4] A formula or statistic is about as persuasive to a postmodern heart as an interpretive dance would have been to a modern mind.

Not that postmodern folk are anti-intellectual. Rather, they have expanded their respect for the God-created human mind beyond the narrow confines of rational analysis to intuition,[5] imagination, and aesthetics. For them, the appreciation of

3. Patrick Sherry, *Spirit and Beauty: An Introduction to Theological Aesthetics* (Oxford: Clarendon Press, 1992); Frank Burch Brown, *Religious Aesthetics: A Theological Study of Making and Meaning* (Princeton, NJ: Princeton University Press, 1989).

4. Steve Turner, *Imagine: A Vision for Christians in the Arts* (Downers Grove, IL: InterVarsity Press, 2001).

5. Some people define intuition as the same as "precognition" or "knowing something without knowing how we know it" or "knowing something and forgetting that we knew it." We now have "scientists of intuition" like Dean Radin of the Boundary Institute

beauty (along with goodness) is as essential to the pursuit of truth as was the scale or slide rule to the modern scientist.[6]

In ministry, this means that ugly is out: ugly buildings, ugly bulletins, ugly sermon outlines (the nine P's of Philippians), ugly hymns.

People get ugly in ugly spaces.

Don't be confused here: Don't assume that this sensitivity to beauty means postmodernity is about a "politically correct" niceness and saccharine sweetness. We are talking about *beauty*, not "niceness" or "prettiness." Full-bodied beauty can contain discord, clash, burn, sting, ugliness. For example, as works of art, Steven Spielberg's *The Color Purple* and *Amistad* and *Schindler's List* are beautiful, yet each contains horrific ugliness. What is the difference between the ugly violence in *The Color Purple* and the ugly opulence in, say, a religious broadcast on cable TV (aside from the hairstyles)?

> Beauty will save the world.
>
> —DOSTOEVSKY, *THE IDIOT*

As you prepare a sermon, therefore, you ask yourself, "Where's the beauty?" As you design the landscape or interior decor for your building, you ask, "Where's the beauty?" As you select singers or musicians or actors or dancers for public worship, you lead them into an understanding that beauty is not simply an adornment or attraction added to our message; beauty is essential to the message itself, because there is a

---

(www.boundaryinstitute.org), who does scientific research into what he calls "information transfers." He uses the example of slowing down at an intersection even though there is no evidence you need to slow down. As you do so, a truck crashes through a red light.

6. See John W. de Gruchy, *Christianity, Art and Transformation: Theological Aesthetics in the Struggle for Justice* (New York: Cambridge University Press, 2001), for an excellent outline of a "theological aesthetics," especially his chapter on "The Redemptive Power of Beauty," 97–135.

beauty to holiness, and the concept of "glory" itself is hard to extract from beauty.

Maybe beauty seemed optional in the modern matrix, but no longer. The old aphorism about cleanliness may never have been true; maybe it should have said that beauty is next to godliness.

B is for Be-living

Yes, we realize that *be-living* isn't really a word—yet. (Postmodern pilgrims will doubtless need to coin a number of new words to help us in our journey.)

Modernity was preoccupied with correct beliefs and believing, but only in a narrowly defined sense. For moderns, so enthralled with rational, conceptual correctness, "believe" was normally married to the conjunction "that," rather than the preposition "in." It was above all important to believe *that* . . . , the word to be then followed by any number of propositions and formulations. Meanwhile, Jesus seemed more concerned that we *believe in*, or more precisely that we simply *believe him*. Jesus' use of the word *believe* conveys something closer to words like "confide in" or "have confidence in" or "trust." The difference, though subtle, is significant.

> But why didn't God just give us a systematic theology book instead of a book of stories, poems, and letters? Why did God gift us with 10,000 years of Jewish and Christian history—and many of the greatest minds ever born trying to examine it all—if he just wants us to simplify his steadfast love for us into a list of propositions?
>
> —TONY JONES[7]

7. Tony Jones, *Postmodern Youth Ministry: Exploring Cultural Shift, Creating Holistic Connections, Cultivating Authentic Community* (Grand Rapids: Youth Specialties/Zondervan, 2001), 127.

Taken to the extreme, *believing that* can lead us into a false security, suggesting that as long as we hold the correct "beliefs," opinions, or doctrinal formulations, we're in like Flynn, safe at home, and otherwise certifiably okay. This might be called "salvation by getting the right formulations" or "salvation through correct opinions," an approach that doesn't square well with the teachings of either Luther or Jesus. Jesus' teachings are not values or propositions to be listed, conceptually affirmed, and checked off as "believed" in order to live a more spiritual life. The modern era succumbed to Satan's third temptation of Jesus. The checkpoint road to spirituality doesn't lead to changed lives.

Do you believe? Do you even believe that God raised Jesus from the dead?

No big deal! Even Satan believes that. You can believe something and not act on it. Authentic Christianity is a full faith, not thin beliefs. We are saved by grace through faith, not by beliefs. If you have faith in something, it transforms how you live. You cannot *not* act on it. Satan *believes in* God. But Satan doesn't *believe* God. Believing God is living faith. That's *be-living*. The social and spiritual implications of be-living are massively more far-reaching than believing.

Interestingly, the word *believe* is a favorite word of John's gospel (again, generally accompanied by "in" and not just "that"). Many modern Christians emphasize "belief" because they have memorized so many key verses from that gospel (3:16; 5:24; 6:40; 6:47; 7:38, etc.). However, the synoptics, rather than emphasizing "believe in me," seem to emphasize "follow me."

This presents an interesting challenge. Do the synoptics present a different gospel, a gospel of following, while John presents a gospel of believing?

Or is it possible that "believe in me," meaning "have confidence in me," is simply John's way of rendering the same meaning as "follow me," and vice versa? In other words, rather than distinguishing the two formulations, would we be wiser to conflate them, or augment each with the other, so we hear

Jesus saying, "Have enough confidence in me to follow me"?
This seems wise, because no one will follow a leader in whom
they lack confidence, and any sort of belief about Jesus that
doesn't result in following Jesus seems to fall far short of the
kind of devotion and commitment John (or Jesus!) calls us to.

That is why we like the word *be-living*. We don't expect it to
catch on, if for no other reason than spell-checkers will mark it
as errant. But as we move beyond modernity, any concept of
believing that doesn't include following is errant in a more
serious way. If you are *believing* in the gospel, you'd best *be-living*
it as well, and if you are *believing* in Christ, you'd best *be-living* as
his devoted follower too.

Be-living moves us beyond privatized beliefs (forcing us to
explore the social implications of the gospel), and it propels
us beyond a defensive belief also. "Defending the gospel" is a
rather odd idea anyway, when you think about it. Can we trust
God with the gospel? Or do we think we must defend a fragile
God, Bible, and faith? Our job is not to defend the faith but to
live the faith. That is the ultimate "defense" anyway—a good
offense. Peter understood this (see 1 Peter 2:12). The ultimate
apologetic is *us* . . . belivers!

"I'm a be-liever," moderns sang.

Anybody up to writing a new version: "I'm a be-liver"?

B is for Belonging

For spiritual seekers today, "belonging" most often comes before
"believing."[8] In contrast, in the modern world, if you've got your
beliefs right, you could belong. In this emerging world, it is the
process of belonging that helps you get your beliefs (and "be-life")

---

8. For more on this distinction, see George Hunter's provocative book *The Celtic
Way of Evangelism: How Christianity Can Reach the West—Again* (Nashville: Abingdon,
2000) and Brian McLaren's *More Ready Than You Realize* (Grand Rapids: Zondervan,
2002).

in order. Identity is now found less in views than in vows, in visions, in customized ventures.

The main space in church is called "nave," a word that comes from the Latin word for "ship." Disciples are on a journey, sailing toward home. But we don't sail alone. Our highly personalized journeys of faith need co-journers. Believing, becoming, and behaving all require belonging.

B is for Blur

The status quo has been replaced by the fluxus quo. Everything is in constant motion. Nothing stands still. Movement precedes stability. The name for this phenomenon is "blur" or "speed."[9]

To survive in a blur world, the fittest are the fastest. It's the Quick or the Dead.[10]

The Blur Rule of Cisco Systems is this: If you can't execute a project within three months, don't do it. If it's too big to do in that amount of time, break it up into smaller steps.

A fluxus quo, survival-of-the-fastest world is bad news for churches who cherish traditionalism and idolize unruffled feathers. You have probably heard the joke:

> Q: How many Baptists (or Methodists or whomever) does it take to change a lightbulb?
> A1: CHANGE? WHO SAID ANYTHING ABOUT CHANGE???
> A2: A hundred. One to change the lightbulb, and 99 to mourn the loss of the old one.
> A3: None. Those newfangled lightbulbs always stop working eventually, so why bother changing them? Let's go back

9. James Gleick, *Faster: The Acceleration of Just About Everything* (New York: Pantheon, 1999); Stanley M. Davis and Christopher Meyer, *BLUR: The Speed of Change in the Connected Economy* (Reading, MA: Perseus Books, 1998).

10. See, for example, Bob Davis's new biography, *Speed Is Life: The CEO of Lycos Reveals His Secrets to Surviving and Thriving on Internet Time* (New York: Currency, 2001).

to the way we used to do it. Kerosene lanterns were good enough for my grandfather, and they're good enough for me!

But the need to change habits of living and thinking is intrinsic to all living systems. Motility is the name given the tendency of the body to change positions. Even when one is in a lying, sitting, or resting posture, the body wants to move. Lack of motility causes improper circulation, corpulence, and bedsores.

Modern churches are in denial no less vicious than that of the hardened alcoholic: "We don't need to change! We shouldn't change! We can't change!"[11] That statement is a pathetic self-delusion. We don't see that the very act of resisting change changes us. (That sentence may merit double-underlining, in red pen if possible, with a star in the margin and a fold-over at the top of this page.) In fact, the act of habitually resisting change inevitably turns us into a slow, stodgy, stagnant, entropic (and thus suicidal) organization. The question is never whether we should change, but rather which of the available change options will lead to a desirable future.[12]

Yes, there are changes that can be dangerous, even fatal. So the .000013% of churches that habitually change too quickly should definitely ignore this item. For everyone else, remember: Quick, or dead?

B is for Body

The concept of "body" has largely replaced "mysticism" in the academic literature of religious studies.

11. For more on the need to come to terms with change, see Doug Murren, *Leadershift* (Ventura, CA: Regal Books, 1994); republished as *Leader Shift: How to Avoid Paradigm Shock* (Mansfield, PA: Kingdom Publishing, 1999).

12. For excellent resources for churches coping with change, see Tom Bandy, *Coaching Change: Breaking Down Resistance and Building Up Hope* (Nashville: Abingdon, 2000), and Mary Jo Leddy, *At the Border Called Hope: Where Refugees Are Neighbors* (Toronto: HarperCollins, 1997).

This emerging culture is body fixated. That's why body-centric items like fountain pens and nonverbal theological activities like iconography have a great future.

People need to have body and soul integrated into a seamless whole.[13] Worshiping God "in spirit and in truth" requires body language. Say "embodiment" and postmoderns get a buzz.[14] In modernity we dissected bodies. In postmodernity we decorate bodies and develop them. The body is the storyboard of choice.

It was moderns, however, who discovered the body and the concept of the "individual." Medieval Man and Medieval Woman had only blurred images of one's body and being. Blown-glass mirrors were not manufactured on a commercial scale until in the early 16th century in Venice. Plate-glass mirrors weren't available for mass consumption until early in the 18th century. The very concept of "comfort" (as in "Is that chair comfortable?") had little meaning to medieval people. (Have you ever seen pictures of their hard-back chairs?) The increase in autobiographies, private diaries, and portraits demonstrates the modern "discovery" of the self.

But where moderns would "make up" their face (mascara, lipstick, rouge, earrings), postmoderns "make up" their body (tattoos, piercings, theatrical muscles, nail stenciling, decorations like jewelry, trinkets, amulets, cross chains, crystals). The more virtual and unreal the culture, the more the body

13. A lovely little book on the body as the dwelling place of God is J. Philip Newell, *Echo of the Soul: The Sacredness of the Human Body* (Harrisburg, PA: Morehouse Publishing, 2001).

14. Robert Webber summarizes the postmodern sensibility in these words: "The kind of Christianity that attracts the new generation of Christians and will speak effectively to a postmodern world is one that emphasizes primary truths and authentic embodiment. The new generation is more interested in broad strokes than detail, more attracted to an inclusive view of the faith than an exclusive view, more concerned with unity than diversity, more open to a dynamic, growing faith than to a static fixed system, and more visual than verbal with a high level of tolerance and ambiguity" (*Ancient-Future Faith: Rethinking Evangelicalism for a Postmodern World* [Grand Rapids: Baker Books, 1999], 27).

becomes a palette, of colors and cuts, for postmoderns to tell the story of their lives and the values by which they live. Don't be surprised if your postmodern Christian sons and daughters want to display all sorts of religious tattoos and piercings on their bodies. Average age at first tattoo? Fourteen years.[15] The church of the future will be filled with people who have both made-up faces and made-up bodies.

The emerging culture is developing complex body rituals memorializing life's events and relationships. Faith communities that are serious about reaching them are reconceiving their rites of passage (such as confirmation or bar mitzvah), strengthening them with retreats, assigned mentors, service projects and community service requirements, tribal initiations, and incorporating body rituals.

It is interesting to note how Dallas Willard, a professional philosopher, has reintroduced many modern Christians to the primal spiritual disciplines, body-oriented practices largely forgotten or ignored by modern Christians who tended to live in the head more than either heart or body.[16] Willard describes the disciplines as teaching your body habits. In fasting and celibacy, you teach your body that all its cravings don't need instant gratification. In silence, you teach your body that it doesn't need to talk. In solitude, you teach your body that it doesn't need to be noticed by others. In simplicity, you teach your body that it doesn't always need to be adorned or comfortable, and so on.

The so-called spiritual disciplines turn out to be surprisingly physical: "The use of our body for positive spiritual ends

15. Robert P. Libbon, "Dear Data Dog: Why Do So Many Kids Sport Tattoos?" *American Demographics* (September 2000), 26. In the year 1997 tattooing was the 6th-fastest-growing retail business; in 1994, 16.4% of Texas teens surveyed already had tattoos.

16. For books more on "how to believe" than "what to believe," see Dorothy C. Bass, ed., *Practicing Our Faith: A Way of Life for a Searching People* (San Francisco: Jossey-Bass, 1997), and Brian D. McLaren, *Finding Faith: A Self Discovery Guide for Your Spiritual Quest* (Grand Rapids: Zondervan, 1999).

is a large part of our share in the process of redemption."[17] Of Jesus, Willard says,

> The fact that he was human just as we are ensures that we must likewise share the disciplines with him—not because he was sinful and in need of redemption, as we are, but because he had a body just as we do. His understanding with his father was: "Sacrifice and offering thou hast not desired, but a body hast thou prepared for me" (Heb. 10:5 RSV). He shared the human frame, and as for all human beings, his body was the focal point of his life.[18]

Of our neglect of the body in modern Christian thought, Willard says, "It is precisely this appropriate recognition of the body and its implications for theology that is missing in currently dominant views of Christian salvation or deliverance. The human body is the focal point of human existence. Jesus had one. We have one. Without the body in its proper place, the pieces of the puzzle of new life in Christ do not realistically fit together, and the idea of really following him and becoming like him remains a practical impossibility."[19]

Emerging Christian leaders must grapple again with the reality that human beings happen in bodies—sexual bodies, hungry bodies, tired bodies, aging bodies, electrochemical and genetic and environmentally sensitive bodies. As Christians, we will see ourselves as far more than minds (or spirits) that temporarily need bodies (mere throwaway containers, an embarrassing concession to the material world) to get around. Instead, we will grapple again with the ancient Jewish insight that when God made us, God made us as bodies, and pronounced those bodies very good.

17. Dallas Willard, *The Spirit of the Disciplines: Understanding How God Changes Lives* (San Francisco: HarperCollins, 1988), 30.
18. Ibid., 29.
19. Ibid., 29–30.

And more: The ancient Christian insight that when God invites us beyond this life, it will not be as disembodied, platonic souls, but as fully embodied persons . . . with bodies even more glorious than these in which our life now pulses, breathes, hungers, and yearns.

By the way, the devout mystic Henry Suso (a.k.a. Heinrich Seuse, 1295–1366) inscribed the name of Jesus on his breast with a stylus.

B is for Branding

What religion was to most moderns, brands are to many post-moderns. In fact, brands are becoming the new religions. Brands are less about products than about ways of life. The two primary means by which many postmoderns build their identities is through brands and bands. Clothes and music are now less something that conveys identity than constructs it.

One of the world's largest ad agencies has concluded that "belief in consumer brands has replaced religious faith as the thing that gives purpose to people's lives. . . . The brands that are succeeding are those with strong beliefs and original ideas. They are also the ones that have the passion and energy to change the world."[20] Through the promoting of a product as a "sign of me," a brand becomes a signal to others of our status, values, and beliefs. Some of the top "uncompromising belief brands" in the emerging culture are Calvin Klein, MTV, Nike, Gatorade, Yahoo, Virgin, Disney.

Through branding, products become signs. So a pair of jeans signifies youthful sex appeal, or a refrigerator becomes identified with happiness. The process of branding establishes an emotional connection with the set of values the brand

---

20. Ad agency Young and Rubicam, as quoted in Richard Tomkins, "Brands Are the New Religion, Says Ad Agency," *Financial Times* (1 March 2001), 4.

represents. What you buy tells others about who you are. Stuart Ewen has called this appropriation of personality by the acquisition of goods "the assembling of the commodity self."[21]

In other words, "I shop therefore I am."

Or, in the Christian deconstruction of that phrase, "You are what you trash."

Brands became part of the mythology of modernity.[22] The right to purchase became as important as the right to vote; disenfranchisement is now as much economic as political. But whereas the modern world branded "goods" through logo and symbol, postmoderns are branding experiences and environments (DisneyWorld, NikeTown, LegoLand). Brands are no longer simply about products, but about ways of life and identity formation.

The most current postmodern "branding" is creating your own brand. The No. 1 brand of postmoderns is the brand of one. In the modern world, to be "trendy" was to be like everyone else. Postmoderns don't want to be "trendy"; they want to be true to themselves. That's why the hottest places to shop for many "tweens" are Good Will Industries stores and A Buck a Pound stores. The most recent crop of postmoderns are not so much into superbrand logos or non-logos as "My Logo"—creating their own logo, their own brand of one, their own one-of-a-kind style. They could care less about how famous your brand is. You have one minute to connect with them and gain their trust. Some are even predicting that "trustmarks" will replace brands in the future.[23]

21. See Stuart Ewen, *All Consuming Images: The Politics of Style in Contemporary Culture,* rev. ed. (New York: Basic Books, 1999).

22. Bill Bryson points out, "In nineteen out of twenty-two product categories, the company that owned the leading American brand in 1925 still has it today—*Nabisco* in cookies, *Kellogg's* in breakfast cereals, *Kodak* in film, *Sherwin Williams* in paint, *Del Monte* in canned fruit, *Wrigley's* in chewing gum, *Singer* in sewing machines, *Ivory* in soap, *Campbell's* in soup, *Gillette* in razors." See Bill Bryson, *Made in America: An Informal History of the English Language in the United States* (New York: Bard, 1994), 242–43.

If Christians wear brands, it is important to tell them that there is a big difference between what you buy and who you are. In fact, the concept of branding comes from marking cattle or sheep with a hot iron and tattoo. Throughout history, criminals were branded, "fixed with a mark of infamy"—the source of the expression "branded a liar." Branding was the curse of Cain (Gen. 4:15). Our late-modern identity as branded consumers should unsettle us and drive us to ask deeper questions about who we are in the bigger economy of God's kingdom.

Having acknowledged this profound and pervasive danger, we must also acknowledge that branding is a fact of life in the emerging culture, no less real than empire or coliseums in the ancient world or jousting and feudalism in the medieval world. For people engaged in postmodern ministry, the question presents itself: What is our brand? Too often in the modern era, like it or not, we branded ourselves as the elite group that prided itself on being pure, right, and superior in doctrines and church practices, in character and intelligence. Each denomination had its own spin, its own pride, its own brand identity.

Now, as we move into the emerging culture, our elitist branding has been discredited. Like Firestone tires after their most recent safety debacle, or like the old Bell Telephone Company that became Verizon, or like Andersen Consulting that became Accenture, we need to realize that the "Christian" label for many means religious broadcasting craziness: weird shouting, bizarre beliefs, big hair, and fake eyelashes drooping with crocodile tears. For others, it means oppression or ugly bourgeois smugness or racism or anti-Semitism or anti-intellectualism.

Changing our name may be tempting, but it won't help. We will need to change ourselves and decide what we believe a good Christian really is, then seek, by God's grace, to actually

23. Kevin Roberts, CEO of Saatchi & Saatchi, quoted in Alan M. Webber, "Trust in the Future," *Fast Company* (September 2000), 212. See *www.fastcompany.com/online/38/roberts.html.* Accessed 4 April 2001.

become those kinds of people, thus rebuilding trust in our brand. We need brand-new Christians and a brand-new church. Facing a challenge like that, we should neither be bored nor be preoccupied with less important matters.

The apostle Paul seemed to see the persecution-inflicted wounds in his body as brands showing his ownership by Christ (see Galatians 6:17; see **Body**).

EPICtivity B: Branding

Stress relief, memory enhancement, energy to leap small buildings—you hear all kinds of promises when you enter into the wellness drink zone. It's not the taste that sells; it's all about the experience the drink promises to provide.

Purchase an assortment of wellness drinks for your next team meeting. You may also include some of the more standard drinks, like Coke. Don't tell your team they are in the middle of this experiment until they have looked over the options, made their selection, and sipped from the refreshing herbal nectar of their choice. Then ask each person these questions:

- Why did you choose the drink you did?
- What does your drink promise, based on its advertising and packaging?
- Do you believe what is being promised? Why or why not?
- How does this product try to become an experience?
- How does it create an identity, a "brand" of person? Does this image match you?
- What values does your ministry brand provide? What are outsiders saying about your particular brand?
- What does your brand promise? Do your promises align with what you are currently delivering? What gaps exist?

• What experiences are you attaching to your ministry brand?
• What experiences do you think should be present?
• What does this discussion make you want to change, do, stop, or start?

B is for Buts

⬤ What religious leaders need to get off of:

"But we never did it that way before"
"But I might lose my job"
"But what will the moderns think?"
"But, but, but, but …"

"Yes, but" is a classic sign of a predicament as opposed to a problem.[24] A problem has a solution ("How do I get to church?"). A predicament is a situation in which a person or church (or whatever) is torn between competing values, pulling in rival directions, and thus can become paralyzed or lost. Problems can be solved with information. Predicaments can be resolved only by making choices.

This primer presupposes not a problem, but a predicament—a predicament that won't let you rest on your buts.

> In everyone's life there is one big "but."
>
> —PEE-WEE HERMAN IN THE FILM *PEE-WEE'S BIG ADVENTURE*

24. The following section draws heavily from Paul Welter's *How to Help a Friend* (Wheaton, IL: Tyndale House, 1978). See especially his chapter on assessing your friend's state of need, "Levels of Need," 51–54. Thanks to Rhonda Cushman for pointing us to this source.

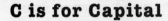

C is for Capital

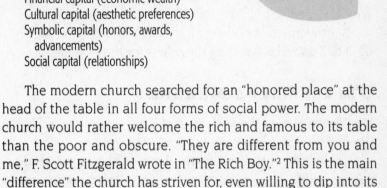

The interplay of these four forms of social power defines your "place" in postmodern society:[1]

Financial capital (economic wealth)
Cultural capital (aesthetic preferences)
Symbolic capital (honors, awards, advancements)
Social capital (relationships)

The modern church searched for an "honored place" at the head of the table in all four forms of social power. The modern church would rather welcome the rich and famous to its table than the poor and obscure. "They are different from you and me," F. Scott Fitzgerald wrote in "The Rich Boy."[2] This is the main "difference" the church has striven for, even willing to dip into its capital reserves rather than live off the interest if the possibility arose.

Will emerging churches do the same? If they do, they will lose their spiritual capital, which is what the church turns all other forms of capital into.

Regions high in social capital tend to have better health, greater affluence, and less crime and violence than those areas low in social capital.[3] But new forms of social capital are required, which will be the real sources of wealth in the future.

1. We have been obviously influenced by Pierre Bourdieu here and his magnificent *Distinction: A Social Critique of the Judgement of Taste* (Cambridge. MA: Harvard University Press, 1984).
2. This is the first short story in the collection of stories published by Fitzgerald as *All the Sad Young Men* (New York: Charles Scribner's Sons, 1926).
3. Robert Putnam has found that states with high social capital (Scandinavian Minnesota and North Dakota are among the leaders) have better health, better education, less crime and violence, and more affluence than those with low social capital (Mississippi, with its plantation pedigree, and Louisiana are among the lowest). See Robert D. Putnam, *Bowling Alone: The Collapse and Revival of American Community* (New York: Simon & Schuster, 2000), 401, and Michael Barone, "Doing Your Own Thing by Yourself," *TLS: Times Literary Supplement* (23 February 2001), 5.

Some have called these the "four currencies" of social capital: "equality, mutual respect, dignity, and self-worth." The new capitalizations and accumulations are those of trust, wisdom, and deeper relationships. Information flow is already a value on a par with material possessions.

And now there abides capital that is financial, cultural, symbolic, and social.

But the greatest of them all is . . . spiritual capital, which is what one gains by investing the others for the kingdom of God.

C is for Carpe Mañana

What "then" was to the ancients and "now" was to the moderns, "there" is to the postmoderns.

Ancient people lived in the land of the Past.[4] Modern people lived in the land of the Present.[5] Postmodern people live in the land of the Future first, but also in the lands of the Past, Present, and Future simultaneously.[6]

> Most people skate to where the puck is. I skate to where the puck is going to be.
>
> —HOCKEY GREAT WAYNE GRETZKY

Anyone who's selling anything is selling us a future: their version and vision of the future. We buy futures all the time whether we invest in hog innards, hides, or Tide.

4. There was no word for "future" in English until Chaucer used it in *Troilus and Criseyde* in 1374, "Futur tyme er I was in the snare," as quoted in the *Oxford English Dictionary*. See also John Burrow, "The Third Eye of Prudence," in *Medieval Futures: Attitudes to the Future in the Middle Ages*, ed. J. A. Burrow and Ian P. Wei (Rochester, NY: Boydell Press, 2000), 37.

5. According to the *Oxford English Dictionary*, the word *modern* comes from the Latin word *modo,* meaning "just now."

6. For a good example of this, check out the playful highlighting of anachronisms in two 2001 movies: *The Knight's Tale* and *Moulin Rouge.*

In the emerging culture, nothing stands still. Everything is moving. The only way you can hit a moving target is to get ahead of it. To Carpe Diem (seize the day) is to play catch up or put down. Only Carpe Mañana (seize tomorrow) can advance the cause of Christ.[7] It's important for leaders to realize that in the emerging culture, the chief advantage lies with the offense (anticipatory leadership), not the defense (reactive leadership).

But *mañana* can mean "not today" as well as "tomorrow"— delay and procrastination. That is why Carpe Manna is at the heart of Carpe Mañana. Seize tomorrow using the fresh supply of resources and foodstuffs God has given you each day.

Buffalo and cattle handle storms in a revealing fashion. Cattle turn their back on a storm and try to outrun it. Buffalo turn their heads into the oncoming storm and race toward it. They engage it and get through it while the cattle run and hide in fear.

When you are whitewater rafting and you hit the rapids, the worst thing you can do is slow down or back up or procrastinate. Paddle forward! Furiously! Keep moving!

Similarly, "do not worry about tomorrow" by seizing tomorrow because "each day has enough trouble of its own" (Matt. 6:34 NIV). Leaders are charged with an epic task: to put their faces, not their backs, to the future, and to prophesy (not plan) the way forward. A biblical prophet was someone who went slightly ahead of everyone else and got there first. Prophetic ministry takes the lead, goes ahead, envisions multiple scenarios of what might be, and of the alternative scenarios laid out, picks the Spirit-guided preferred future to bring to pass. To Carpe Mañana means to choose and create your future by prophesying your way forward.

The direction of Carpe Mañana leadership is described best, not by the words "natural" or even "supernatural" as by

7. For more, see Leonard Sweet, *Carpe Mañana: Can Your Church Seize Tomorrow?* (Grand Rapids: Zondervan, 2001), and Carl F. George, *Prepare Your Church for the Future* (Tarrytown, NY: F. H. Revell, 1991).

8. This borrows the phrase of Pat Kane in "There's Method in the Magic," *New Statesman* (23 August 1996), 27.

"futurenatural."[8] "Futurenatural" thinking replaces certainty with prophecy: *not* unpredictability or uncertainty, but prophecy and predictability. Predictability is based not on guessing what will happen, but getting ahead of what is happening and directing it. In prophesying you create the future: The fastest way to get something to come true is to act as if it were true. Instead of a self-fulfilling prophecy, make it a God-fulfilling prophecy: prophesy (not plan) your way forward, and bring about desired futures by creating those futures. (See **Scenario Thinking.**)

> Don't get sick on an unripe tomorrow.
>
> —NINA MASSON

Unfortunately, much of the church doesn't have a sense of the future; instead, it's knocked senseless by change, *left behind* in apocalyptic paralysis, devoid of a hopeful vision of the future. This distorted form of Carpe Mañana fantasizes about an apocalyptic escape from a future it cannot face via Second Coming and Rapture. By contrast, a true and faithful-till-he-comes Carpe Mañana seizes the future for the gospel.

C is for Categorical Imperialism

You may have heard of the categorical imperative. Now you need to be aware of—and beware of—categorical imperialism. A categorical imperialist is one who sanctifies the categories and canons of modernity and imposes them on other cultures, including postmodernity.[9]

9. For the best examples of categorical imperialism, see Douglas Groothuis, *Truth Decay: Defending Christianity Against the Challenges of Postmodernism* (Downers Grove, IL: InterVarsity Press, 2000), Marva J. Dawn, *Reaching Out without Dumbing Down: A Theology of Worship for the Turn-of-the Century Culture* (Grand Rapids: Eerdmans, 1995), and Os Guiness, *Time for Truth: Living Free in a World of Lies, Hype and Spin* (Grand Rapids: Baker, 2000).

The hazards of categorical imperialism are illustrated in the true story of a farmer from Gaston County, North Carolina, who sold a large parcel of his farm to a developer who paid him exactly what he asked for it. Patting himself on the back, the farmer bragged to a friend in town how he had "shown that developer." When told how much he got for his land, the friend was aghast.

"Why did you let that developer take advantage of you?"

"Take advantage of *me*? Are you kidding. I feel guilty for asking as much for it as I did. That land was worthless. What good is land that butts up right next to the road?"

If you're raising livestock, of course, the land next to the highway is the worst land you own. Your cattle can get loose and get killed on it. But if you're not raising cattle, if you're building houses—if the categories have changed—the land next to the road is the most valuable land you can possess.

If you want to do ministry among postmodern people, whose traditional categories have been unraveled by the emerging culture, you've got to drop your old categories. Jesus challenged the Pharisees to do this again and again. For example, the woman who washed Jesus' feet at Simon the Pharisee's home was, to Simon, a simple garden-variety species in the category of "sinner." To Jesus, she was in a different category: one who was forgiven much, and therefore loved much. Can we similarly reconsider our favorite modern categories, like liberal/conservative, absolutist/relativist, natural/supernatural, maybe even saved/lost?[10]

The church has said to postmoderns: We want you to become a disciple, but first we have to culturally circumcise you; first you have to give up your native culture. On one level, modernizing may mean giving up your native style of dress for a late-20th-century style. In this regard, humorist P. J. O'Rourke

---

10. For a fictional look at the inadequacies of both the liberal and conservative alternatives, see Brian D. McLaren, *A New Kind of Christian: A Tale of Two Friends on a Spiritual Journey* (San Francisco: Jossey-Bass, 2001).

says that the message most churches give to kids is "Pull your pants up, turn your hat around, and get a job."

On a deeper level, modernizing may mean giving up your native style of thinking, speaking, planning, organizing, and presenting yourself. For example, postmodern standards of "excellence" are very different from modern standards of "excellence." That's why when moderns judge postmodern worship, it most often gets attacked for being a "dumbing down" of the gospel, when in fact there is a new standard of excellence: What seems like "dumbing down" is really "drawing in."

Of course, it could be said that the Incarnation sets a pretty strong example of dumbing down. But saying so, while true, still coddles the modern superiority complex. One must ask: Is the modern category of excellence necessarily the superior one?

For example, "pursue excellence" over time can easily degenerate into "put forward a good image." Many postmodern people have been so disgusted by the superficial image-consciousness of modernity that they have adopted a "put your worst foot forward" approach—defy the categories of excellence expected by moderns and look much worse than you are. Putting your worst foot forward ruins the first impression, but it vaccinates against hypocrisy. Being a little messy, profane, or unrehearsed is part of the message, saying, "You don't have to be perfect or powerful or polished to be here, because we're barely holding it together ourselves." Again, this isn't the only legitimate way to do things, but it does have a certain resonance with a Savior who shows up in a makeshift crib, with no fanfare, in prickly hay and in the presence of manure.

C is for Celebrity

● The ultimate commodity. What sells newspapers or magazines—even Christian ones.

Who would want to inhabit a world without heroes? But celebrities are not heroes; they are merely famous for being "famous," a word that "transforms everything without changing anything."[11] Andy Warhol, the Pope of Pop Art, promised 15 minutes of fame for everyone. His prophecy is being realized all around us.

Charles Dickens was perhaps the first modern "celebrity" author. When Dickens came to America in 1841, he was hounded by people who had never read his books but who got caught up in the media frenzy. Some "fans" even leaned ladders against his hotel room to peek into his windows.

Contrast this with "stardom," which could be conferred only by those who had actually read and appreciated an author's books (e.g., contemporary William Wordsworth). A "star" is someone who is actually good at something and has accomplished some mission. Nine-Eleven created stars, not celebrities.

What makes a celebrity? Ask overworked blurb writers or tabloid columnists and trash journalists: Celebrity culture feeds on gossip and scandal. To be fair, tons of junk have always been dumped into our minds daily by the media. Genuine "stars" like George Washington were accused of gambling, reveling, horse racing, and horse whipping. Thomas Jefferson was called effeminate, an adulterer, an atheist, and an illegitimate son of a prostitute. Abraham Lincoln was portrayed by cartoonists as a baboon, and his wife was accused of treason. In his *Autobiography*, Malcolm X complains about media distortions: "If I had said 'Mary had a little lamb,' what probably would have appeared was 'Malcolm X Lampoons Mary.'"[12]

> Nobody believes the official spokesman ... but everyone trusts an unidentified source.
>
> —RON NESSEN, FORMER PRESS SECRETARY TO PRESIDENT GERALD FORD

11. Richard Appignanesi and Chris Garratt, *Introducing Postmodernism* (New York: Totem Books, 1995), 40.
12. Malcolm X with Alex Haley, *Autobiography of Malcolm X* (New York: Grove Press, 1965), 245.

Christian "celebrities" abound. Where are the "stars"?

Postmoderns will tend to trash the idea of the "Christian celebrity" (which generally elevates the wrong people) and will instead look for true "stars"—people worthy of a place in the firmament of the "communion of saints." For example, a Roman centurion, a widow giving her last quarter to the offering, a Syrophoenecian mother spunky enough to push back on Jesus, a Calcutta nun who held to her breast those dying of AIDS as if they were Jesus himself . . . and a host of other shooting stars who bathe us for centuries in their afterglow.

The greatest heroes, the greatest stars in the future, are not those who are the greatest celebrities, but those who are the greatest persons. So, for example, 80-, 90-, 100-year marriages will be achievements as monumental and as celebrated by postmoderns as the Eiffel Tower or the Guggenheim Museum.

C is for Choice Culture

Moderns: I think, therefore I am (Descartes).

Postmoderns: I choose, therefore I become.

Postmodern culture is a Choice Culture. You and I are the sum of our choices. The essence of the postmodern Renaissance: the right to define ourselves by the choices we make. We can choose what to put on our CDs. We can choose what to experience in life. We can choose what age we want to appear. Part of our choice now is place: We are rushing to "rural Valhallas,"[13] fleeing from those places that are aesthetically challenged. We can even choose our futures. (See **Carpe Mañana.**)

Have you read any hyperfiction yet? In hyperfiction you don't so much read as make choices. Everything is based on interactions and multiplex reactions. One reads hyperfiction spatially rather than linearly—which may help explain why postmoderns

---

13. According to the 2000 Census, the states with the highest growth rates were Idaho, Colorado, Nevada, Oregon, Wyoming, Utah, Montana, Arkansas, Tennessee, and Iowa, in that order.

aren't reading the mainstream press or watching the evening news—which they find too much like church: noninteractive, one-way, unexciting, smug.

This is what is truly revolutionary about the emerging culture. Heretofore humans lived a WYSIWYG life: what-you-see-is-what-you-get. Their choices were very limited. Humans can now increasingly live a WYCIWYG life: what-you-choose-is-what-you-get. More than everything else, WYCIWYG living is what is behind the "P" in EPIC.[14] It's a Participation Culture. (See **Karaokees**.)

For Christians, choice culture poses threats and opportunities. The threat? That "my" faith becomes my personal choice for my personal comfort and my personal convenience, where my spirituality is a commodity that I acquire like a hot tub, a fine leather couch, or a state-of-the-art entertainment center. This commodification of the faith turns churches into vendors of "religious goods and services,"[15] rendering pastors into shopkeepers with an enticing line of soul candy, or marketing reps for elite lines of "teaching styles" and "worship experiences" that deceive "customers" into thinking they are actually learning the ways of Christ and worshiping God when really they are indulging in a kind of spiritualized narcissism.

This choice-culture spirituality, like choice-culture marketing in general, often delivers a product that doesn't live up to its advertising. For example, even though one of the "spiritual products" I may choose to acquire is community, the very act of choosing to acquire community as one would acquire a haircut almost guarantees that I won't experience it.

14. For an explanation of EPIC (Experiential, Participatory, Image-rich, Connective), see Leonard Sweet, *Postmodern Pilgrims: First-Century Passion for the 21st-Century World* (Nashville: Broadman & Holman, 2000).
15. An apt and repugnant phrase from the Gospel and Our Culture Network, *www.gocn.org*.

Why? Because when I encounter conflict or disappointment or some other dimension of real life that doesn't "feel" like the experience of community that I wanted ... then I'll simply choose to leave that shop and seek elsewhere. (See **Love.**) If there is one thing that's certain about community, it is this: Community (like communication with others in general) is a lifelong pain—missed chances, missed boats, mistakes, misunderstandings at every turn.

Real community is only experienced by people who stay and learn forgiveness in the midst of conflict, endurance in the midst of missings. (This commodification of life, by the way, should probably not be seen as a feature of postmodernity, but rather of high modernity, which is reaching its zenith during this transitional time, and which will bequeath itself to the postmodern world as an inheritance that may be more curse than blessing.)

On the other hand, choice culture offers significant opportunities for Christians who live by mission rather than acquisition. I can choose where to live based on service as well as comfort, and I can choose downward mobility as well as upward. I can choose to make a lot of money and give a lot away, or make little and live simply. I can choose a new denomination or stream of Christian life and service, and in fact, I can, if I wish, spend a decade each in an Anabaptist church, a Presbyterian one, an Anglican, and a storefront Pentecostal church ... rounding out my faith with a wealth of varied experiences, and bringing to each new setting the enrichment gained from the previous ones.

It is as true with choices as it is with any other blessing: To the one who has been given much, much is expected. A big part of ministry today is getting people to take responsibility for the choices they make, and to make the right choices. "It's my life. I have chosen this way, and I will be judged by God accordingly." An old Indiana Jones movie said it well: "Choose wisely."

C is for church (lowercase)

● The worst form of community ever devised, except for all the others.[16] Mark Oakley confesses to a "soap-dish doctrine of the church where what is cleansing and vital is from time to time . . . held by something . . . unpleasant to handle."[17]

● Too often, sociological structures filled with pachyderms solving problems that no longer exist, or answering questions that no one is asking.

In Amsterdam in the early 1990s, postmoderns were asked whether they were interested in God: 100% answered yes. Then they were asked whether they were interested in church: 1% answered yes, 99% answered no. If you look on the bright side, you'll say that at least the church isn't competing with God. If you look otherwise, you'll cry.

> Jesus hated church, too.
>
> —BILLBOARD FROM TENTH PRESBYTERIAN CHURCH, PHILADELPHIA

C is for Church (uppercase)

● The body of Christ—an organic being.

● The communion of saints.

● A spiritual portal into the kingdom of God.

Note: not temple. It was not until Stephen suggested that the church was a body and not bricks ("The Most High does not live in temples made with hands," Acts 7:48 NKJV) that he was martyred.

---

16. A paraphrase of what Winston Churchill said about democracy.
17. Mark Oakley, *The Collage of God* (London: Darton, Longman & Todd, 2001), 29.

C is for Cloning

● Another word for the mass-copying of organisms and a nightmare world of perpetual sameness. Cloning is already routine among animals (mice, sheep, goats, pigs, even a rare Asian guar—a wild ox—have been cloned). You can even place an order for a cloned cow on the Net. A high school girl working at a Wisconsin animal-cloning company cloned a cow.[18]

● Another word for treating genes like Play-Doh, shaping and molding them according to human preferences and designs.

● What the church hates in a biological sense; what the church loves in a spiritual sense—a community of people who think alike, act alike, and look alike.

● The opposite of God's design for creation, which is increasing differentiation and diversity.

● One of the lesser biotech ethical dilemmas of postmodern culture. A human clone is inevitable, if not already accomplished.[19] Singapore, India, Russia, and Brazil (among others) have not outlawed human-cloning research.[20]

Naturally occurring clones—called twins—remind us that clones are never clones. No matter how genetically identical, even clones experience life and turn out differently.

If your church develops something effective in postmodern ministry, please make a solemn pact with God *not* to develop a conference or seminar or notebook to teach other churches how to become little clones of yourself. Share your breakthrough, by

18. Brian Alexander, "(You)^2," *Wired* (February 2001), 126. See *www.wired.com/wired/archive/9.02/projectx.html?pg=1&topic =&topic_set=*. Accessed 4 April 2001.

19. Saddam Hussein has already approached a cryonics society in the U.S. to find out whether his sperm could be cloned. As reported in PRI's "In Brief" review of Robert M. Youngson and Ian Schott, "Medical Blunders," *TLS: Times Literary Supplement* (19 July 1996), 32.

20. Only five U.S. states have laws banning reproductive cloning (Missouri, Michigan, Louisiana, California, and Rhode Island).

all means; spread it far and wide. But see your success not as a clonable product, but rather as an inspiration for others to create, adapt, develop, improvise, and discover new possibilities in their locale.

C is for Coaching

Personal coaching: Postmoderns will want and need their own personal spiritual coaches. The duties of a spiritual coach are to bring out the best in a player. Coaches cannot play the game for their people, but they can teach, correct, discipline, motivate, mentor, inspire, and praise their players to spiritual greatness. A personal spiritual coach helps disciples of Jesus to realize God's dream for their lives, maximize their soul's potential, and lead faithful, abundant lives true to the gospel. Pastoral counselors will need to reinvent themselves as personal spiritual coaches and divest themselves of the "therapist" model if they are to have a future. A spiritual director is now part artistic director, part interior designer, part coach,[21] part cheerleader, part shaman.

Team coaching: One of the most difficult jobs imaginable. Why? Because building a team is an art form that harmonizes superstars and team players. Teams need prima donnas and can't survive without them. But prima donnas need to work as a team and can't shine as prima donnas without the backlighting of the team.

In modern ministry, the hero was the star—the prima donna preacher, the singer, the broadcaster, the author, the speaker. In postmodern ministry, the hero is the coach—the one who develops his or her players and deploys them wisely, the one

---

21. Anita Schamber, "The Leader as Coach," *Christian Management Report* 25 (January/February 2001), 7–10. See the websites of Coach U (*www.coachu.com*), the Coaches Training Institute (*www.thecoaches.com*), or the Academy for Coach Training (*www.coachtraining.com*). Accessed 23 July 2001.

who scouts for needed new talent, the one who inspires discipline and sacrifice, the one who calls—at just the right time—the right plays and the needed time-outs, the one who seeks to give rather than earn praise, and the one who makes sure the players get the credit due at the end of the game.

Modern leaders seeking to transition to a postmodern world will have to ask themselves some probing questions about coaching: Do I want the place of fame and acclaim on the field or the place of service and true significance at the sidelines? Do I want my team to outshine me? Do I need the spotlight?

EPICtivity C: Coaching

Every Thursday the CEO and cofounder of TalentFusion, a recruitment outsourcing agency, takes his 45 staff members out for a company soccer game. What began as a way to blow off some steam is now a part of the company's DNA.

"We use the game as a way to channel our energy while communicating our company vision to our staff," says David Pollard, 40, who plays the position of striker. "Titles mean nothing on the soccer field. I love when people are able to focus on how to win the game, not on the company hierarchy."[22]

Pollard uses the game to experience the beauty of team and collaboration. You could play soccer or basketball or Nintendo or . . . you could try something really different: golf-cart polo.

Golf-Cart Polo

1. Rent five golf carts (two-passenger type). One golf cart is for the referee.
2. Purchase a Nerf soccer ball and croquet mallet for each player.

22. Erika Germer, "Not Just for Kicks: Meeting I Never Miss," *Fast Company* (March 2001), 70. *www.fastcompany.com/online/44/minm.html*. Accessed 17 May 2002.

3. In an unused outdoor parking lot, set up two cones on each end as goals.
4. Play for 45 minutes to one hour. If there are a lot of participants, you can have two-minute periods.
5. Have a blast—and be sure not to run into each other!

Dialogue about the game:

• What do you think was absolutely essential to scoring goals?
• What hindered your team from making goals?
• What would you do differently if you were to play the game again?
• Based on what we learned in this game, how can we function better as a team in our current ministry?
• What obstacles are keeping us from being a better team?

C is for Community

● An overused word in recent Christian vocabulary. (See **Love.**) (Also see the EPIC*tivities*.) To experience "community," see almost anything *but* Community.

C is for Complexity

Many people in pastoral ministry were ordained for "Word, Sacrament, and Order." As well as a "Law and Order" ministry, postmodern ordinations need to embrace a "Grace and Love" ministry, perhaps even a ministry for "Word, Sacrament and Chaos." After all, it was in the interest of decency and order that Jesus was put to death.

In the Genesis picture of God's Spirit hovering over the primeval chaos, God created the world *ex complexio* (Gen. 2) as well as *ex nihilo* (Gen. 1).[23] Complexity theory is a new field of science that studies the emergence of life from self-organization, a newly discovered law of life. In complexity sciences, an important incubator of scientific advances in the 21st century, the truth is in the complexity. Messiness is essential for birth, creativity, and even structure. The greater the disturbances to a self-organizing system, the greater the structure.[24] In fact, some scholars argue (although we don't agree) that the sacred is *only* found in the chaos, not in the world of order, which is of human construction (e.g., Georges Bataille).[25]

> ... it is the ability to self-organize,
> more than anything else, which promotes and
> enhances our life in the universe.
>
> —DIARMUID O'MURCHU[26]

Postmoderns are not afraid of complexity and, indeed, embrace it. Their family lives are complex—step-siblings, step-mothers, eight grandparents, networks of relatives and friends. The "five shortcuts to" or "seven habits of" or "twelve rules in"[27] no longer cut it.

In the modern era we were taught to respect and trust the big and the simple. In the postmodern matrix we are learning to have confidence in the cellular and the complex.[28] In fact, the smaller you get, the more complex things become. Bigger

23. See Catherine Keller, "The Lost Chaos of Creation," *The Living Pulpit* 9 (April-June 2000), 4–5.

24. John Polkinghorne, *Quarks, Chaos, and Christianity* (New York: Crossroad, 1996).

25. Georges Bataille, *Theory of Religion,* trans. Robert Hurley (New York: Zone Books, 1989).

26. Diarmuid O'Murchu, *Quantum Theology* (New York: Crossroad, 1997), 96.

27. Around 1800 every British cottage had a copy of the "Twelve Good Rules" of King Charles II.

28. In *Christian Chaos: Revolutionizing the Congregation* (Nashville: Abingdon, 1999), Thomas G. Bandy appropriates chaos theory and relates it to the church.

means simpler. Smaller means screwier and more fickle, more conscious and more spiritual. An electron is in many ways more complex than a spaceship or a battleship. Big things obey simple mechanical laws. Masses of people are predictable— they follow certain statistical rules. Individuals are annoyingly unpredictable.

When Einstein said we need to make everything "as simple as possible—but not simpler," he was anticipating a world of bits-bites-bots where you can be small and global at the same time. Small things can have big effects. Mega-ministries are built on mini-mindsets.

> The world is so complicated, tangled, and overloaded that to see into it with any clarity you must prune and prune.
>
> —Novelist Italo Calvino[29]

The greater the complexity of the system, the greater the need for simplicity. Why McDonald's? We sometimes need to put our minds in neutral when the thousands of choices and fast-food franchises threaten to derail us. Why Coke? It "allows us to disconnect from connectivity," and that's "what makes [super-brands] transcendent across reality barriers."[30]

Complex adaptive systems are open systems. And open systems have great advantages over closed systems.

This preference for complexity and open-endedness can give industrial-age and industrial-strength religious institutions the bends. Can you imagine a church or denomination that has two or three different doctrinal statements all functioning synchronously? Are Lutherans better off for refusing all

29. Italo Calvino, *If on a Winter's Night a Traveler*, trans. William Weaver (New York: Harcourt Brace Jovanovich, 1979), 244.
30. Watts Wacker and Jim Taylor with Howard Means, *The Visionary's Handbook: Nine Paradoxes That Will Shape the Future of Your Business* (New York: HarperBusiness, 2000), 18.

pastoral candidates except those who have been filtered through the Lutheran screening system? Could a half-dozen humble Mennonite pastors (or a dozen highly charged Pentecostals) help a Presbyterian judicatory by "complexifying" it?

In general, modern churches had amazingly complex doctrinal statements and stunningly simple discipleship protocols (i.e., "attend church services and learn more of the Bible"). What would be lost—and gained—if your church or denomination reversed that pattern, dropping its entire doctrinal statement and replacing it with the Apostles' Creed, or the Great Commandment . . . and becoming far more sophisticated in its approach to helping people grow as disciples?

Søren Kierkegaard said that the two great mental faults are laziness and impatience: laziness (refusal to abide the complexities and unknowns), and impatience (refusal to not have it all now). How lazy and impatient will your church be?

> *Melins est dubitare te ocultis, quem litigare de incertis.*
>
> Better to doubt what is obscure, than dispute about things uncertain.
>
> —AUGUSTINE OF HIPPO

C is for Connectivity

The Plains Indians were known for the smoking ceremony. At the conclusion of the sharing of the pipe, all the participants would say in unison: "We are all related."

The experience of the self as a part of others—"We are all related"—is one of the most spiritual of experiences. Everything is related. Nothing exists in isolation.

The basic unit of the future is not the isolated individual, not the communal collective, but the interdependent collective.

The more interdependent we become, the more important our individual uniqueness becomes. The interplay of the individual and the interdependent yields a third entity: the connective self. You can hear it in the U.S. Army commercial "An Army of One." Postmodern people seek new ways of fitting together, not of fitting in.[31]

The clamor for connectivity that haunts postmoderns can be heard in Rodney King's soul-cry, "Can't we all get along?" Connectivity is partly a response to the decline in social capital, civic engagement, and social connections to other people—to partners, family, friends, and strangers.[32] But there is something else at work as well.

All the connections—between human beings, between humans and nature, between humans and God—are being rewired. Concepts of connectivity have replaced notions of geographic centrality. The whole of integrated connection is now more the focus than the component parts of self-sufficient separateness.

31. For more of these insights in a Gen-X framework, see Steve Rabey, *In Search of Authentic Faith: How Emerging Generations Are Transforming the Church* (Colorado Springs: Waterbrook Press, 2001); Ken Baugh and Rich Hurst, *Getting Real: An Interactive Guide to Relational Ministry* (Colorado Springs: NavPress, 2000); Richard W. Flory and Donald Miller, eds., *Gen X Religion* (New York: Routledge, 2000); Clarence E. McClendon, *The X Blessing: Unveiling a Redemptive Strategy for a Marked Generation* (Nashville: Thomas Nelson, 2000); Andrea Lee Schieber, Ann Terman Olson, and Richard Webb, *What's Next: Connecting Your Ministry with Generation X* (Minneapolis: Augsburg Fortress, 1999), with video companion; Tom Beaudoin, *Virtual Faith: The Irreverent Spiritual Quest of Generation X* (San Francisco: Jossey-Bass, 1998); Tim Celek, *Inside the Soul of a New Generation: Insights and Strategies for Reaching Busters* (Grand Rapids: Zondervan, 1996); Kevin Graham Ford with Jim Delaney, *Jesus for a New Generation: Putting the Gospel in the Language of Xers* (Downers Grove, IL: InterVarsity Press, 1996); Alan Roxburgh, *Reaching a New Generation: Strategies for Tomorrow's Church* (Downers Grove, IL: InterVarsity Press, 1993).

32. Robert Putnam attributes 25% of the decline in social connectedness to television. The other 75% is largely due, he argues, to generational issues. "The declines in church attendance, voting, political interest, campaign activities, associational membership, and social trust are attributed almost entirely to generational succession." The GI generation is the champion of social capital. See Robert D. Putnam, *Bowling Alone: The Collapse and Revival of American Community* (New York: Simon & Schuster, 2000), 229, 265.

The greater the communication, the greater the hunger for connectivity.[33] The church must connect people through communication in community for communion through both physical and virtual venues.

Shortly after the massive hydroelectric Norris Dam was built in the hills of East Tennessee, a night-shift worker observed something odd. As he looked across the lake, he could hear behind him the humongous dynamos humming powerfully in the quiet of the night, generating fabulous amounts of electricity. But in front of him, every cabin in sight was lighted not by electrical energy, but by kerosene lamps.

When he inquired why, he discovered that the transmission lines had not yet been laid. Here were people living in the shadow of a power source sufficient to light up whole cities, but they could receive none of its power because they were not connected to it. Power surrounded them, but they were not plugged in.[34]

Wiredness means three things for emerging ministry. First and foremost, are you "plugged-in" to the Spirit, to the power supply that God has provided to supply your every need? Second, are you plugged-in to digital culture, both in terms of your ministry goals and personal gadgets/toolkit? Third, are you socially wired—connected to other creatures (both human and animal)?

The threads of a spider's web are drawn out from within the spider's very being. The threads in the web's concentric circles are sticky. The threads leading to the center are smooth.

For the way to be made smooth to life's only true center—Jesus the Christ—the circles of life must be gluey with connections. In the word *consciousness* is hidden this

33. Larry Crabb, *Connecting: Healing for Ourselves and Our Relationships: A Radical New Vision* (Dallas: Word, 1997).

34. James W. Moore, *Some Things Are Too Good Not to Be True* (Nashville: Dimensions for Living, 1994), 122–23.

mystery of connectivity: To be conscious means to "know with" (*sci* + *con*). Christian leaders must increasingly remind people of what a wise Midwestern pastor repeatedly wakes up his congregation with: "Individual Christian, the Bible takes no notice of you."

If we are not connecting people in community—so they know together ("together with all the saints" as Paul says in Ephesians 3:18) and grow together and serve together and suffer together and rejoice and cry and feast and fast and give and live and fall and rise together—then we are spinning our wheels in terms of authentic Christian ministry, whether modern or postmodern or whatever.[35] In modernity we thought "knowing" was something that happened in an individual's mind; now we begin to see that knowing is a connective experience, not unrelated to loving.[36] In the words of one postmodern,

> Worship that is relevant, that "speaks to me," is worship that is
> > Personal yet communal
> > Emotional yet instructional
> > Inspiring yet practical
> > Spiritual yet tangible.[37]

"Dare to connect" has replaced Kant's famous motto of the Enlightenment, "Dare to know." (See **Mysticism.**)

---

35. For new ways of building connections, see Randy Frazee, *The Connecting Church: Beyond Small Groups to Authentic Community* (Grand Rapids: Zondervan, 2001).

36. For the role of small groups among postmoderns, see Jimmy Long, *Generating Hope: A Strategy for Reaching the Postmodern Generation* (Downers Grove, IL: InterVarsity Press, 1997), and Jimmy Long et al., *Small Group Leaders Handbook: The Next Generation* (Downers Grove, IL: InterVarsity Press, 1995).

37. Richard P. Schowalter, *Igniting a New Generation of Believers* (Nashville: Abingdon, 1995), 80.

C is for Contemporary Worship

● Another name for 1970s worship, i.e., worship that is 30 years behind the times instead of 150 to 300 years.

When people talk about making their worship "more contemporary," it most often means dimming the lights or accelerating the beat or changing the music to make it more hip-hop than bebop. Never mind (for now) that worship is much more than singing. Even restricting ourselves to the musical dimension of worship, we are missing the point.

In the emerging culture we would be better to drop the term "Contemporary" and move this entry to "F" for "Fresh Worship" or "I" for "Intentional Worship." Fresh and intentional worship beyond modernity can easily draw on the most ancient of resources; in fact, we expect that it will increasingly do so. The real attraction of contemporary worship wasn't its trendiness; it was its freshness—different, new—and its powerfulness and purposefulness.[38]

We have two unacceptable options today, it seems. In "traditional worship" we too often have lyrics that are meaningful ("Here I raise mine Ebenezer" or "Bring forth the royal diadem") but not very understandable to the uninitiated. (We could just as well be singing "Totus tuus sum, mundi salvataris" or "Khvalite imya Gospodne," which, though meaningful in Latin or Russian, are thoroughly incomprehensible to speakers of contemporary English.) In "contemporary worship" our lyrics are understandable but far less rich in meaning, poetry, texture, and depth. Something that's contemporary and meaningless is not a great improvement over something that's meaningful but not understandable; something that is understandable and meaningful is a big improvement over both.

38. Sally Morgenthaler, *Worship Evangelism: Inviting Unbelievers into the Presence of God* (Grand Rapids: Zondervan, 1995).

Similarly, contemporary isn't necessarily a great achievement. To prove our point: Attend 52 Sundays at a contemporary church that sings for 45 minutes each week using standard contemporary songs. After singing these songs for 2,340 minutes (or 39 hours), there is one certainty: You will be bored. Even though the songs are contemporary, nearly all of them lack freshness after 39 hours. True, the songs are contemporary, but they use the same standard chord progressions, the same predictable melodies, the same clichéd lyrics. Being in contemporary style doesn't keep them from becoming stale contemporary songs.

Give us songs that are meaningful (which requires that they be understandable), and we will sing with joy. Give us songs that are fresh, and we will sing with sustained enthusiasm.

Songs are to growing a healthy soul what produce is to growing a healthy body. Lettuce, broccoli, carrots, and potatoes have a short shelf life. Only a few "classic" songs and products ("Amazing Grace," "As the Deer," "Pepsi," "Frosted Flakes") deserve passing on from generation to generation. Savor the classics, and then sing a new (fresh, meaningful, understandable) song to the Lord.

C is for Converts

● What the church has too many of, as opposed to disciples, which the church has too few of.

Conversion has gone from being a U-turn off a self-driven rut and onto a God-driven highway to a choice of which highway to take to get where *you* want to go (as evident in the Christian bumper sticker "God is my *co*-pilot").

Witness the greatest "conversion" story of the 20th century, which is also one of the greatest genocide stories of the time. By 1994, 85% of Rwandans called themselves "Christians." In one month in 1994, 100,000 Hutu "Christians" killed about 1,000,000 Tutsi "Christian" neighbors for no other reason than that they were Tutsi.[39] These Hutu Christians were "born again, but still-born," as Christian British poet Geoffrey Hill would put it.[40]

Didn't Jesus give us all the same mission statement? "Go and make disciples." It has two parts: "Go" and "make disciples."

That one word *disciples* tells us who we are as Christians and what our calling is. Making converts is not enough. Discipleship is a *cultivated* art.

C is for Creation

● What modern secularists called "nature" (a term that turned a sacred work of art into a profane source of "raw materials") and what modern Christians always linked with "versus evolution" (thus turning a sacred mystery into a profane and misguided argument).

● What ancient Christians viewed, along with Holy Scripture, as one of God's two primary sources of self-revelation.

● What emerging Christians will cherish as God's art gallery in which we live and of which we are a part and for which we were created as planetary trustees and caretakers.

The Bible could not link the story of life to the story of the earth any more intimately than is implied in God's creation of Adam out of *adamh*—the dust of the earth.

In ancient Greco-Roman culture, there was the custom of kissing the earth to honor the earth. The most-used New Testament word for "worship" is *proskuneo*. It comes from *pros* ("towards") and *kuneo* ("kiss").

For postmoderns, it's "Mother Earth," holy ground tragically portrayed in the words of James Merrill: "Father Time and

---

39. See John A. Berry and Carol Pott Berry, eds., *Genocide in Rwanda: A Collective Memory* (Washington, DC: Howard University Press, 1999). According to the Berrys, 92% are Christians (p. 27).

40. Geoffrey Hill, *The Triumph of Love* (Boston: Houghton Mifflin, 1998), 46. Hill has been called "the finest British poet of our time." His Christian musings have been called "the major achievement of late 20th century verse."

Mother Earth, / A marriage on the rocks."[41] No wonder the word *environment* is used less and less; it's too cold a word for this theology of "holy ground."

If our humaneness is most manifest in our relationships—with swallows and snails, with friends and enemies, with the Father, Son, and Holy Spirit—the modern world needed marriage counseling big-time. The willingness to sacrifice living systems for commerce has meant that the lungs and other vital organs of Mother Earth are being cannibalized to the point where "natural" disasters are no longer "natural" but induced.

The mad weather patterns of the past decade are a byproduct of disappearing forests (at current rates of deforestation, Ecuador will be totally barren of trees in 20 years), disappearing healthy air, and disappearing ecosystems. Moderns had trouble thinking in systems and relational terms. The very concept of ethnobotany (the study of the relationship between people and plants) or biocolonialism was at best a joke. In the emerging culture, ecology is all about systems and relationships and quality of life. In the words of Henry David Thoreau, "What is the good of having a nice house without a decent planet to put it on?"

The hunger today is for a culture of "leavers" rather than "takers."[42] The sustainability movement, called "the fastest growing and most powerful movement in the world today,"[43] offers a shared understanding of planet Earth that the church

---

41. James Merrill, "The Broken Home," in *Nights and Days: Poems* (New York: Atheneum, 1976), 28.

42. These are Daniel Quinn's words in *Stepping Lightly: Simplicity for People and the Planet* by Mark A. Burch (Gabriola Island, BC: New Society Publishers, 2000), 168. For a 12-week study (available on video with participants manual and leader's guide) for congregations on this subject, see Charles R. Foster, *Steward: Living as Disciples in Everyday Life* (Nashville: Abingdon Press, 2000). See also Thomas Sieger Derr with James A. Nash and Richard John Neuhaus, *Environmental Ethics and Christian Humanism* (Nashville: Abingdon, 1996).

43. Paul Hawken, "The Resurgence of Citizens' Movements," *EarthLight: The Magazine of Spiritual Ecology* (Winter 2001), 10; see also his *The Ecology of Commerce: A Declaration of Sustainability* (New York: HarperBusiness, 1993).

should have provided. The whole concept of a "green belt," for example, is straight out of the book of Numbers. Cities given to the Levites were to be surrounded by a *migraash*, an inner belt of open space extending 1000 cubits in every direction and reserved for animals, movable possessions, and public amenities. An outer belt of 1000 cubits was for fields and vineyards.[44]

For modern people, "outdoors" means the sliver of Creation experienced between your front door and driveway, between your parking lot and office, and at the service station where you filled up your gas tank and emptied your trash. For postmodern people, "Creation" has a sacred sound because of its relation to "Creator," and to be outdoors feels holier than being in a cathedral.[45] Caring for Creation is, for the emerging culture, caring for the cathedral God built. There are now over 130,000 religion and ecology projects in operation worldwide.[46] Unfortunately, very few of them are emanating from evangelical churches.

One postmodern image of heaven? The place where, when you die, all the cats and dogs you've ever owned come running to greet you.

> Live simply, that others may simply live.
>
> —Dorothy Day

44. For more such ideas, see Mary Elizabeth Moore, *Ministering with the Earth* (St. Louis: Chalice Press, 1998). Also Jay McDaniel, *With Roots and Wings: Christianity in an Age of Ecology and Dialogue* (Maryknoll, NY: Orbis Books, 1995).

45. You can feel this in the Earth Charter web page, *www.earthcharter.org*, where the entire Earth Charter statement is accessible in multiple languages. Accessed 17 May 2001.

46. See Libby Bassett, John T. Brinkman, and Kusumita P. Pedersen, eds., *Earth and Faith: A Book of Reflection for Action* (New York: Interfaith Partnership for the Environment, 2000). Also Tony Campolo and Gordon Aeschliman, *50 Ways You Can Help Save the Planet* (Downers Grove: InterVarsity Press, 1992).

C is for Cultural Syndromes

Cultural syndromes consist of shared attitudes, beliefs, norms, role and self definitions, and values of members of each culture that are organized around a theme.[47]

Two of the biggest syndromes in the emerging culture are "individualism" and "collectivism," distinctions developed by the cross-cultural researches of Harry S. Triandis at the University of Illinois at Urbana-Champaign.

The modern world has witnessed a massive shift from collectivism to individualism. This is due to the increasing complexity of cultures, affluence, urbanism—all of which leads to increasing individualism.

Individualism: Individual goals precede group goals.
Collectivism: Group goals precede individual goals.
The Ideal of Individualism: Doing one's thing.
The Ideal of Collectivism: Doing one's duty.

In individualism, the base referent is the individual and personal goals. Attitudes are more important than norms. Identity derives less from emotional attachments to others than from personal preferences, cost-benefit analyses, experiences, accomplishments, skills, and possessions. The self is distinct from the in-group and may be coterminous with the body. Child-rearing customs stress creativity, independence, and initiative.

In collectivism, the base referent is relationships and social space is "cut up" into groups.[48] Either no distinction is made between personal and collective goals, or the latter trumps the former. Norms are weightier than attitudes. Identity derives from family identity, and behavior is shaped by common norms. "Norms are more important determinants of social

47. Harry C. Triandis, "The Psychological Measurement of Cultural Syndromes," *American Psychologist* 51 (April 1996), 407–15.
    48. Ibid., 409.

behavior in collectivist cultures, and attitudes are more important in individualist cultures."[49] The self flows from the in-group and may even be coterminous with the group (such as the family or tribe), and the focus is on groups. Child-rearing practices stress obedience, duty, "correct behavior," and sacrifice for the larger whole. Social distance is much shorter than in individualist cultures.[50]

Ancient Mediterraneans had a collectivist self, not an individualist self like USAmericans have today.[51] By the end of the 20th century, Triandis observes, 70% of the world's population is collectivistic, while the remaining 30% are individualistic.[52] In other words, what is most important in North America—individualistic values—is least important in the rest of the world.

Postmoderns are at the beginning stages of moving away from the hyperindividualism of high modernity and toward a bringing of the self and society together in new configurations. In talking about the self as a cultural syndrome, there are three aspects of the self to keep in mind: private self, public self, collective self. "The private self is an assessment of the self by the self. The public self corresponds to an assessment of the self by the generalized other. The collective self corresponds to an assessment of the self by a specific reference group."[53]

49. Harry C. Triandis, Christopher McCusker, and C. Harry Hui, "Multimethod Probes of Individualism and Collectivism," *Journal of Personality and Social Psychology* 59 (1990), 1007.

50. Ibid., 1018. For example, "Greeks, who are collectivists, tend to ask 'intimate questions' of people they have just met, with whom they would like to establish a friendship. . . . They ask, for instance, 'How much money do you make per month?' of a person they have just met."

51. For an excellent summary of the differences between the two (although we have otherwise profound disagreements with this book's attempt to reduce Jesus to a political action committee leader), see Bruce J. Malina, *The Social Gospel of Jesus: The Kingdom of God in Mediterranean Perspective* (Minneapolis: Fortress Press, 2001), 119–39.

52. Harry C. Triandis, "Cross-Cultural Studies of Individualism and Collectivism," in *Nebraska Symposium on Motivation,* ed. John J. Berman (Lincoln: University of Nebraska Press, 1990).

53. Harry C. Triandis, "The Self and Social Behavior in Differing Cultural Contexts," *Psychological Review* 96 (1989), 506–20, 507.

The private self becomes rich and complex when based on "finding yourself."

The public self becomes rich and complex when based on "what others think about you."

The collective self becomes rich and complex when based on belonging: "Remember: You are a member of this family; don't ever forget that you're a Christian."

C is for Culture

● "One of the two or three most complicated words in the English language," according to Raymond Williams.[54]

● One of three sources (the other two being tradition and, most importantly, Scripture) for constructive theological reflection, according to Stanley J. Grenz and John R. Franke.[55]

The "I Am" sent his only Son to say this to every culture: "I'm In." Much of the church is trying to get out of what Jesus is trying to get into: culture, whatever it is.

Culture is an essential concept in the centering doctrine of the Christian faith: Incarnation. Lesslie Newbigin said words that shock modern hearers: "We must start with the basic fact that there is no such thing as a pure gospel if by that is meant something which is not embodied in a culture. . . . Every interpretation of the gospel is embodied in some cultural form."[56]

Christians in the emerging culture must relearn what Christians of modern times only sometimes knew: Jesus did not come to impose a culture on people or to drive a culture from people, but rather to drive from every culture the sin that

54. Raymond Williams, *Keywords: A Vocabulary of Culture and Society* (New York: Oxford University Press, 1976), 76.
55. Stanley J. Grenz and John R. Franke, *Beyond Foundationalism: Shaping Theology in a Postmodern Context* (Louisville: Westminster John Knox, 2001).
56. Lesslie Newbigin, *The Gospel in a Pluralist Society* (Grand Rapids: Eerdmans, 1989), 144.

besets it, and into every culture bring the life, joy, grace, peace, and freedom of God.

Modern Western Christians tend to forget that they are living an enculturated gospel; their familiarity with modern Western culture makes it invisible to them. When people say, "I don't want to be a modern Christian or a postmodern Christian; I just want to be a *biblical* Christian," they are expressing a perhaps admirable ideal that is, nevertheless, naive and therefore dangerous. God's people across the storyline of Scripture lived, worshiped, trusted, and obeyed in many cultural settings—from hunter-gatherer tribes to nomadic pastoral patriarchies, to tribal confederations, to monarchies, to refugee subcultures, to provisional cultures as exiles and slaves, and so on. To be biblical means to live in a culture, including modern or postmodern, and seek to be an agent of Jesus Christ there. Of course, to be Christ's agents in a culture will make us in many ways countercultural. But even so, we are still living out an interpretation of the gospel, as Newbigin said, in "some cultural form." Those ministering in postmodern contexts need a heightened sensitivity to issues of gospel and culture.[57]

C is for Cyborg

● What we all have become: part "born," part "made."

The question now is not What is cyborgian? or What is not cyborgian?[58] The question now is, What does it mean to be human? What is nonhuman? The everyday cyborgization of humans (contact lenses, pacemakers, breast implants, artificial limbs) is proceeding faster than we know.[59]

57. For more, see John Docker, *Postmodernism and Popular Culture: A Cultural History* (New York: Cambridge University Press, 1994), and David Harvey, *The Condition of Postmodernity: An Enquiry into the Origins of Cultural Change* (New York: Blackwell, 1989).
58. Check out the Cyborg Manifesto at various websites.
59. For more, see Chris Hables Gray, *Cyborg Citizen: Politics in the Posthuman Age* (New York: Routledge, 2001).

In fact, the "born" and the "made" are now artificial distinctions. They are coming together, as the code on a microchip parallels the DNA code within a cell and as our digital creations are evolving and moving beyond their creators' control. Many people in the scientific community believe that our children, who will write the story of the 21st century, will see "conscious machines." The question is how soon. John Holland (University of Michigan) thinks not for 100 years. Bill Joy (chief scientist, Sun Microsystems) thinks in 30 years.

Postmodern culture is in the midst of an identity crisis. Or, in the words of one scientist (Douglas Hofstadter, professor of cognitive science at Indiana University), "Who will be we in 2093?"[60]

The Fifth Amendment to the U.S. Constitution protects what's inside our bodies. But part of my brain is now outside my body. My PC is an extension of my brain—a less pretty one, and more linear, to be sure. Should someone be able to get a court order to read my mind?

> I have not lost my mind; it's backed up on
> disk somewhere.
>
> —ANONYMOUS

The Turing Test dominated modernity: If you can't tell the machine from the human after five minutes of typed conversation, then the computer is thinking well enough to be called human. Parenthetically, and pathetically, the big problem with the Turing Test is that "judges" almost never mistake a computer for a human being, but they often mistake a human being for a computer.[61]

---

60. See Doug Hofstadter's "Spiritual Robots" presentation at the 1999 Stanford Symposium "Will Spiritual Robots Replace Humanity by 2100?" *www.technetcast.com/tnc_play_stream.html?stream_id=256.* Accessed 17 May 2002.
61. Alexander Fiske Harrison, "A.L.I.C.E.'s Springs: Do Computers Really Converse?" *TLS: Times Literary Supplement* (9 June 2000), 14.

C is for Cyborg

— • • —

The Moravec Test is dominating postmodernity: The test of whether a machine is human is not whether it can think or the level of its artificial intelligence, but whether it can achieve consciousness.[62]

62. Hans Moravec, *Robot: Merer Machine to Transcendent Mind* (New York: Oxford University Press, 1999). The Moravec Test was compiled by Hans Moravec, head of the Robotics Institute at Carnegie Mellon University.

Deconstruction

- One of the most important philosophical/interpretive concepts of postmodernity.

- Also, one of the most difficult for outsiders to understand.

- An approach to interpretation of literary texts (and film and other media) that begins by questioning many of the assumptions of traditional interpretation. For example, traditional interpretation assumes that the author's conscious intent is a (or the) primary concern in interpreting a text. Deconstruction asks, "Might the author have had subconscious motivations at work that express meaning even deeper, and perhaps more interesting, than his or her conscious intents?" Or deconstruction might ask, "Might the author have been expressing broader cultural ideas or emotions or conflicts that he or she wasn't even aware of and that therefore lie deeper than conscious intent and are an essential dimension of meaning of the text?"

Traditional interpretation generally assumes a logical structure and deep coherence of texts; in other words, the author meant to say something sensible and did so in a coherent way. Deconstruction looks for points of inherent tension, contradiction, and incoherence. It doesn't see these features as flaws or failures in the text, but rather as interesting elements that are essential to the meaning of the text. Perhaps because it believes that reality itself is mysterious and it defies comprehension, and perhaps because it fears that simplistic systems may obscure truth rather than clarify it, deconstruction seems to treasure these inherent tensions and incoherences as sparks of genius and insight.

Moreover, traditional interpretation has worked within the larger modern worldview in which language is believed to correspond quite strongly and neatly with reality. In this view, our words correspond to things in reality outside of our minds in a simple, commonsense way. With this confidence, as modern scholars work with words, they believe they are working with reality.

Deconstruction sees this confidence as naive. Deconstructionists believe that scholars (including deconstructionists!) participate in communities that speak to one another in words that refer to other words, which in turn refer to other words, and so on ... and that the connections to reality outside the discourse of the community are not obvious, straightforward, or clear. The fabrics or patterns of words that communities use tacitly, without even being aware of them, are commonly called worldviews or theories; these are the "constructs" that deconstructionists are trying to dismantle so that (a) the assumed theories themselves can be surfaced, seen, and evaluated, and (b) the information contained in those theories can be seen afresh from outside the theoretical matrix in which it had been embedded.

In other words, deconstructionists tend to see communities as being removed from reality "out there" through many, many layers of translucent (or perhaps even opaque) veils of interwoven words, while traditional modern interpreters tend to see words as one very thin and transparent layer between the scholarly community and reality.

Traditional modern interpretation, then, is fond of finding the one "true" meaning in a text, while deconstructionists do not give any one reading privileged status, but rather are interested in hearing the interplay of many interpretations that arise from within many different interpretive communities. This interplay increases the possibility for new and deeper understandings, deconstructionists believe, since the perspectives of many communities are brought to the table. (See **Simultaneity.**)

Traditional interpreters may see this deconstructive approach as a dangerous and destructive abandonment of truth as a goal or pursuit, and sometimes their critique appears valid. But many deconstructionists might respond to this critique by saying something like this: "Our acknowledgment of the complex relationship between reality, language, and communities that use language in certain ways is itself a pursuit of truth. We haven't given up on truth, but we have come to believe that truth is a lot harder to find than our traditional colleagues seem to acknowledge. We have become aware of how easily communities of interpretation can create a bubble where they are certain they are in touch with reality, but to those on the outside, it doesn't look that way at all. (Think of the Taliban, white supremacists, the Flat Earth Society, for example.) We are trying to avoid becoming such a self-deluded community."

The implications of deconstruction are staggering for Christians doing ministry in the emerging culture. For example, every time preachers or authors seek to interpret Scripture, they make it clear by their assumptions and method which interpretive community they belong to. By driving for "the one true interpretation," for example, they disenfranchise postmodern readers for whom deconstruction is as much the mother tongue as traditional interpretation is for modern people. Will modern Christian leaders demand that deconstructionist hearers "convert" to their traditional mode of interpretation? Is such a demand an act of faithfulness to Scripture and our Christian tradition, or is it merely faithfulness to modernity?

When modern Protestants feel afraid of opening the door to this new approach to interpretation, when they feel that deconstruction is the first step on a slippery slide to nihilism and chaos, then at that moment modern Protestants probably understand how medieval Catholics felt 500 years ago when the Reformers argued for a then-new approach to biblical interpretation.

While deconstruction feels to moderns like chaos and nihilism, it feels to postmoderns like honesty and liberation. While moderns feel deconstruction yields readings that are unclear, slippery, unserious, and unscientific, postmoderns feel that deconstructive readings are meaningful, interesting, playful, rich, honest, rewarding, and inclusive.

Learning to understand and respect deconstruction may be the hardest challenge of all for modern Christian leaders, and this may be the most difficult entry in this primer. Readers will probably learn more about deconstruction through a single thoughtful viewing of the movies *The Matrix* and *The Truman Show* than through re-reading this entry a hundred times.

D is for Dedicated Server

If you can't think of yourself as a "minister," this is what you are: a dedicated server. Don't let the world steal our best lines. "Even God can't work when the servers are down."

All disciples of Jesus are ordained to dedicated service. The church has no volunteers, only ministers and dedicated servers. In a success-oriented culture, the church incarnates a server-oriented culture. Christian greatness comes through service.

Asked what he did for a living, one man routinely said: "I'm an ordained plumber."

What do you do? Whatever it is, you are an ordained minister in that area. You're an ordained chef. An ordained contractor. An ordained teacher. An ordained doctor. The *www.Ginghamsburg.org* website has an Olan Mills–type church directory with pictures of members and "day job" and "real job" entries—*both of which* are bonafide aspects of serving God and neighbor:

John Doe: Day Job—Dentist
Real Job—4th Grade Sunday School Teacher

> Writing is a sacred calling—but so are gardening, dentistry, and plumbing—so don't put on airs.
>
> —WRITER/RADIO PERFORMER GARRISON KEILLOR[1]

1. As quoted in Katherine Kurs, "Voices of a New America," *Spirituality and Health* (Spring 2001), 30.

In the modern world only those things that could be measured were deemed worthy and successful. In the postmodern world there is a growing awareness that the deepest and most successful things in life can't be measured. The purpose of life is not to measure. The purpose of life is to matter.

What multiplies your "mattering" is the biblical principle of "service" to "others"—treating everyone as a subject (i.e., putting "others" first), and treating what you do as a resource for them. This focus on mobilizing people for service and mission is more than an ecclesial parallel to literary theorists like Roland Barthes, who, way back in the 1960s, concentrated on the position of the reader rather than the author in relation to the work. Lay mobilization is a biblical and theological issue. The church of the future will be led, not by top-down visionaries, but by lay-led missionaries.[2] If a pastor must lead the charge, then leadership has degenerated from a process to a person.

This new concept of ordination means that in the emerging culture, your pastor isn't the only ordained one. Rather, he or she is the one who trains you to faithfully and fruitfully do your ordained work of dedicated service in the world into which you have been sent.[3] In fact, the paradigm of "church growth" rather than "dedicated service" may itself be another expression of the church being held hostage to a modern mentality.[4]

"Clergy" who have been cursed by modernity's "lay/clergy" distinctions will be threatened by this shift in roles. They will see elevating the laity to ordained status as a demotion for themselves. Wiser dedicated servers will realize that by giving up ownership of ministry they are actually being promoted—promoted to the

2. Loren Mead, *Once and Future Church: Reinventing the Congregation for a New Mission Frontier* (Washington, DC: Alban Institute, 1991); Leonard Sweet, *11 Genetic Gateways to Spiritual Awakening* (Nashville: Abingdon, 1998).

3. For more on "servant evangelism," see Steve Sjogren, *101 Ways to Reach Your Community* (Colorado Springs: NavPress, 2001).

4. This is the argument of Mark A. Olson, *Moving Beyond Church Growth: An Alternative Vision for Congregations* (Minneapolis: Augsburg Fortress, 2001).

level of seminary presidents and bishops, training ordained dedicated servers for vital ministry not only in the church, but everywhere they go.

By the way, try to find an account in the New Testament where one pastor leads a congregation.

D is for De-Words

Success in the modern world went to those who mastered the centripetal forces—those who could push power towards the center, the via media, the mass, those who could garner control and harness authority.

Success in the emerging culture goes to those who master the centrifugal forces—those who can push power from the center toward the edge, the marginal, the borders; those who can disperse control and distribute authority. The most powerful centrifugal force at work today? The Internet, especially P2P (Peer to Peer) sharing.[5]

The modern era was structured around "re" words. The doors of the postmodern era are being opened up to new experiences and expressions by "de" words. The prefix "de" signifies the push to regionalized and localized autonomy. Three of the biggest "de" words for postmodern ministry are devolution, decentralization, and deconstruction.

1. *The Devolution Revolution*: Authority structures are devolving to relationship structures—the pyramid ("stovepipes," "silos," "chimneys") has become a pancake.[6] Hierarchical "multistory" bureaucracies are being flattened into "single-story" networks: from hierarchy to lowerarchy. The paper-based world

5. Check out *www.groove.net*. Accessed 17 May 2002.

6. For an excellent look at a functional rather than hierarchical structure, based on shared authority, team strategies, and stewardship as a management model, see Peter Block, *Stewardship: Choosing Service over Self-Interest* (San Francisco: Berrett-Koehler, 1993).

of modernity created an infrastructure that is now increasingly obsolete in an electronic world. Standard modern authority relationships, power relationships, and leadership relationships are all giving way. The clergy-dominated church is an expression of hierarchical, elitist patterns inherited from the Enlightenment and before.[7] To say that the Enlightenment project is dead is also to say that many things it has taught us about organizations need to be buried.

The devolution revolution has led to the disintermediation of all professionals: "amateurs" become "experts" through self-education and expect a partnership with professionals as well as a synthesis of "guilded" and self-guided learning. Some 3000 educational institutions are now offering Web classes.

Does this mean that there will be no clergy in the future, or that all pastors should take secular jobs and do ministry as unpaid "amateurs"? This kind of either/or thinking is dangerously unhelpful (although "amateur"—meaning someone who works for *amar* [love], not just money—is a word that should describe even the highest-paid pastor, no doubt). The point isn't to replace one mandated structure with another, but rather to realize that structures need to be created, adapted, outgrown, replaced, and reinvented as needed. And the point isn't to replace hierarchical leadership with no leadership or weak leadership or underpaid leadership or disrespected leadership. (Hierarchy may be bad, but is anarchy any better?) The point is to develop leaders who equip other leaders who equip others and so on, so that ministry happens and God's will is done on earth as it is in heaven.

7. Of course, when some feminist critics of the Enlightenment describe Newton's *Principia* as a "rape manual," and others object to science as an "assault upon women" because of its "vertical" and "phallocentric" thinking, it is almost enough to make one defend the old scientific method. For other such stories, see Gertrude Himmelfarb's review, "A Sentimental Priesthood—*Who Stole Feminism? How Women Have Betrayed Women* by Christine Hoff Sommers," *TLS: Times Literary Supplement* (11 November 1994), 20. Sommers's book is published by Simon & Schuster, 1994.

2. *Decentralization*: In the Babel story we see God's response to human attempts at centralization.

The modern world created bell-shaped middles with cathedral centers. In the postmodern souffle, all middles are sagging. What economist F. A. Hayek predicted is coming true: the unraveling of centralized structures in classic barbell fashion—a mitosis of all middles and a build-up of the extremes. Hayek was one of the first to see that centralized planning institutions are flawed because they presuppose on the part of the planners knowledge that is unavailable to them because it is dispersed throughout society, often in practical and local forms.[8]

With decentralized transactions, however, comes the necessity of hypercentralized activities. De- and hypercentralization are opposite sides of a coin. The more our secondary relationships get decentralized, the more highly centralized become our primary relationships. The demonstrators against the World Trade Organization in Seattle in 2000 called for greater local autonomy (decentralization) while demanding universal standards (hypercentralization).

Denominations face another de-word in this regard: demotion. Rather than ruling as centralized planning and regulatory institutions, denominations may only survive by descending to a lower place, becoming servants and encouragers of local vision. Rather than stepping in to impose control and mandate plans, they will need to step down to exercise Christlike servant-leadership, washing the feet of local pastors, encouraging them, resourcing them, serving them. Ironically, of course, denominational structures may in this way find that the way down ultimately leads up to a better future.

8. See, for example, Hayek's 1976 lecture to the Canberra Branch of the Economic Society of Australia and New Zealand, "Socialism and Science," in *The Essence of Hayek*, ed. Chiaki Nishiyana and Kurt R. Leube (Stanford, CA: Hoover Institution Press, 1984), 115–27.

> There are more than 22,000 denominations in the world. How lucky you are that you happen to be in the one that is right!
>
> —Argentinian evangelist Juan Carlos Ortiz[9]

3. *Deconstruction*: Another way of talking about what medievals called the *via negativa*[10]—the negative way of knowing—in contrast to the *via positiva*. This medieval distinction offers another reminder that postmoderns must learn from premoderns.

Deconstruction is disassembling anything that has acquired a pat and patent set of meanings for the purpose of reassembling in new ways. It means allowing the interpretation of a familiar text, image, or experience to unravel and become unstable so that new insights and old revelations can be found and reclaimed.[11] To get free of molds, we need indirection and detours. (See **Deconstruction.**)

Existing Christian leaders face devolutions, decentralizations, and deconstructions so great that many will choose to stay on their side of the divide and leave postmodern ministry to their children or grandchildren. And their children or grandchildren may sorely disappoint them, because although they will love Jesus no less, they will probably love the denominations and other structures they inherit much less.

What would your denomination or local church look like if it were devolved, decentralized, and deconstructed by your children or grandchildren? Your children and grandchildren will either show you, or leave your structures (if they're courageous enough).

9. As quoted in Wolfgang Simson, *Houses That Change the World: The Return of the House Churches* (Waynesboro, GA: OM Publishing, 2001), 10.

10. Ilse Nina Bulhof and Laurens ten Kate, eds., *Flight of the Gods: Philosophical Perspectives on Negative Theology* (New York: Fordham University Press, 2000).

11. See David W. Odell-Scott, "Deconstruction," in A. K. M. Adam, ed., *Handbook of Postmodern Biblical Interpretation* (St. Louis: Chalice Press, 2000), 55–61.

D is for Disabled

● Those who, from Stephen Hawking (who has amyotrophic lateral sclerosis, or "Lou Gehrig's disease") to Stevie Wonder (who is blind), can produce our greatest artistic and intellectual achievements.[12]

The share of people with disabilities is 23% among 45–54-year-olds and 37% among people aged 55 to 59. After 59, the proportion of the population just with "severe disabilities" is 25%. Those figures suggest that if you don't consider yourself disabled now, just wait a few years.

Some who are most "disabled" at technological and intellectual achievements are often most enabled at human and spiritual achievements (like love, joy, peace, temperance, mercy, hope, and trust).

● Another word for the "human condition." Another word for where God wants to do God's greatest work in your life. If you know your spiritual gifts, you know where you are strongest naturally and will make your easiest contributions. If you know your spiritual weaknesses and disabilities, you know where you can be strongest supernaturally and where God's power and strength will be made most known. In the shadow of our weakness is our strength, and in the shadow of our strength is our weakness. Or in other words, disciples of Jesus are strongest in the broken places.[13]

Postmodern Christians must start from the premise that we are all disabled in one form or another. In fact, the term *disabled* itself reinforces the oppressive modern idea that to depart from

12. Stephen Hawking, who was stricken with ALS while in graduate school in 1962, became a teaching fellow at Cambridge University's Gonville and Caius College—which historically had not admitted handicapped students—now writes and communicates using a head- or eye-movement-operated computer program that allows him to compose 15 words a minute.

13. See Leonard Sweet, *Strong in the Broken Places: A Theological Reverie on the Ministry of George Everett Ross* (Akron: University of Akron Press, 1995).

"normal ability" is to let us all down by failing to conform to what Phyllis McGinley, in her poem "In Praise of Diversity," calls "some imagined norm."[14]

EPICtivity D: Disabled

Rent or borrow a wheelchair (or two), and as a team, with one or more of your team members taking the role of a wheelchair-bound person, attend a public event together—a baseball game, an amusement park, an art gallery, a shopping mall, a concert, or a pastors' conference.

After the event, reflect on the experience. Ask the disabled person to share what the experience made him or her feel, think, experience, and realize. Have the friends of the disabled person similarly share. Then discuss the following:

- How does our ministry treat people with disabilities? Which disabilities do we accommodate, and which do we reject?
- In what ways does each member feel "subnormal," and in that way, compared with other team members, how does each member feel disabled in some way?
- What spiritual and team advantages could flow from these disabilities?

D is for Disciplines

● Habits that become habitations of the Spirit. Postmoderns often prefer the language of "spiritual practices" (prayer, fasting, Bible study) to "disciplines."

---

14. See Phyllis McGinley, "In Praise of Diversity," in *The Love Letters of Phyllis McGinley* (New York: Viking, 1954), 14.

Whatever the terminology, the emphasis is on Christianity as a way of life rather than merely an intellectual belief system.[15] (See **Be-living; [The] Way.**) Thirty minutes of aerobic exercises three times a week are essential for a healthy life. When done religiously—come hail, come sleet, come high water—exercise gets you one more year of life. Spiritual practices add life to all your years, and beyond.

Practice makes perfect. (See **Holiness.**)

> Indeed, the most interesting conversations—about religion or anything else—take place among people who disagree and, while trying to understand their disagreements and learn from one another, are willing to defend their own points of view.
>
> —WILLIAM PLACHER[16]

D is for Discourse

● Conversation—what we should count instead of conversions, because if we seek to "get" conversions, we won't, but if we simply engage in respectful discourse and gentle, caring spiritual conversations, conversions will naturally result.

● What replaces modern debates, arguments, and theologies. The forum replaces the classroom. Just look at the phenomenal growth of talk radio in the past 15 years.[17]

For the Christian, the main conversation partner is Scripture, but also seated at the table are various communities

15. For an attempt at a Christian "world-life," not just a "world-view," see Leonard Sweet, *SoulSalsa: 17 Surprising Steps for Godly Living in the 21st Century* (Grand Rapids: Zondervan, 2000). For a spirituality of technology, see William John Fitzgerald, *Blessings for the Fast Paced and Cyberspaced: Parables, Reflections, and Prayers* (Leavenworth, KS: Forest of Peace, 2000).

16. William Placher, *Unapologetic Theology: A Christian Voice in a Pluralistic Conversation* (Louisville: Westminster John Knox, 1989), 144.

17. In the first half-decade of the 1990s, talk radio stations went from 308 to 1,028.

of interpretation, most authoritatively the full-faith community of the past 2000 years. Of course, seated at the head of the table is the still-alive Christ, who is always up to new things. (Other religions are our conversation partners, too, of course.)

Postmoderns don't know what they think until they hear themselves say it in discourse. Thinking is a group process, and truth emerges from the give-and-take of dialogue and discussion with input from as many angles as possible. You can't quote what one of them says in a conversation and get away with it because the entire conversation is the quote.

Moderns and postmoderns need to become "conversant" with each other and "conversational" toward each other's discourse. Much of the conversation between the two has orbited in an abstract stratosphere. (Watch the television forum program *Crossfire* for an example of moderns not talking *to* one another but *at* one another.) When "moderns" have a conversation, the Miranda rule applies: Whatever you say can and will be used against you. When postmoderns discourse, every participant is given blanket immunity.

The need for discourse to become "poly-lingual" culturally, musically, theologically, and traditionally applies more to moderns than postmoderns. Why?

1. Because postmoderns are already well schooled in poly-lingual discourse. It is an ingrained habit of their mental habitat.
2. Because the role and rule of authority has been altered. Children are now teaching parents.[18] Adults don't have all the answers anymore. Parent-child relationships are being redrawn around conversation and dialogue rather than authority and obedience.

18. Douglas Rushkoff, *Playing the Future: How Kid Culture Can Teach Us to Thrive in an Age of Chaos* (New York: HarperCollins, 1996).

For the first time in history, kids have the skills that adults
need to run the world.
—QUEENSLAND-BASED EDUCATION EXPERT DALE SPENDER[19]

Jesus told it straight: Learn from a child (Mark 10:13–16).

It is amazing how the doctrinal debates of the 16th and 17th centuries, although recondite and often repellent in tone to us, were part of the everyday conversation and currency of common people who had no formal education. Theology was not the preserve of the elite, but the bread and butter of the people. Contrast that with today's disciples who grew up in a church culture where theological education was largely lost in the local church from 1960 to 1990.

An alert for pastors, teachers, youth group leaders, evangelizers, neighbors, and others engaged in postmodern ministry: How many conversations have you had this week? Is your church helping every member to become a conversant theologian? Is your common discourse "common" (literally "shared by all")? What forums and open discussions are you sponsoring?

D is for Double Ring

The emerging culture turns everything it touches into something else—its very opposite. But these are not dichotomous realities or duplicitous realities; they are duplicate realities. Contrary things now happen at the same time that aren't contrary. In fact, polarity means attraction. When you aim for both margins at once, you get something interesting.

19. Quoted by Diana Bagnall in "Born to Be Wired," *The Bulletin* Sydney, NSW, Australia. (15 August 2000), 25.

Danny Hillis designed the fastest computer in the world ("Connection Machine"). Danny Hillis also designed the slowest computer in the world ("10,000-Year Clock"). Postmoderns always ring twice.

> I have no belief
> But I believe
> I'm a walking contradiction
>
> —FROM GREEN DAY'S "WALKING CONTRADICTION"[20]

All incarnational ministry embodies this double ring: this mutual exchange between the gospel and the culture, the Word and the world.[22]

> I'm a total mystic and a total rationalist. I'm a complete truth nut yet embrace confusion. I'm radical but totally balanced. I'm humbly human and boldly spiritual. I'm a Jesus person but hate Christianity.
>
> —EMAIL FROM POSTMODERN LEADER TONY BRIGSTOCK[21]

● Another way of talking about modernity's either-or culture having given way to a "both-and" culture and increasingly an "and-also" culture. We agree with Richard Nesbitt ("high-tech/high-touch") and Robert Nozick: The more time we spend in virtual worlds, the more thirst we will have for reality. In

20. "Walking Contradiction," Green Day, *Insomniac, www.angelfire.com/biz3/foo/lyrics/insomniac.html.* Accessed 3 May 2001.

21. For more on what Brigstock is up to, check out *www.christiancitychurch.com; www.globaltribe.com; www.christiancitychurch.org.*

22. In his *Transforming Mission: Paradigm Shifts in Theology of Mission* (Maryknoll, NY: Orbis Books 1991), 454, David G. Bosch writes, "Inculturation suggests a *double movement*: there is at once inculturation of Christianity and Christianization of culture. The gospel must remain Good News while becoming, up to a certain point, a cultural phenomenon." The other great missions text of the last half of the twentieth century is Andrew Walls', *The Missionary Movement in Christian History: Studies in the Transmission of Faith* (Maryknoll, NY: Orbis, 1996).

Nozick's words, "We refuse to see ourselves as merely buckets to be filled with happy experiences."[23]

Symbols of the double ring? Mobius Strips, Klein bottles, and the Interrobang (which combines the question mark and the exclamation point).

> Don't blame me. I voted for BOTH of them.
>
> —FLORIDA BUMPER STICKER AFTER 2000 PRESIDENTIAL ELECTION

Jesus' birth, life, death, and resurrection resounded in double rings. Jesus was born poor, as close to the earth and animals as he could get, with simple shepherds all around, yet he was attended by angels and visited by wise men bearing royal gifts. Jesus taught a double-ring theology and both-and discipleship ("Give to Caesar what is Caesar's, and to God what is God's"; "be wise as serpents and innocent as doves," etc.). The greatest double-ring document ever delivered was the Sermon on the Mount, especially the Beatitudes. Jesus' concept of heaven elaborated the Hebrew concept of heaven, which is based on a double ring.[24] The greatest symbol of this double-ring union of opposites? The cross, which bridges heaven and earth and centers the square and the circle.

Orthodoxy is paradoxy. One/Three; Transcendent/Immanent; Human/Divine; Saint/Sinner; Revealed/Hidden; Ascension/Presence. (See **Paradox.**) Jesus' death was present in his birth—the

---

23. Richard De Grandpre doesn't subscribe to the double-ring concept. He predicts that all we will be left with is "a dead world exhausted of nature and one all-too-soon-real real virtual machine." See Richard De Grandpre, *Digitopia: The Look of the New Digital You* (New York: Random House, 2001), 4; also at *www.AtRandom.com*.

24. The word *heaven* in Hebrew is the meshing of fire and water; *shamayim* is Hebrew for heaven. The *Midrash Rabba* for Genesis tells us that *shamayim* is composed of *esh* (fire) and *mayim* (water). "R. Abba b. Kahana said in Rab's name: The Holy One, blessed be He, took fire and water and beat them together, and from them heaven was made." *Genesis*, trans. Rabbi H. Freedman, 3d ed., vol. 1 of *Midrash Rabba*, trans. and ed. H. Freedman and Maurice Simon (New York: Soncino Press, 1983), 32.

cloths that swaddled him in birth imaged those that would swathe him in death. Jesus left physically so that he could be intimate with all of us spiritually.

Biblical truth is found in getting both extremes to kiss each other (Ps. 85:10). Or in the words of Ecclesiastes 7:18: "It is good to grasp the one and not let go of the other. The man who fears God will follow them both."[25]

The ultimate in both/and, however, is *both* Both/And and Either/Or. Here are some Either/Or's.

> "Choose you this day whom you will serve..."
> Choose God or Mammon.
> Choose life or death.
> Choose heaven or hell.

> You are the most hidden from us and yet the most present amongst us.
>
> —AUGUSTINE OF HIPPO[26]

25. The final phrase is an alternative reading of the phrase "avoid all extremes," as noted in the NIV margin.

26. Paraphrase of Augustine, *Confessions*, bk. 1, pt. 4. See Augustine, *The Confessions*, ed. John E. Rotelle, trans. Maria Boulding (Hyde Park, NY: New City Press, 1997), 41.

E is for e=mc³

The formula that opens many mysteries of the universe, according to Albert Einstein, is $e=mc^2$. E equals energy. M equals mass. C squared is the constant—in this case, the speed of light. When the constant is present, energy and mass (spirit and matter) become different ways of talking about the same thing.

The formula that opens many mysteries of the spiritual universe is $e=mc^3$ E equals the energy of a spiritual awakening.[1] M equals the mass density of knowledge about the Word and world that has become wisdom. C cubed is the constant of the J-Factor (see **J-*Factor***), which is raised to three dimensions: the depth of trusting faith, the height of connectivity, and the breadth of mission. Every spiritual awakening in Christian history has been the deployment of this spiritual formula.

The church's ministry needs more brain, more backbone, and more muscle and nerve energy.

E is for Economics

The rule of economics has replaced the rule of politics as our primary power paradigm.

In premodern times, religious levers controlled the mechanisms of power. Lord Acton's famous remark about "absolute power"[2] was written, not about politicians, but about Reformation popes.

In the modern world, political levers were the fulcrums that ruled the world. This is how far politics has sunk. None of the

---

1. For more on this formula, see chapter 10, "The Fast Learning/Unlearning Gene" in Leonard Sweet, *11 Genetic Gateways to Spiritual Awakening* (Nashville: Abingdon, 1998), 42–54.

2. "Power tends to corrupt and absolute power corrupts absolutely" (letter to Bishop Mandell Creighton, 3 April 1887).

Big Three television networks still had a correspondent based in Paris when Princess Diana died there. The "foreign correspondents" contingent has shrunk, but the number of economics correspondents has risen to an all-time high.

In this postmodern world governed by economics, being a consumer is now more primary than being a citizen (at least in Western societies). Instead of looking for political "saviors," we are looking for economic saviors, a variety of which have come and gone in the last twenty years alone: the Japanese TQM, the European social model, the Asian miracle, the Internet. The latest "savior," the American Way, is now turning round the bend and going out of sight.

> The business enterprise is now the major actor on the world stage and the global marketplace is a key driver of the U.S. economy. With the end of the Cold War, we have witnessed the shift from superpowers to supermarkets. The initiative today comes more from companies than from capitals. In effect, the new Commanding Generals are companies such as General Electric, General Motors, General Mills and General Dynamics.
> —MURRAY WEIDENBAUM[3]
> MALLINCKDRODT DISTINGUISHED UNIVERSITY PROFESSOR, WASHINGTON UNIVERSITY

If current predictions prove accurate, by the year 2025 the world's cities will accommodate 60% of its population.[4] Postmoderns will have moved, not just to cities, but to posturban city-states, a new global, poly-centered political metroplex built on economics that work. The expanding role of corporations in

3. Murray Weidenbaum, "A Key Driver for the U.S. Economy: Global Economy: Superpowers to Supermarkets," *Vital Speeches of the Day* 1 (June 1999), 506.
4. See the "Agenda 21" document that emerged from the Rio de Janiero environmental summit sponsored by the United Nations Conference on Environment and Development (UNCED) in 1992.

our lives is the lesser story. The big story is the way economic entities such as corporations are replacing nation-states as the primary political entities. Global units are emerging that are economic, not political.

It is time for the church to emerge from the economic stone age and to start thinking of itself as a global economic entity. Even those few Marxists left are admitting that market institutions are inevitable. But who defines the varieties and forms of those market institutions? Will the limits of market functions be constrained to protect communities and individuals?[5]

It is also time for the church to ask its members some probing economic identity questions: Are you consumers? Are you citizens? Are you Christians?

If you are the first, your economics revolves around the question, Is this the best deal for me? If you are the second, your economics revolves around the question, Is this best for the nation? If you are the third, your economics revolves around a very different question, Is Christ calling me to do this?

E is for Emergence

● An approach to science that is sensitive to the ways a whole can become more than the sum of its parts. For example, an ant colony possesses and passes on knowledge that no individual ant could possess. Beehives, slime mold colonies, and human cities do the same.[6]

There are six functions to self-organizing systems:

1. Self-propagation
2. Self-nourishment

5. Two recent titles published in Routledge's Radical Orthodoxy Series seek to address this issue: D. Stephen Long, *Divine Economy: Theology and the Market* (London: Routledge, 2000); ibid., *Theology and Economics: Values, Protests, Virtues* (London: Routledge, 2000).

6. John H. Holland, *Emergence: From Chaos to Order* (Reading, MA: Addison-Wesley, 1998).

3. Self-education
4. Self-governance
5. Self-healing
6. Self-fulfilling

When "perturbations" take place, the self-organizing system is shaken up and begins to reshuffle the deck. New connections are made and new holons (see **Holarchy**) emerge. But this can only happen when the sharing of information within the system is maximized. Open information generates positive energy.

Emergence has two key components:

1. "We make it up as we go along." (This was true all along in the modern world, but kept secret.)
2. "The whole is greater than the sum of its parts."[7]

In the same way that water is very different from the gases of oxygen and hydrogen of which is composed, so systems have emergent characteristics and properties different from their components.[8] The Internet and the Web are emergent entities.[9] So is the church as the Body of Christ.

● One postmodern way of explaining how humans behave in altruistic and self-sacrificing ways that make no "evolutionary" sense: Love and virtue *emerge* from the chaos of selfish competition and the vicious struggle for survival.

● A postmodern way out of the science versus Scripture, creation versus evolution ("evil-ution") wars. Emergence theory incorporates into an intellectual and spiritual framework ancient and

7. For the sensitivity of some scientists to the power of emergence to point us to God, see Gary Lachman's addendum to this statement: "The whole may be greater than its parts, but it, and its parts, are made of the same material. As the physicist Murray Gell-Mann said, 'We don't need something else in order to get something else'" (Gary Lachman, "Edging Out of Chaos," *TLS: Times Literary Supplement* [12 March 1999], 27).

8. Tony Gill, *About Systems Thinking* (London: Verso/Phronesis, 2001), 1. See *www.phrontis.com/systhink.htm.* Accessed 14 July 2001.

9. Jennifer Cobb, *Cybergrace: The Search for God in the Digital World* (New York: Crown, 1998), 86.

recent arguments of intelligent design (focusing on diversity and complexity) with certain aspects of evolution (natural selection and the fossil record).[10] In this view, part of the goodness of Creation is an inherent potential to generate new possibilities so that more and more goodness can emerge.

Emergence is a faith-friendly view of the world that dethrones reductionist thinkers the modern world adjectivalized: Freudian, Darwinian, Marxist.

E is for Entropy

Entropy rhymes with *atrophy* and means about the same thing.

All organic systems run down without new sources of energy and new supplies of life, according to the second law of thermodynamics. Creation is either being spurred forward into new forms and vitality or slipping back into formlessness and randomness. Creation returns to chaos without fresh breaths of life. If you don't wash your body, it will decay and deteriorate. If you don't brush your teeth, they will fall out. If anything is not re-energized and re-breathed—including the church—it will die.

Inertia: The "hold-on-till-(Jesus/retirement/whatever)-comes" mentality. Another name for lack of faith. The difference between inertia and homeostasis: Inertia is stagnation and safety; homeostasis is gestation and balance.

10. For more on Intelligent Design, see *Science and Evidence for Design in the Universe: Papers Presented at a Conference Sponsored by the Wethersfield Insistute, New York City, September 25, 1999*, ed. Michael J. Behe, William A. Dembski, and Stephen C. Meyer (San Francisco: Ignatius, 2000); William A. Dembski, *The Design Inference: Eliminating Chance through Small Probabilities* (New York: Cambridge University Press, 1998); ibid., *Intelligent Design: The Bridge between Science and Theology* (Downers Grove, IL: InterVarsity Press, 1999); Michael Behe, *Darwin's Black Box* (New York: Free Press, 1996). For evolutionary theorists and their opposition to ID see Kenneth R. Miller, *Finding Darwin's God: A Scientist's Search for Common Ground between God and Evolution* (New York: Cliff Street Books, 2000); Richard Dawkins, *Unweaving the Rainbow: Science, Delusion, and the Appetite for Wonder* (Boston: Houghton Mifflin, 1998); Ernst Mayr and William B. Provine, ed., *The Evolutionary Synthesis: Perspectives on the Unification of Biology* (Cambridge, MA: Harvard University Press, 1998).

Acedia: Shorthand for absence of newness and lack of energy to start afresh and be open to change.

> I'm all for progress. It's change I don't like.
> —MARK TWAIN

COD: Shorthand for "Change or Die." One medical definition of death is a body that does not regenerate. A body not constantly regenerating life and taking fresh breaths is a dead body.

Church: Too often, the equivalent of hospices—safe places for the dying—and presided over by private chaplains or "clan priests" overwhelmed by their own ennui, effete bureaucratic rituals, and entropy.

Christian leaders need to ask several important questions about themselves and the organizations they lead: What overcomes entropy? What renews us? What re-energizes us? What drains us? What makes us feel like giving up?

Many dutiful Christian leaders become unintentionally suicidal in terms of ministry. They slog away at the draining, depressing, defeating tasks day after day, postponing the renewing, reenergizing, reinvigorating activities as extravagant luxuries that they don't deserve or can't afford. The reverse is actually true: They can't afford *not* to recharge. They act as if Sabbath and feasts and singing and celebration were the devil's idea rather than God's command.

While God may call you to martyrdom, God is not inspiring you to ministry suicide. Wise leaders intercept entropy as early as possible and take remedial action quickly. And that remedial action—whether it be throwing a party or hosting a feast or declaring a rest period or giving out awards or scheduling a sabbatical or suspending draining committees or canceling needless meetings—will probably feel a lot like fun.

Don't feel guilty. Fun trumps entropy.

E is for EPICtivities

Turn every activity into an EPICtivity.[11]

(See **Experiential; Participatory; Image-Rich; Connectivity.**)

If you would like to bring others in on the kind of thinking stimulated by this book, here are some EPIC activities for you to try. How about . . .

- Using an EPICtivity to begin each of your leadership team meetings for the next year?
- Developing a retreat around some of these EPIC-tivities?
- Using an EPICtivity at your small group meeting?
- Inviting a group of pastors to try some EPICtivities together?

Remember: The surprise factor (see **Abductive Method**) is essential for these EPICtivities to be successful. Please don't explain anything about the purpose of the activity before leading people into it. Don't even give the EPICtivity a name. Build suspense, and trust that all the clarity that is needed will emerge as the EPICtivity progresses. If you make a mistake, make it in the direction of giving *too little* explanation.

These are only starters. After you have some experience, you will start getting ideas for EPICtivities of your own. That's when the fun really begins.

EPICtivity E: EPICtivities

1. Visit the following websites and evaluate them, according to the following criteria:

- How did you experience the site? How many of your

---

11. This concept is developed in Leonard Sweet, *Postmodern Pilgrims: First-Century Passion for the 21st-Century World* (Nashville: Broadman & Holman, 2000).

senses did the site involve? Would you like to repeat the experience?

- How could you participate in the website? Did it invite your participation?
- What images did the site employ? What do those images communicate to you? Can you imagine other images that could have been used?
- Viewing websites is normally an isolated, individual experience. How could these websites be used to draw you into community? Could you interact with those who are behind the site, or with others who visit the site?

    www.ginghamsburg.org
    www.geocities.com/gacbloomington/
    www.ststephen-stow.com
    www.holycrossnj.org
    www.vurch.com
    www.wuzzupGod.com
    www.emergentvillage.com
    www.leonardsweet.com

2. P is for participatory! Watch a portion of *Who Wants to Be a Millionaire* or a similar television game show. Also borrow a set of Pokemon cards from a child, and ask the child to explain the whole world of Pokemon.

- During their peak, what do you think made these two forms of entertainment successful?
- What makes Pokemon cards different from other collectible cards?
- What generation is the game show reaching?
- How can you make your ministry more multi-generational?
- How can you make your ministry more participatory like Pokemon cards and *Who Wants to Be a Millionaire*?

3. I is for Image! Go to five or six restaurants and collect (or borrow) menus from each. Also ask for kids' menus if available. Compare all the menus.

- Which menus are easiest to use?
- Which menus are the most difficult to select from?
- What suggestions would you offer these companies regarding the way they lay out their menus?
- In your area of ministry, what can you *picture* instead of *say*?
- Brainstorm images for your small-group, children's and youth ministries, and vision statement.
- What can your organization learn from restaurant menus?

E is for Eschaton

● The end of entropy.

In the postmodern matrix there is a good chance that the world will reverse its chronological polarity for us. Instead of being bound to the past by chains of cause and effect, we will feel ourselves being pulled into the future by the magnet of God's will, God's dream, God's desire. This magnetic "future-natural" orientation differs wildly from the mechanistic modern view of the world set in motion by a Prime Mover who made and wound up the clock long ago and ever since has let it unwind naturally, occasionally intervening with a small correction.

This new vision sees the universe as only partially created, an unfinished symphony, a masterpiece in progress. In this eschatology we are invited to be part of God's creative team working to see God's dream for the universe come true (in other words, working to see God's will be done on earth as in heaven). In this way our relationship with God is more than interactive; it is collaborative. It is more than just a matter of God interacting with us; it is a matter of God inviting us to be creative partners (subcontractors, if you will) in the construction of a world as it could be from the world as it is so far.

In the new eschatology, modern charts, bizarre predictions (a tired and tiring game for anyone who knows church history), and apocalyptic novels pretending to something more than purely fictional status will be *left behind.* (See **Hope.**)

As people who are being pulled toward an "all-things-new" world to come, we bear the fresh scent of the approaching spring, not the stale cologne of the fading winter.

E is for Evangelism

Best-Case Scenario: Inviting others into a relationship with God, so that the Holy Spirit can make Christ come alive and live in them, so that they can live in God's fullness and providence, so that they can participate in God's missional community, so that God's will can increasingly be done on earth as it is in heaven.

Worst-Case Scenario: Forcing unwilling Christians to force their beliefs on unwilling people for the sake of the church, because it needs more seats filled; teaching people to communicate an authentic message of the Good News in forced and artificial ways.

Evangelism is the modern term for the middle part of the disciple-making process, which occurs between what was formerly (in modernity) called pre-evangelism and what was formerly called "follow-up" or discipleship.

The onramps to outreach have changed. Whereas come-to-church evangelism was effective in the modern world in getting people to come to Christ, in the postmodern world come-to-Christ evangelism is what gets people to come to church. Modern churches built ministries and devised strategies to draw people in. Postmodern churches design ministries to release the Spirit inside its members and send them out.[12]

Modern evangelism led to a decision. Evangelism in the emerging culture leads to a long-term journey. Mennonites call this "non-violent evangelism." Evangelicals call this "relational evangelism." Some mainliners call this "process evangelism" or "hospitality evangelism." Others call this "post-colonial," "cross-cultural," or "user-friendly" evangelism.[13] Whatever one calls it, this form of evangelism is based on a few key premises:

1. *Trust*: Modern evangelism was dominated by the notion that we brought Jesus to people through "show-and-tell" strategies and spiritual laws. Now, it seems arrogant to think that we are the ones bringing Jesus to anyone. (Isn't Jesus already there?) We must trust that Jesus has intersected with people's lives long before we ever did.

2. *Relationship*: Unless we value and appreciate all sorts of people and enter into relationships with them, we are treating them as objects, not as subjects whom Jesus loves and died for. The foremost question of a disciple is this: Am I growing in my relationship with God and others?

3. *Listen and Learn*: Our first task is not to tell anything but to listen and learn (hear into speech) what Jesus is already doing in a person's life. As with all true relationships, we must be open to what this person can teach us about how God works, what God is doing, and how to discern signs of God's presence ("God-sightings") in our own lives.

4. *Pray*: Ask God to reveal what God is already doing in a person's life to bring that person to wholeness. Pray that God

12. For new ways of reaching postmoderns, see Rick Richardson, *Evangelism outside the Box: New Ways to Help People Experience the Good News* (Downers Grove, IL: InterVarsity Press, 2000), and Brian McLaren, *More Ready Than You Realize* (Grand Rapids: Zondervan, 2002).

13. Bertil Svensson, "Crosscultural Evangelism in a Post-Colonial Time: A Swedish Perspective," *International Review of Missions* 84 (1995), 427–31; Robert G. Tuttle, "Cross-Cultural Common Denominators: Tools for a More User-Friendly Evangelism," in *Global Good News: Mission in a New Context*, ed. Howard Snyder (Nashville: Abingdon, 2001), 176–89.

will make manifest how God is already present and accounted for and what God is up to. Pray also that what you say will not be your words only, but also the Spirit's words.

5. *Connect*: Help people connect the dots between their story and the Jesus story. Then help them make connections between faith and life. "In every generation—*bachol dour va dour*," says the Passover Seder text in its most important sentence, "every Jew must feel as if he himself has come out of Egypt." The essence of evangelism is connection-making: "This is *my* story, this is *my* song." Or in the resonating words of Rector Paul Abernathy:

> We do not recount the record of our redemption simply to recall ancient biblical texts. No. We retell the story so that it takes deeper root in us. We retell the story so that we become the story, the church seasons becoming active verbs in our lives. We retell the story so that we always "advent," being alert to the coming of Jesus to us. We retell the story so that we always "christmas," being animated by the birth of Jesus in us. We retell the story so that we always "epiphany," being awake to the revelation of Jesus in us for the world. We retell the story so that we always "lent," being aligned to the death of Jesus for us in our dying to sin. We retell the story so that we always "easter," being alive to the resurrection of Jesus for us and in us. We retell the story so that we always "pentecost," being afire with the empowering presence of the Holy Spirit.[14]

6. *Be a Third Testament*: Live "the gospel according to me" until your life is a "living epistle" where Jesus' presence can be read, researched, sealed with the stamp of the Spirit.

Ironically, corporate culture has embraced modern, colonialist ways of evangelism and even the phrase "evangelist."

---

14. Paul R. Abernathy, "When Will It End?" *The African American Pulpit* 1 (Fall 1998), 6.

- Some of the biggest names in the worlds of science and business (Kevin Kelly, Tom Peters, Guy Kawasaki, Jonathan Bulkeley) are calling for leaders ("new revolutionaries") to become "evangelists" and "evangineers."[15]
- Howard Schultz, when asked what he does as CEO of Starbucks, replies, "I'm a coffee evangelist."
- A front-page lead article in the *Wall Street Journal* referred to one of its subjects as "a long-time evangelist for the commercialization of space."[16]
- One of six questions asked by Russell Reynolds Associates to determine whether or not you have "Web DNA" is, Are you more evangelical than Matthew, Mark, Luke, or John?[17]

Like the rest of church life, evangelism must embrace both virtual and physical meeting places (or what Andrew Careaga calls "e-vangelism").[18] Place-based churches and organizations will always be necessary. Jim Forest states, "The Catacombs bear witness that wherever Christians prayed, they sought to create a visual environment that reminded them of the Kingdom of God and helped them to pray."[19] But the coming together of virtuality and materiality will be raising "space-and-place" metrics to unprecedented positions. Here is one question church planters, evangelists, and architects will need to face on every front: Is this building really necessary?

15. Kelly, *New Rules for the New Economy* (1998); Peters is quoted in *Fast Company* (September 2000), 106; Kawasaki, *Rules for Revolutionaries* (1999); Bulkeley, CEO of *BarnesandNoble.com,* argues that "leaders today must be evangelists for changing the system—not for preserving it."
16. The *Wall Street Journal* (16 June 2000), A8.
17. "Web DNA," *Fast Company* (July 2000), 170.
18. Andrew Careaga, *E-vangelism* (Lafayette, LA: Vital Issues Press, 1998). See also his *Eministry: Connecting with the Net Generation* (Grand Rapids: Kregel, 2001).
19. Jim Forest, *Praying with Icons* (Maryknoll, NY: Orbis, 1997), 4.

E is for Evil

The world has changed much in some ways. The world has changed little in others. Where the world has stayed most the same is in this four-letter word—EVIL.

Sin is an unacknowledged sociological category. Humans spin off sin the way a caterpillar entombs itself in a silken shroud. But the cocoon of sin is a casket from which no butterfly emerges unless grace liberates.

This emerging culture will invent new kinds of sin and elevate old ones. Douglas Coupland offers a catalog of "new temptations" for postmoderns:

Instant wealth
Emotionally disengaged sex
Information overload
Belief in the ability of ingested substances to alter
   the aura of one's flesh or personality architecture
Neglect of the maintenance of democracy
Willful ignorance of history
Body manipulation
Willful rejection of reflection
Body envy
Belief that spectacle is reality
Vicarious living through celebrities
Rejection of sentiment
Unwillingness to assign hierarchy to values[20]

The no. 1 postmodern blind spot? The Babelian bind of "nothing will be restrained from them, which they have imagined to do" (Gen. 11:6 KJV). The snake in the Garden of Eden was smart and right: "You shall be like God." Twenty-first century people have become like gods. And gods don't think they can sin.

20. Douglas Coupland, *Polaroids from the Dead* (New York: Regan Books, 1996), 156.

> Female, male, inanimate, plant. I think God is everything. Human beings created the punitive, vengeful deity who considers us to be innate sinners.
>
> —POP SINGER ALANIS MORISSETTE[21]

Prime consumers are treated as prime ministers used to be. Every ad that exists tells postmoderns, "You're a god." Every commercial pummels into the mind and heart, "You're in control" or "You're in charge" or "You're number one" or "You deserve it." Some commercials are not even subtle: "For the goddess in you."

A whole genre of computer games are god-simulation games that let you play the role of an omnipotent deity. You can be evil or good. You can harass and kill your own people, or you can heal them and help them. You can be kind and forgiving to those who don't believe in you, or you can wreak vengeance against them.

For a culture that is teaching people to "be gods," the church must help them to hear those same words but with a different meaning: to move from "be gods" to the way the late singer/composer Rich Mullins signed his books and CDs: "Be God's." The little shift of an apostrophe takes us from EVIL into reverse: LIVE. (See **Holocaust.**)

E is for Exercise

● A physical or spiritual practice essential for a healthy life. (See **Disciplines.**)

E is for Experiential

● The Holy Grail of the emerging culture.

21. As quoted in Elizabeth Weitzman, "A Gig Called God," interview with Alanis Morrissette, *Interview* magazine (1 November 1999), 106.

People today are experience gatherers. They don't know it when they see it; they know it when they experience it and enact it. In the words of the *Chicago Tribune* reviewing a Blue Man Group show, "THE PERFECT ENTERTAINMENT . . . So much fun it must be experienced to be believed." Experience is the major currency in this "experience economy."[22] Experience (which includes reason and more) trumps reason alone.

Companies have abandoned promoting their products and instead are giving people an experience around provocative images that raise awareness, provoke discussion, and chart the future. Don't believe there is such a thing as the "experience economy"? Ask Dennis Tito, who spent $20 million for a space vacation at the International Space Station. Can't come up with a story to surround and experientialize a product? Manufacture one. Hence "The Ernest Hemingway Collection," five categories of furniture being made by Thomasville Furniture to match the five homes that Hemingway worked out of: Paris, Havana, Key West, Ketchum (ID), and Kenya.[23]

Postmoderns define the meaning of life in terms of the integrity of relationships and the intensity of experiences. For them, intensity, not clarity, is the dominant concern.

Moderns were "seekers." Postmoderns are finders who are open to new discoveries and new experiences. For better or worse, they often become putty in the hands of anything that draws them deeper into the experience—whatever that experience may be. The facts are not as important as the feelings, and postmoderns tend to "feel after him" (Acts 17:27 KJV).[24]

22. James H. Gilmore and B. Joseph Pine, *The Experience Economy* (Cambridge, MA: Harvard Business School Publishing, 1999).

23. See www.*thomasville.com/hemingway* for more. Accessed 17 September 2000.

24. This is one reason for the phenomenal growth of Pentecostalism. See Harvey Cox, *Fire from Heaven: The Rise of Pentecostal Spirituality and the Reshaping of Religion in the Twenty-first Century* (Reading, MA: Addison-Wesley, 1995), and David Martin, *Pentecostalism: The World Their Parish* (Malden, MA: Blackwell, 2002).

> The old paradigm taught that if you have the right teaching, you will experience God. The new paradigm says that if you experience God, you will have the right teaching.
>
> —PASTOR/NAE PRESIDENT LEITH ANDERSON[25]

Whereas moderns were greedy about accumulating money and things, postmoderns are greedy about accumulating experiences and relationships. And this greed is self-fueling: The more you have, the more you hunger for more. (Note: Spiritual postmoderns can be equally greedy for pleasant spiritual experiences, which may in fact be a deterrent to authentic disciple making.)

The current quest for identity through experience is creating a culture and cult of sensation. Modernity made *sensible* synonymous with *rational*. Postmodern worship must become "sensible" again in the original meaning of the word—both "perceiving or feeling" as well as "that which can be felt or perceived, perceptible by the senses."[26]

But with the promise of "sensible" worship comes the great peril of postmodern worship: the inversion of the Emperor's New Clothes. Remember Hans Christian Andersen's fable about the emperor who was deluded into thinking he was wearing new clothes when in fact he was buck naked and everyone was afraid to tell him? In the postmodern inversion of that story, we have churches whose worship is fully adorned in the latest fashion—robes outfitted with all the buttons and bells, smells and electronic whistles—but without any Emperor: no Lord of Lords and King of Kings.

---

25. Leith Anderson, *A Church for the 21st Century* (Minneapolis: Bethany House, 1992), 21.

26. Two excellent resources for this are Tex Sample, *The Spectacle of Worship in a Wired World: Electronic Culture and the Gathered People of God* (Nashville: Abingdon Press, 1998), and Kim Miller and Ginghamsburg Church Worship Team, *Handbook for Multisensory Worship* (Nashville: Abingdon Press, 1999), supplemented with *The Handbook for Multisensory Worship Interactive CD-ROM* (Nashville: Abingdon, 1999).

So we must remember: Faith cannot be reduced to experience.

In fact, "experiencing God"—if by it we mean attaining a certain pleasant feeling—may become an idol, a narcotic, and a substitute for serving God, obeying God, or experiencing *obedience* to God. How is God most glorified? Ask the prophets like Amos or Micah. Does it happen through our worship, or through our obedience and service?[27] What God wants most is a living sacrifice, not praise songs or provocative dramas or PowerPoint sermons (Matt. 28:9; Rev. 4:10).

A parable: One day after dinner, while finishing dessert, a father sent his boy out to cut the lawn. Smiling broadly, the son said, "No, Father, I just want to stay here experiencing your presence, expressing my love for you, my dear Father." The father frowned and said, more firmly this time, "Actually, Son, I would rather you go out and cut the lawn." But the boy acted as if he didn't even hear his father, and he replied, "Dad! Guess what? I just wrote a song expressing my love for you!" The son began to sing, his eyes closed in sincerity and intense emotion, and the father left the table to go watch TV. The boy didn't notice, but kept singing, with tears streaming down his face.

At that point the father wanted the boy to experience *obedience* (which may entail heat, sweat, thirst, sunburn, strained muscles, hunger, endurance, and fatigue) even more than the warmth of his *presence*.

Apprised of the danger of seeing experience as a narcotic, postmodern Christian leaders nevertheless realize that human

27. This provocative argument from Kirk Hadaway is worth discussing: "We don't actually worship God. God does not require that we bow down and worship him. Instead, what we do in our worship is communion with God in Christ as God's people. The purpose of worship is to come together as God's people, as the body of Christ, and be what we are in praise of God's glory and celebration of what God has done. What worship does is to let us practice being what we are, seeing the world as God sees it—recognizing and realizing the Realm of God in our midst. Through such practice the community is formed, and we as individuals are transformed into members of it." See Kirk Hadaway, *Behold I Do a New Thing: Transforming Communities of Faith* (Cleveland: Pilgrim Press, 2001), 99.

beings abhor boredom as nature abhors a vacuum, so they seek to transform boring experiences into learning experiences. For this reason, postmodern Christian leaders must become students of experiential learning, as opposed to that odd modern creation, "classroom learning"—a model of learning with limited value, based on the assembly line and factory model of human manufacturing. Someday we may look back on modern children's classrooms with the same regret with which we now look back on child labor in high-Industrial-Age factories or chimneys or mines.

F is for Festivals

The highest honor any scholar or intellectual can receive is what is called a Festschrift (a celebration in writing, putting the scholar's work in perspective and advancing it). It used to be that *Festschriften* were considerably more *Fest* than *Schrift*. In the modern world, a *Festschrift* became almost all *Schrift* and no *Fest*.

In yet another way in which postmodern will be more premodern than modern, the premodern world wasn't a flood of words. It was a festival of metaphors, songs, dance, rituals, stories, ceremonies, and parties. Until the modern era, Christians averaged one day out of four in some kind of festivity related to the church's calendar.[1] Jesus himself never attended a meeting, but loved "meatings." The New Testament word *deipnon* (dape-non) means literally a "lingering meal." Jesus loved deipnons. His ministry was fundamentally a ministry of deipnons.[2] In fact, according to house church theologian Wolfgang Simson, "The Lord's Supper was actually more a substantial supper with a symbolic meaning, than a symbolic supper with a substantial meaning."[3]

As much as people today long to live a festive life, they don't know how to relax. The art of accidentalness, naturalness, spontaneousness needs both space and time. Leisure time is down about 16.5 hours a week in recent decades. We are working about a month's time more per year than was the norm in the 1960s. Little wonder increasing numbers suffer from a newly diagnosed syndrome called "leisure sickness"—the inability to

1. See Barbara Ehrenreich's forthcoming book on the role of festivity on social and political movements, as described in *www.inf.uoregon.edu/notable/ehrenreich.html*.

2. For more on this, see Leonard I. Sweet, *The Jesus Prescription for a Healthy Life* (Nashville: Abingdon, 1996), especially the chapter "Set the Table," 113–34.

3. Wolfgang Simson, *Houses That Change the World* (Cumbria, UK: OM Publishing, 2001), xxii, 82.

unbend and unwind.[4] The medical cure for "leisure sickness"? Whole days of rest.

At the same time that we live in a world that goes at the "speed of light," we need to learn how to live at the speed of life. We need spaces for rest and refreshment and reflection. Life takes time. Living things require time. Relationships require time. In the haunting words of Margaret J. Wheatley, "What do we lose when we're out of time? We lose each other."[5]

Sabbath-keeping is a mandate for ministry in the emerging culture.[6]

F is for Forms

Everywhere we go, people are asking what form the postmodern church will take. Our answer: all forms. Remember, this is *post*modern ministry we're talking about. We're beyond the "one-size-fits-all" formulas of modernity.

If the modern church structured itself like an armadillo, the postmodern church will structure itself like a jungle with all kinds of animals. We believe there will be postmodern megachurches and house churches, postmodern liturgies and nonliturgies, postmodern postdenominations and nondenominations. And all of them will come and go, just as the first form of Christianity (the Jewish church in Jerusalem) came and went in A.D. 70. Postmodern churches will meet in living rooms and ancient cathedrals, in storefronts and high-tech auditoriums,

4. "Leisure Sickness," *Trend Letter* 20 (21 May 2001), 2.

5. Margaret Wheatley, "Organic Leadership," plenary remarks at the "Exploring off the Map" leadership conference in Denver on 25 May 2000. For more of Margaret Wheatley, see her classic management text *Leadership and the New Science: Learning about Organization from an Orderly Universe*, rev. and enl. (San Francisco: Berrett-Koehler, 2000).

6. For more on Sabbath-keeping, see Marva Dawn, *Keeping the Sabbath Wholly: Ceasing, Embracing, Feasting* (Grand Rapids: Eerdmans, 1989), and chapter 13, "Declare a Sabbatical: Soul Artists Create Rest Spaces in Their Days," in Leonard Sweet, *SoulSalsa: 17 Surprising Steps for Godly Living in the 21st Century* (Grand Rapids: Zondervan, 2000).

online and in person, in robes and in jeans, in the presence of incense and candles and in the presence of coffee and bagels.[7] As for leadership styles and structures, we anticipate all possible combinations of seminary-trained/not seminary-trained, formally and informally mentored, paid and unpaid, structural chaos and anarchy and "chaordy."[8]

So, on the one hand, we are sympathetic with Wolfgang Simson, who decries modern formulas of worship that can degenerate into repetitive, mechanistic routines:

> Since Jesus is a person, the idea of having each meeting with that person structured around the same old pattern seems to be as creative and inventive as a bridegroom bringing his future bride each day the same set of flowers, singing the same songs, and declaring his ardent love with the same poems. I suspect after a short time she would be less than excited to receive him and listen to his program.[9]

On the other hand, we are sympathetic with Robert Webber, who anticipates a postmodern return to ancient liturgy and ritual. Their very repetitiveness, familiarity, and predictability can make them capable of a kind of transparency, thus enhancing worship by not drawing attention to themselves.[10]

If you want to give moderns the heebie-jeebies, tell them that worship is a time when "anything can happen and probably

7. For resources that meet postmoderns where they are, see Jim Thomas, *Coffeehouse Theology* (Eugene, OR: Harvest House, 2001), and Leonard Sweet with Denise Marie Siino, *A Cup of Coffee at the SoulCafe* (Nashville: Broadman & Holman, 1998).

8. For more on "chaordic" institutions, see Dee Hock, *Birth of the Chaordic Age* (San Francisco: Berrett-Koehler, 1999) and the recent audio cassette set, *The Positive Side of Chaos Revisioning Organization* (Ukiah, CA: New Dimensions Foundation, 2000). See also the chapter "Get Chaordic—'Chaordic' Churches and 'Chaordic' Leaders," in Leonard Sweet, *SoulTsunami: Sink or Swim in New Millennium Culture* (Grand Rapids: Zondervan, 1999), 71–106.

9. Simson, *Houses That Change the World*, 140.

10. Robert Webber, *Ancient-Future Faith: Rethinking Evangelicalism for a Postmodern World* (Grand Rapids: Baker, 1999).

will." If you want to give postmoderns tingles up their spine, tell them that worship is a time when "anything can happen and probably will." Then be sure to remind them that one of the things that can happen and probably will is the resurgence of ancient forms.

The biggest difference we anticipate is not that new forms will replace old forms, but that a new relativism about forms will replace the old absolutism about forms.

The dance between content and form will continue to challenge the church to keep moving to a changing rhythm. In Jesus, God married content (divinity) and form (humanity). Fusion only happened once, and it can only happen once. But we can use the power of that fusion to authorize form and content to dance together in artistic and surprising ways.

The church as Christ's bride is called to be the ultimate fusion of form and content on earth.[11]

F is for Foundationalism

● One of the most powerful and seductive constructions of the modern world.

● One of the ways the Christian church in the West became most worldly. (Doubt this? Ask ten modern Christians what the foundation of their faith is, and then compare their answers with 1 Corinthians 3:11; Ephesians 2:20; and 1 Timothy 3:15.)

In the pre-foundationalist world, people assumed that life was a mystery, full of "secret things" that "belong to the LORD" (Deut. 29:29). What God reveals is a precious treasure that is to be received as a gift.

In the foundationalist world, people assumed that through careful reason, logic, and research a complete structure of

11. For an excellent essay on form and content from an artist's perspective, see Makato Fujimura, "Form and Content: That Final Dance," in *It Was Good: Making Art to the Glory of God*, ed. Ned Bustard (Baltimore: Square Halo Books, 2000), 49–60.

knowledge could be erected and mysteries could gradually be replaced with knowledge. This knowledge would accumulate like bricks cemented on a foundation, and assuming the foundation is secure and certain, humans could have rock-solid certainty from the bottom up. Modern secularists tended to rely only on sensory data for their "bricks," while modern Christians mined their bricks from the Bible, which was assumed to be intended by God as a source from which propositions could be extracted. In either case, it was assumed that knowledge was like a wall or building engineered upon an undoubtable, unshakable foundation.

Just as medieval Christians built stone cathedrals that they believed would last forever, modern Christians seemed to believe that their conceptual structures would stand forever. Just as medieval cathedrals are beautiful but often unused artifacts of a past era, so modern conceptual systems will be seen as the remembered but often unused artifacts of modern Christianity.

In the post-foundationalist postmodern world,[12] people will generally feel a greater affinity to pre-foundationalists, sharing with them this awareness: The more we learn, the more we know that we don't know, and the more aware of mystery we become. In the words of Rodney Clapp, arguing the case that everyone is "better off" repudiating foundationalism,

> One of the better reasons for abandoning it is that the abandonment will enable us to be more devout Christians and less devout liberals.... To put the matter metaphorically, it is as if foundationalists are on the playground of knowledge and insisting that everyone frolic only on the slippery slide. They believe that only there can knowledge be safely found.

12. We are well into a post-foundational world, according to Nancey Murphy, *Beyond Liberalism and Fundamentalism: How Modern and Postmodern Philosophy Set the Theological Agenda* (Valley Forge, PA: Trinity Press International, 1996), and Stanley Grenz and John Franke, *Beyond Foundationalism: Shaping Theology in a Postmodern Context* (Louisville: Westminster John Knox, 2000).

Foundationalists fear that, freed from the slide alone, some relativistic children may tire of any restrictions and wander into the street. But I think foundationalists need to admit that there is no such thing as safely and absolutely secured knowledge. Knowledge is particular and perspectival, and as such is always contestable. And it is after all not entirely safe living atop the slide, which is why those who do so are obsessed with slippery slopes. Dismounting it, we are at least freed to accurately assess danger in all its varieties. And we are freed to admit that danger is inescapable in a finite (and fallen) world.[13]

F is for Fractals

● The way in which the whole is replicated in miniature in every part.

"Fractal teams" were introduced by Wayne Cordeiro of New Hope Christian Fellowship in Honolulu. Each team is composed of five leaders: a team leader and four others who each spearhead one area of responsibility. Each of these four heads up a subteam also divided into four areas of responsibility, whose leaders in turn spearhead subsidiary teams. It goes on until everyone in the church is a part of a team ministry.[14]

F is for Fundamentalisms

Whether of Jewish, Muslim, Christian, or market variety, surging fundamentalisms are the hypermodern reaction to postmodern

---

13. Rodney Clapp, "How Firm a Foundation: Can Evangelicals Be Nonfoundationalists?" in *The Nature of Confession: Evangelicals and Postliberals in Conversation,* ed. Timothy Phillips and Dennis Okholm (Downers Grove, IL: InterVarsity Press, 1996), 82, 89.

14. Wayne Cordeiro, *Doing Church as a Team* (Ventura, CA: Regal Books, 2001), 176–95. The two best resources on team ministry are George Claddis, *Leading a Team-based Church: How Pastors and Church Staffs Can Grow Together into a Powerful Fellowship of Leaders* (San Francisco: Jossey-Bass, 1999), and E. Stanley Ott, *The Power of Ministry Teams* (San Francisco: Jossey-Bass Pfeiffer, 2001).

culture, the "panic interface of postmodernism."[15] In the face of frightening change, humbling mysteries, and unwanted ambiguities, fundamentalists seek stability, clarity, and certainty, sometimes at the expense of honesty, humility, and charity. "The frenzy of different forms of fundamentalism in our world," writes Celtic Christian theologian Philip J. Newell, "speaks of the fear that surfaces in us when it becomes clear that the Mystery cannot be controlled but only adored."[16]

Fundamentalists are those who outmodern the modernists in their reading of sacred texts.

Note: Fundamentalists are found in two subspecies: liberal and conservative.

F is for Fusion-Fission

Twenty-first century society is a fusion-fission society: Loosely coupled communities are constantly forming, unforming, and reforming around both virtual and physical spaces linked by relational agenda.

> Give me ambiguity or give me something else.
>
> —BUMPER STICKER

F is for Fuzzy

● The adjective that describes the highest forms of logic, computer science, technology, and theology.

Pure and true art is in the fuzz—in the ambiguities of thought and emotion that transform the transparent into the transcendent.

---

15. Richard Appignanesi and Chris Garratt, *Introducing Postmodernism* (New York: Totem Books, 1995), 159.
16. Philip J. Newell, *Echo of the Soul: The Sacredness of the Human Body* (Harrisburg, PA: Morehouse Publishing, 2000), 16.

In modernity, clarity was all. Everything wrong with modern culture is symbolized by fluorescent lights, which make all beneath them look clean, pale, and dead. By late modernity, sensitive souls began to realize that a light that banishes all shadows and mists has its drawbacks. For example, if you have one clear theory of the Atonement, you have the advantage of being able to draw crisp diagrams and drive to the same clear formula in sermon after sermon. But when you recognize that the Bible seems to suggest at least a half-dozen or so theories of the Atonement, you realize that holding these varied views simultaneously yields something better than clarity: profundity. It is only the shallow water that maintains clarity; the deeper the water you peer into, the greater the fuzziness.

> A clear idea is therefore another name for a little idea.
> —EDMUND BURKE

If maximum fuzz is when a set or a concept equals its own opposite,[17] Jesus (fully divine, fully human) is maximum fuzz. Chris Hughes, a doctoral student at Drew University, calls the doctrine of the Trinity (God is One, God is Three) "fuzz cubed."

EPICtivity F: Fuzzy

Give everyone a copy of your church's or denomination's doctrinal statement. Ask the members to "vote off" one item from the statement, and then ask them what effects (negative or positive) losing this statement would have on your church.

Continue the exercise until you have eliminated all of the items in your statement.

---

17. As suggested by Bart Kosco in *Heaven in a Chip: Fuzzy Visions of Society and Science in the Digital Age* (New York: Three Rivers, 2000), 12.

Then read the Great Commandment (Matt. 22:34–40), the New Commandment (John 15:12), and the Great Commission (Matt. 28:18–20). Ask this question: What would be the advantages and disadvantages of having these three statements replace our current doctrinal statement?

Conclude with this question: If you could only be clear on one set of statements (your doctrinal statement, or the three statements of Jesus), which would you choose, and what would be the consequences?

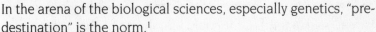

G is for Genetic Predestinationism

There is one notable exception to the warming of science-faith relations. The reign of *theological predestinationism* has been replaced by a *scientific* or, more precisely, *genetic predestinationism*. In the arena of the biological sciences, especially genetics, "predestination" is the norm.[1]

The theological consequences of biological research are startling and scary. Geneticists have discovered specific genes for Alzheimer's disease, cystic fibrosis, and colon cancer—and even genes for behavioral traits like aggression, alcoholism, and adultery are being located and "marked." Some are saying that cancer itself is a disease of the genes. Thrill-seeking is supposedly 59% heritable; happiness 80% heritable; assertiveness 60% heritable; most personality traits are said to be heritable at around 50%.[2]

Neurologists have named fifteen religions leaders who supposedly had epilepsy (including Paul, Mohammed, and Joan of Arc). That is enabling some of them to claim that the brain's temporal lobes are the place where you can find God. In 1994 other neurologists announced their belief that every healthy brain has a moral center located in the frontal lobes at the top of the brain. In other words, those who are morally awry have a haywire frontal lobe.

More recently, scientists have discovered two small "knots" of neuronal tissue above each ear they have nicknamed "god spots." These "knots" seem to mediate peak experiences in religion, creativity, and intuition. When these "god spots" are stimulated, the person feels at one with the universe, "in touch" with the divine.

1. Ted Peters, *Playing God? Genetic Determinism and Human Freedom* (New York: Routledge, 1997).

2. Kevin Sharpe with Rebecca Bryant, "Genes and Predestination: The Cracked Skull," *Science and Spirit* 11 (March/April 2000), 11.

Trying to find a "God spot" on the brain, or understanding spiritual experience as a quantum vacuum or an electrical charge in your skull, could be a sincere search for truth, or it could be the latest modernist rantings of reductive naturalism and scientific materialism, the source of the new predestinationism that robs us of our ability to be in relationship with wholeness and truth.

To say that spiritual experience has a biochemical locus in the brain could imply that spirituality is an illusion and that only the brain chemicals are real (the old modern reductionism at work again). Or it could simply mean that the human brain has developed faculties to interpret and respond to real spiritual data, just as eyes developed to interpret light, color, and beauty (an approach beyond reductionism).

Reductionism—a view of the world that assumes the complex realities can be fully understood by breaking them down (reducing them) to smaller parts—had been a powerful force in modernity, and although its dominance is being challenged by systems thinking and emergence theory, it is not dead yet.

Despite the claims of reductionist modern science, God is not a neural knot. Spirit is not a genome. Religion is not an outcome of neurobiology. True, humans are hardwired for religious experience, but it's a valid spiritual hardwiring, not just a reductionist biological one.

For those doing ministry in the emerging culture, this delicate area—comprising neurobiology, philosophy of mind, psychopharmacology, and theological anthropology—will call us to practice both confidence and humility. We will need the confidence (the courage of our convictions) not to be cowed into silence or capitulation by exaggerated claims of deterministic science. If they are partly right—that *much* of our behavior is limited, if not determined, by genetics and biochemistry—then we will need the humility not to repeat the naïve or arrogant mistake made by the church in the days of Copernicus and Galileo. (By the way, if their most extravagant claim is right—that *all* human behavior is determined by genetic or biochemical mechanisms—then they can't help believing what they believe, any more than you can help believing in God!)

What if some people are, as some scientists suggest, genetically more predisposed to adultery and others to impotence, some to violence and others to indolence, some to homosexuality and others to heterosexuality, some to clever dishonesty and others to simple stupidity?

Wouldn't this just be more reason for us to

1. Not judge (as we've already been told, since only God is able to judge)
2. Be gracious and patient (since we don't know what heavy burdens others may be bearing simply to do as well as they're doing), and
3. Work hard and encourage others who work hard, in a true scientific labor of love, to find whatever therapies we can to help people afflicted genetically, just as we would help people who are afflicted in some other way?

Isn't this just another way of saying that we need to continue to love our neighbors and do for them as Christ has done for us?

> Behind every crooked thought there lies a crooked molecule. Every sadness is chemical.
>
> —Neurosurgeon Ralph Gerard

Against a backdrop of chaos, we are naturally prone to emphasize the power of God over chaos. But what do we emphasize against a backdrop of genetic determinism? Perhaps this: that God, a free Being of glorious dignity, has created us as free beings in his image, and that freedom and dignity have emerged in his universe, just as one would expect—meaning that genetic determinism (a late product of reductionistic, mechanistic modern science) doesn't have the last word. (See **Emergence.**)

G is for Globalization

For the first time in human history, the world is forging an awareness of our existence as a single entity, a *Unum Humanum*. The people of Planet Earth are having the same experiences at the same time around the same events and the same people, creating a planetary consciousness. Each person with a screen now has the whole world at his or her fingertips. No wonder globalization has been called "the most ambitious collective experiment ever undertaken by the human race."

Whaling was the first truly global industry. But the whole world is now being *wired*—encased in a neural net that creates a "space-time compression." That's why boundaries and borders are becoming less significant and why the market state is replacing the nation state. (See **Economics.**) Global factors now account for the lion's share of stock market fluctuations, an integration that increases dramatically during times of high volatility in share prices. What happens on Wall Street can explain 80% of price movements in Europe, for example.[3]

For some, the word *globalization* means the universalization of Western values.[4] But like it or not, globalization means that Eastern ideas become global property too.

Think you can escape globalization? Think again. There is nothing more global than the anti-globalization movement. The only question for us is, Will the church be a "global player"?

When advocates of local cultural and regional identity fight adherents of globalization, the ensuing struggle is little more than shadowboxing. There is evidence to suggest that, rather than wiping out cultural differences, postmodern globalization heightens differences and plurality. Popular culture (especially

---

3. See Robin Brooks and Luis Catão, "The New Economy and Global Stock Returns," *IMF Working Paper 206* (December 2000). See *www.imf.org/external/pubs/ft/wp/2000/wp00216.pdf.* Accessed 10 April 2001.

4. The "silent takeover" is what Cambridge don Noreena Hertz calls it. See Hertz, *The Silent Takeover: Global Capitalism and the Death of Democracy* (London: William Heinemann, 2001).

pop music) is a prime example of the mixing and matching of cosmopolitan forms into something original, indigenous, and universal.[5] Also, a growing body of research demonstrates that growth and globalization in fact help the poor, even to the point of raising their incomes substantially.[6]

The perils of globalization, however, must not be under-appraised. There needs to be greater understanding of local concepts such as property, authority, and exchange if globalization is to be a shared experience. The promise of globalization needs to be clarified: Is it prosperity, or is it individual liberty?[7] Sometimes globalization and unfettered capital flows can create an environment hostile to basic liberties[8] or can strengthen antiliberal forces (e.g., Russia). George Soros has observed how deregulated financial markets and free flows of capital can "behave more like wrecking balls than pendulums," making some scholars argue that "there is no systematic connection between globalized markets and liberal values."[9]

The greatest concern for the church over this emergence of a meta-mind ought to be, How do we give it a conscience? Will the gospel have a voice that speaks boldly to this emerging global meta-mind?

5. Two scholars unafraid to handle popular culture are William D. Romanowski and Quentin Schultze, both of Calvin College. See Romanowski, *Eyes Wide Open: Looking for God in Popular Culture* (Grand Rapids: Brazos, 2001), and *Pop Culture Wars: Religion and the Role of Entertainment in American Life* (Downers Grove, IL: InterVarsity Press, 1996); Schultze, *Dancing in the Dark: Popular Culture and the Electronic Media* (Grand Rapids: Eerdmans, 1990). See also Denisoff R. Serge and William D. Romanowski, *Risky Business: Rock in Film* (New Brunsiwck, NJ: Transaction Publishers, 1991).

6. David Dollar and Aart Kraay, "Growth Is Good for the Poor," *www.worldbank.org/research/growth/absddolakray.htm.* Accessed 28 September 2000.

7. For the latter, see John Micklethwait and Adrian Wooldridge, *A Future Perfect: The Essentials of Globalization* (New York: Crown Business, 2000), 332–43.

8. For an example of how globalization can weaken fledgling liberal regimes, remember what happened when markets moved against the South African currency.

9. As quoted in and argued by John Gray, "Does Globalization Bring Liberty?" *TLS: Times Literary Supplement* (17 November 2000), 18.

The local church was the focal point of late modern ministry. In the postmodern world, purely local churches may go extinct or become a backwater. In their place will arise mission-minded churches without boundaries that are thoroughly rooted in their locale, yet thoroughly connected globally. These global/local or "glocal" churches will be linked by shared concerns, mission trips, the Internet, or the exchange of worship groups and pastors and youth groups to churches and needs and resources around the world.

World Relief's motto expresses this well: "Churches helping churches help the hurting." This Christian charitable organization connects churches rich in resources with churches rich in opportunities to serve in areas of need. In this way, World Relief helps both kinds of churches go from local to glocal.

There are many reasons for this identity beyond locality. For example, those doing ministry among the addicted have learned that addicts around the world comprise a definable global culture. Stan Farmer, founder of His Mansion, calls addicts the Fourth World (after Old, New, and Third). Fourth Worlders have much in common—whether they are lawyers in Cincinnati or street people in Calcutta—and so do those who minister to them.

Similarly, those doing ministry among refugees may have more in common with other refugee workers across the globe than they do with the local church around the corner. And people ministering to postmoderns in Boston will discover a parallel affinity to colleagues in Paris or Bratislava or Nairobi or Beijing. Old geographic categories have less and less significance in this globalizing world.

But there is an even more profound reason for churches to go glocal: There is no local place to hide from the juggernaut of global realities—environmental degradation, overpopulation, racial and ethnic hatred, economic exploitation. If God loves the world, and if we love our neighbors, how can we not care about these global issues that will affect all our neighbors, not to mention our children and ourselves? In the same way that Joseph became Pharaoh's God-guided advisor to deal with a regional famine, shouldn't the church become a resource to a world at risk from similarly threatening global realities?

Emerging global realities and spreading global linkups will transform local churches into "glocal" churches, and the flow of blessings will go both ways.

EPICtivity G: Globalization

Gather your group together for the following EPICtivity. Divide into teams of 4–6 people and ask them to talk about your church's mission over the next 100 years. After the brainstorming, distribute the following materials to each team and ask the teams to use them to try to express their vision of the church:

Clay	Scissors
Poster board for a base	Straws
Construction paper	Paper cups
and markers	A small globe or,
Pipe cleaners	map of the world
Any other supplies you can think of	

Afterward, have each team share its image of the future church.

When all have shared their visions, explain that one purpose of this exercise is to see how each team incorporated the symbol of the world (globe or map). How significant was the global dimension of each team's creation?

Then talk about what happens next—what they want to do after having this discussion?

G is for Grace

● A most important word in the Christian vocabulary that is a way of talking about the sheer beauty and bounty of God.

● A word that means what it always meant: God's outstretched hands of "unmerited favor and forgiveness" that reconciles opposites—human sin and divine holiness. The history of Christianity is the story of the redemption of terrible resumes of abominable sin with amazing grace.

> My favorite word is "grace"—whether it's amazing grace, saving grace, grace under fire, Grace Kelly. How we live contributes to beauty—whether it's how we treat other people or the environment.
>
> —DESIGNER CELESTE COOPER

But grace is only an invitation for us to participate. Without our participation in God's hospitality, the energies of the divine are unsatisfied.

What's the worst you can think of? There, *but* for the grace of God (and an accident of birth, an incident of child abuse, or one dysfunctional parent), go you and I. There, *by* grace, go you and I in service and ministry.

H is for Helix

● The model of all living things, the shape of all that is alive. This is the model of DNA, the nucleic acids that contain the human body's 30,00-to-40,000 genes and reside in the body's 70-to-100 trillion cells.

Notice what they are: organic, customized, lapidary, nonlinear.

Notice what they are not:

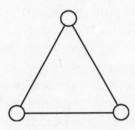

Notice four other things about a helical structure. First, it has a spiral form. The motion of time, the motion of life, is not linear, but spiral. Mate a line with a circle, connect linear to nonlinear, connect analytic to associative powers of the brain, connect past to future—and you end up with a spiral. In spiral dynamics, each level of the past remains curled up inside us (like nested Russian dolls) as we move up to next-level challenges. A spiraling faith is one of timelessness within time, one in which the past is embedded in the future.[1]

---

1. For more on the "ancientfuture" concept, see Leonard Sweet, *FaithQuakes* (Nashville: Abingdon Press, 1995); Gerard Kelly, *RetroFuture: Rediscovering Our Roots, Recharting Our Routes* (Downers Grove, IL: InterVarsity Press, 2000); Robert Webber, *Ancient-Future Faith: Rethinking Evangelicalism for a Postmodern World* (Grand Rapids: Baker, 1999); and Jeffrey C. Pugh, *The Matrix of Faith: Reclaiming a Christian Vision* (New York: Crossroad, 2001).

Second, the phrase "double helix" is a misnomer. A three-dimensional spiral is really a triple helix.[2] We are a thirding combination of nature, nurture, and choice. (For thirding, see **Trialectics.**) How do you create new DNA? Have a baby. How did God give humanity God's own triple helix of DNA? An immaculate conception. How do we acquire God's DNA? A new birth in Christ, in the power of the Spirit.

Third, ascent can be descent, and descent ascent, and it's hard to tell the difference. Only 2-3% of DNA is "genes." The rest is not "junk" DNA, as some argue. The rest is DNA, whose value we don't yet fully understand. There are two kinds of genetic modification: somatic-cell therapy (altering cells of the body to fight disease), and germ-line modification (making inheritable changes to the sex cells, the product of which is often known as "designer children"). Choose the latter, and the ascent can become a descent real quick.

Fourth, understanding DNA tells us another reason why our denominational isolation must come to an end in the post-modern world: Inbreeding guarantees the degradation of DNA. New genes need to brought into the population pool. (See **Entropy; PALS.**)

H is for Holarchy

There is a sacred order to the universe and its web of relationships that combines both hierarchy and heterarchy. It is called *holarchy*.

Esteemed scholar Martin Jacques distinguishes the old order from the new in the following way: The ending world was dominated by "hierarchy, certainty, bureaucracy, homogeneity, class, centralization and the state." The new order emerging is

---

2. Victor G. Henigan, *The Triple Helix: A Harmonic Interpretation of Reality* (Bloomington, IN: First Books Library, 1997). From a biological perspective, see Richard C. Lewontin, *The Triple Helix: Gene Organism and Environment* (Cambridge, MA: Harvard University Press, 2000).

characterized by "market egalitarianism, uncertainty, diversity, heterogeneity, multi-identity, decentralization and confusion."[3]

Hierarchy: Sacred (*hieros*) structure or order (*arche*). The fullest expression of the vertical in the Great Chain of Being (philosophy) and the Vatican (ecclesiology). There are multitudinous hierarchies, such as patriarchy, caste, and "offices" (deacon, elder). Modern hierarchies often became pathological (e.g., clergy-lay hierarchy).

Heterarchy: Other (*hetero*) structure or order (*arche*). The fullest expression of the horizontal (complex relationships) in IT (Information Technology). The problem with heterarchy is that it is "differentiation without integration, disjointed parts recognizing no common and deeper purpose or organization: heaps not wholes."[4] It doesn't adequately reflect the complexity and diversity of life. As Cletus Wessels has said, "Social structures are not flat, and they are not heaps. There are some people who have a deeper sense of the sacred than others, some who have a power of healing, and some who have leadership qualities."[5]

Holarchy: The ordering (*arche*) of holons (*whole/parts*). The word *holon* was invented by Arthur Koestler to describe increasing levels of wholeness in the universe. Every whole is a part and every part is a whole. Everything is a holon.

All quantum systems exhibit the double ring. Matter is both wave and particle. Similarly, humans have a particle component (individual) and a wave component (cultural/communal). We are both self and community, both core and periphery. Holons contain both self-preservation (particle) and self-adaptation (wave).

We are both part and whole. All self-organizing systems are both/and.

---

3. Martin Jacques in *The Oxford Companion to Politics of the World*, 2d ed., ed. Joel Krieger (New York: Oxford University Press, 2001).

4. Ken Wilber, *Sex, Ecology, Spirituality: The Spirit of Evolution* (Boston: Shambhala, 2000), 21.

5. Cletus Wessels, *The Holy Web: Church and the New Universe Story* (Maryknoll, NY: Orbis Books, 2000), 133.

H is for Holiness

Holiness is too often understood as a state that we are expected to attain to some degree on our own, as reflected in the beautiful contemporary worship song

> *Holiness, holiness,*
> *Is what I long for.*
> *Holiness is what I need.*
> *Holiness, holiness,*
> *Is what you want from me.*[6]

In postmodernity, we propose, the last line will be changed to "holiness is what you want *for* me" rather than "from me"— emphasizing that holiness isn't a state of perfection we have to attain *for* God, but rather it is a gift *from* God *for* us, something truly worth longing for (as the song says).

But what is holiness?

We are writing this book (in part) on a software package called WordPerfect.

Question: If WordPerfect truly had been perfect, would it have needed so many upgrades over the last five years, progressing from WordPerfect 5.0 to WordPerfect 9.0?

Question: What is the relationship between perfection and holiness?

The question of holiness seems to be a key theme of Jesus' Sermon on the Mount. Perfection, righteousness, and holiness had been defined by the Pharisees in a constricting, cramped, lifeless way. Jesus, who did "everything well" (Mark 7:37), seeks to upgrade their imperfect understandings of perfection and holiness. For example, when he says, "Be perfect as your Father in heaven is perfect," it is clear from the preceding verses (and from comparing them with the parallel passage in Luke's

---

6. Scott Underwood, "Holiness," as found on the sound recording *Holiness, Why We Worship 2* (Vineyard Music Group, 1998), YMD9280.

gospel) that he does *not* mean merely the "perfect" elimination of legal infraction. Rather, his call to perfection echoes his call to be merciful and compassionate as God is.

Holiness also goes far beyond eliminating taboos, according to Jesus. Your Father in heaven is perfect with a full-bodied merciful perfection, a wholly compassionate perfection, a fully developed loving perfection. In other words, for God, holiness goes beyond word-perfection or legal-perfection to love-perfection.

Holiness is not merely being set apart from, but set aside for. For what? For LovePerfect Living. Holiness is LovePerfect Living.

In translating Jesus' words (originally spoken in Aramaic), Matthew chooses a term from Greek aesthetics, *teleios*, that means "whole, pleasing, having integrity, reaching ultimate completion and full fruition." "If your holiness isn't whole, complete, fully matured enough to include love, compassion, and mercy," Jesus says, "your perfection isn't really perfect and needs a major upgrade."

Mabel Boggs Sweet had a saying: "The good is always the best's worst enemy." So, good isn't good enough. Even good enough isn't good enough.

Remember that in the Creation narrative, on the sixth day God saw all that God had made and said it was "very good" (Gen. 1:31). But "very good" wasn't good enough. "Very good" had to be followed by a seventh day, which made everything holy or whole or perfect. A "very good" sixth day needed the completion of a holy seventh day, which made everything "holy."

So even *very* good isn't good enough. Only holiness is good enough. And to discover that holiness, we may need to do what God did—not work more, harder, longer, under more and more pressure to get it/everything/ourselves technically *perfect*—but rather take a rest, take a sabbatical.

It is in this sense that we use the language of LovePerfect Living for holiness. Our perfection, like WordPerfect's, is unfinished, in process. Perfection for us is a direction, a process of continual upgrading, not a destination. Perfect love is not immaculate actions, but godly aims. Perfection is a maturity and integrity and quality of relationship, not merely a flawlessness of morality or an ideal of sinlessness. To say that we are to be perfect as God is perfect is to say that since God loves completely, fully, wholly, not partially, so we are to love each other fully, wholly, not partially.

> Apollyon, beware what you do; for I am in the King's Highway, the way of Holiness, therefore take heed to your self!
>
> —JOHN BUNYAN'S PILGRIM IN *THE PILGRIM'S PROGRESS*, PART 1

We are all pilgrims on the King's highway of holiness. Postmoderns are hungering for holiness and thirsting after justice—the perfection of being better and getting better and loving better: "It can't get any better than this" equals living the perfect life.

Holiness, then, is wholeness. But even more, it is also wholeheartedness. The doctrine of holiness is this: If you are going to be a disciple of Jesus, be a disciple who goes *all* the way. God is calling us to "go the whole way with me." Isn't anything less than giving your "all" to God a form of rejecting God? Aim for the highest and deepest levels of discipleship. Don't stop with "good enough." Dare to let yourself go completely in faith. Don't rest content "until all of us come . . . to maturity, to the measure of the full stature of Christ" (Eph. 4:13). Make it your ambition to use your gifts to maximum purpose. Don't be satisfied with anything but wholehearted holiness. God has coded our genes and impulses with dreams and abilities that we must use and explore. Who doesn't want the full-meal deal?

Or as they put it in John Wesley's day, aim to be as good a Christian as God can make you.

The gospel calls us to live a life of holiness—a larger life than we thought possible, a life larger than ordinary life.

H is for Holocaust

● The point at which time stopped, modernity collapsed, and nothing could ever be the same again. Auschwitz showed the ease with which reason could become treason (Hitler's propaganda minister, Josef Goebbels, had a Ph.D.); after Auschwitz, people plumped for scientific rationalism less and less. When the heart of the Enlightenment's metanarrative of systematic rationality was opened, there oozed forth a sin-sick, sick-unto-death soul. The Belsen commandants who left their "jobs" of genocide to listen to Bach showed that the arts and sciences can both be tools of violence and inhumanity.

That is why some have talked about "the Enlightenment" (the early modern movement that enthroned rationalism and exiled spirituality) as "the Endarkenment." It is not the time when we "got smart" but when we "got dumb." Enlightenment rationalism dumbed humanity down and disenchanted nature. Philosopher Jacques Derrida says we need to get enlightened about the Enlightenment, and he's right.

> Our wager was, the more enlightened we get about the Enlightenment, the more likely religion is to get a word in edgewise.
>
> —JOHN CAPUTO AND MICHAEL SCANLON[7]

In fact, when postmoderns use the word "enlightenment," it usually has the word "spiritual" in front of it and means almost exactly the opposite of what it did to moderns.

7. John Caputo, Michael Scanlon, eds., *God, the Gift, and Postmodernism* (Bloomington: Indiana University Press, 1999), 2.

For postmodern people, spiritual enlightenment requires a sober, heartbreaking reflection on the horrific, unfathomable darkness that descended on our planet midway through the twentieth century. It requires a kind of civilization-wide corporate repentance that will last for hundreds of years. The way we can be most sure that the post-Holocaust dream "never again" will come true is by repeating the 614th Commandment while repenting, "Never forget, never forget, never forget."

Along with the Holocaust, of course, we remember the other tragedies of modernity, from the slave trade to the racial cleansings of native peoples, from Stalin to Pol Pot, from environmental rape to mass extinctions. Native Americans made 333 treaties with the white man—all 333 were broken. We who benefit from the successes of modernity must, we feel, also mourn the evils of modernity as our own. It is hard to imagine any genuine spiritual enlightenment that would do less.

H is for Hugs

Studies have demonstrated that four hugs a day are necessary for survival, eight are good for maintenance, and 12 for growth.[8]

The more high-tech the culture, the higher those numbers will get.

Coming from a "malnourished love life"[9] at home and in the world, postmoderns won't tolerate a "malnourished love life" at church.

8. Cited and validated by Judith Weisberg and Maxine R. Haberman, "A Therapeutic Hugging Week in a Geriatric Facility," *Journal of Gerontological Social Work* 13 (1989), 181–86.

9. William Mahedy and Janet Bernardi, *A Generation Alone: Xers Making a Place in the World* (Downers Grove, IL: InterVarsity Press, 1994), 96.

I is for Icon

"Theology written in images and color" is Jim Forest's definition of an "icon." Russian iconographer and monk Father Zinon, who paints out of the Monastery of the Caves near Pskov, calls them "holy doors."[1]

Postmoderns have rediscovered the power of symbol. Symbols are thick texts that mediate our understanding and experience of the world. Symbols are indispensable to a healthy spiritual life.[2] Little reaches people today that is unmediated by symbols or metaphors. In the emerging culture, mediating structures are being replaced by mediating metaphors and symbols, especially symbols that become icons.

> Spiritual reality cannot be represented in any other way except through symbols.
>
> —LEONID OUSPENSKY[3]

What power of iconography? Farmers who grow the wheat found in Wheaties cereal get only half as much money as Tiger Woods receives from the boxes that carry his picture.[4]

Every home has an icon corner. Our icon corner may be the garage or a blinking box in the family room or a bursting bank account, or a . . . .

1. Jim Forest, *Praying with Icons* (Maryknoll, NY: Orbis, 1997), 14, 19.
2. The task of the iconographer is to invent and invert symbols that can be aids to worship and instruments of prayer. Every morning, Stravinsky would not compose a note until he had prayed to an icon that he brought from Russia. To paint a virtual icon go to *www.iarelative.com/virgin*. Accessed 17 July 2001.
3. Leonid Ouspensky and Vladimir Lossky, *The Meaning of Icons* (Crestwood, NY: St. Vladimir's Seminary Press, 1982), 27.
4. As quoted in *US Catholic* (October 2000), 11.

The church must help people get the right icon corner—a true center for prayer and adoration and visual meditation—and help them resist the temptation to worship icons.

Go outside to find icons: Look for Christ in the faces of the poor and needy; find the image of God in other people.

Each one of us is an icon, created in the image and likeness of God.

The Taliban in Afghanistan destroyed 3000 years of art history in its iconoclasm. In so doing, it became an icon of ugly, destructive, dangerous fanaticism.

The symbols that have become our icons are ones that connect to shared experience and greater meaning—thematic clips from commonly recognized film scores, a segment of film, a photo image, a desktop icon, a swooping symbol on a ball cap that communicates "Just do it!" with a million images of athletes pushing the limits flashing through your mind—and to shared experience.

> Christianity is the revelation not only of the Word of God, but also of the Image of God, in which His likeness is revealed.
>
> —LEONID OUSPENSKY[5]

I is for Image-Rich

It needs to be said again and again: The church has an image problem. In an image-is-everything culture where images have supplanted words as the cultural vernacular,[6] the church is heavily "logocentric" (i.e., word-based), nervous around images, and

---

5. Ouspensky and Lossky, *The Meaning of Icons*, 27.
6. In a marvelous metaphor, Michael W. Foss argues that we need to figure out the "cultural clues" that enable us to communicate, not just when we travel to a foreign land,

alienated from its own image-rich pedigree. This contrasts with the fact that even children today are extraordinarily learned within a visual tradition.

Of course, words still and should thud and punch. But what principles and points were to moderns, metaphors and images are to people in the emerging culture. Images are now the narrative, words the declarative ("Look at this!" "See how this works!"). Words now support images; they don't create images themselves. Visual ideas rather than scripts set today's story lines.

Metaphors are the masters of postmodern culture, and leaders must offer people master metaphors that offer life rather than death. Virginia Woolf said of Yeats, "Wherever one cut him, with a little question, he poured, spurted fountains of ideas."[7] Cut postmoderns anywhere, and they gush, spurting fountains of images. Focus groups are now not being asked questions so much as being given images (e.g., 400 laid out on a table) and asked to pick them up, respond to each, and relate how they make one feel.

We live by metaphors. Metaphor is the ordinary language of the mind. Far from being the preserve of poets and artists, metaphor is how the mind thinks and is what distinguishes our thinking from the animal kingdom's speech and speculation. One of the foremost linguists of our time, George Lakoff, even argues that image is that from which reason emerges:

> On the traditional view, reason is abstract and disembodied. On the new view, reason has a bodily basis. The traditional view sees reason as literal, as primarily about propositions that can be objectively true or false. The new view takes imaginative aspects of reason—metaphor, metonymy, and

but also when we stay at home. See his *Power Surge: Six Marks of Discipleship for a Changing Church* (Minneapolis: Fortress, 2000), 66–68.

7. Virginia Woolf, describing Yeats, as quoted in Hermione Lee, *Virginia Woolf* (New York: Alfred A. Knopf, 1997), 567.

mental imagery—as central to reason rather than as a periph-
eral and inconsequential adjunct to the literal.[8]

Metaphors are the real thing. Metaphors are mental magic,
the wand that transforms the brain when waved over attention.[9]
"A talent for speaking differently, rather than for arguing well, is
the chief instrument of change," argues philosopher Richard
Rorty.[10]

> He is the image [*ikon*] of the invisible God,
> the firstborn of all creation.
>
> —COLOSSIANS 1:15

The greatest communicators in history have used the wiz-
ardry of metaphor magic. Jesus, the greatest of all time, did not
speak in public without the use of "parables"—an image-based
form of narrative. Dante created physical pictures of hell, pur-
gatory, and heaven that have pestered us ever since. The phenomenal growth of Southern gospel music in late modern
culture is partly due to its Christocentric focus, the genius of
Bill and Gloria Gaither, and Southern gospel's tribal integrity
("O Brother, Where Art Thou") and ingenious, close-to-the-
people use of images and metaphors to convey biblical truth.
Similarly, the success of modern masters of "seven points" and
"eleven principles" like Steven Covey can be attributed in part to
their use of vivid metaphors (e.g., "sharpening the saw," "the fire
within," etc.). How has Los Angeles pastor Erwin McManus been
so successful in building a multicultural, multigenerational,

8. George Lakoff, *Women, Fire, and Dangerous Things: What Categories Reveal
about the Mind* (Chicago: University of Chicago Press, 1987), xi.
9. Marcel Danesi uses the phrase "word magic" to describe metaphor in his *Of Cig-
arettes, High Heels, and Other Interesting Things: An Introduction to Semiotics* (New
York: St. Martin's Press, 1999), 93.
10. Richard Rorty, *Contingency, Irony, and Solidarity* (New York: Cambridge University Press, 1989), 7.

missional church? He masterfully employs vivid images, not just words, to embody Mosaic Church's mission and values. For example: Most churches are "spiritual bomb shelters"; "you can't wash the feet of a dirty world if you refuse to touch it."[11]

While most modern Protestant churches either left their walls unadorned, or adorned them only with words on Scripture plaques, University Baptist Church in Waco, Texas, fills its worship space with artistic touches—from icons to crucifixes to brightly-colored walls—all bespeaking a sensitivity to image.

Modern preachers structure their sermons via analytical outlines with points and subpoints, angled with alliteration and pointed with parallelism. It's all about words, words, words. Meanwhile postmodern preachers pace back and forth, musing and dreaming, seeking to discover and craft vivid, unforgettable, and profound images—like bursting fishing nets and fruited grapevines, swooping crows and resting sparrows, naïve kings and spunky widows.

I is for IQ (Internet Quotient)

Whether you have a high or low IQ will partly determine success or failure in the future.

Postmoderns come to their high IQ's naturally. The Web is a whole new infrastructure for living that they take for granted. The Internet is technology for moderns because they were born before it was invented. The Internet is not technology for postmoderns any more than the book is technology for moderns.

The Internet is a powerful driver of social change in postmodern culture. While Yale computer science professor (and Uni-Bomber victim) David Gelernter is correct in observing how "the Internet is a topic that tends to bring out the fruitcake in

11. For more McManusisms, see his book *An Unstoppable Force: Daring to Become the Church God Had in Mind* (Loveland, CO: Group Publishing, 2001).

people,"[12] it would be difficult to overestimate the impact of the Internet on human culture. There have been three great reinventions of education in the history of learning: (1) invention of the Greek alphabet in the eighth century B.C., (2) invention of the printing press in the 15th century, and (3) invention of the Internet in the late 20th century.

What is the difference between the "Internet" and the "Web"? The Web is only one use of the Net along with email, Instant Message, peer-to-peer sharing (Napster, Groove), and much else that is emerging online. Twenty percent of Internet users in the U.S. get religious and spiritual information online, making it more popular than online banking (18% of Internet users) or online auctions (15%). People today are using their online lives to enrich and expand their offline living, not to substitute for it. There is a richness of social relationships in the digital global network that moderns cannot even begin to comprehend. (See **Categorical Imperialism.**)

If the church is to raise its low IQ, we must be open to the Internet as a whole new delivery system for learning and faith development. We must expand our architecture of sacred space to embrace virtual as well as physical places. Will the church help design the architecture of the social space that everyone is going to live in these next thousand years? Will the church play a role in framing the "Five P's" of the Internet: policing, pornography, privacy, protection, and property?[13] Will the church help decide which will win out—the Internet as a "global village," or the Internet as a "global market"—or whether they are mutually exclusive?

12. David Gelernter, "Fast Enough for You? [Review of George Gilder's *Telecosm*]" in *National Review* (25 September 2000), 50.
13. Note the change of subtitle in these two editions published just four years apart: Frances Cairncross, *The Death of Distance: How the Communications Revolution Will Change Our Lives* (Cambridge, MA: Harvard Business School Press, 1997), and *The Death of Distance: How the Communications Revolution Is Changing Our Lives* (Cambridge, MA: Harvard Business School Press, 2001).

> Sometimes we will use networks to avoid going places.
> But sometimes, still, we will go places to network.
>
> —William J. Mitchell[14]

Many churches are dipping their toes into the Internet world by posting a website that serves as an online brochure or calling card. That is a start. But what about online or emailed daily devotionals (and responses), or small groups that meet not in church buildings or living rooms, but chat rooms? What about online giving (via credit cards) and new forms of membership? Could a church in Baltimore have members in Calgary who enjoy public worship online (in real time, or downloaded later), keep up with church news online, vote as members online, participate in a group online (with members in eleven countries, maybe?), tithe online, sign up for mission trips online, and book tickets online for in-real-life participation at an annual retreat, where face-to-face time and nonvirtual hugs happen? Could this kind of membership be more intense, personal, and rewarding than the casual membership of 97% of church members in traditional off-line settings?

If we are ready to go further in developing our IQ, perhaps we will grapple with this question: When are we going to stop yanking promising young leaders out of real ministry so they can go to seminary and get "trained" for theoretical ministry? A few seminaries are leading the way, offering online courses to people currently in lay ministry so they can be trained and resourced and linked with other students online, even while these people do frontline ministry in their own settings.

Wouldn't these online seminarians be among the best candidates for "professional" ministry, learning on the job, in the saddle, in the middle of life, just as Jesus' disciples did, and

14. These are the closing words to William J. Mitchell's *"e-topia: Urban Life, Jim—But Not As We Know It"* (Cambridge, MA: The MIT Press, 1999), 155.

getting a track record and building real-life experience as they study, interact, read, and discuss online?[15] Nobody says this has to be an either/or deal; exciting combinations of onsite, short-term intensives can be interwoven with an ongoing online training experience.

Exciting new possibilities come into view when our IQ improves!

EPICtivity I: IQ (Internet Quotient)

Purchase a videocam and software for each person on your team to connect to his or her personal computer. (To save money, you can pair up people. The cost is approximately $80 per computer package.)

Have a team meeting, Bible study, or small-group meeting using the software.

After the experience (in person, or still online) discuss the following questions:

- Describe your videocam experience. What were its strengths and weaknesses? How many of those weaknesses can be resolved through improved technology?
- What possibilities do you see for using this form of technology in your ministry setting?

15. Ralph E. Moore reminds us that "seminary, as the threshold to pastor ministry, is a recent innovation in the United States. Prior to the establishment of seminaries, there were three predominant training patterns for pastoral ministry: Congregational and Presbyterian churches used a system of apprenticeship following college. Methodist in-service training coupled circuit-riding apprentice preachers and lay leaders in home meetings. The circuit rider, while being discipled by a more established pastor, showed up for one sermon a month. The lay leader was the actual shepherd and ran the rest of the meetings. Finally, Baptists in the South ran their *tent-making ministries*. This was used most effectively in the South and on the frontier" (Ralph E. Moore, *Friends: The Key to Reaching Generation X* [Ventura, CA: Regal Books, 2001], 86).

• What are some of the drawbacks? What other elements could you combine with this technology to resolve some of the drawbacks?

At the end of your IQ session, have everyone go to the "last page" of the Internet: *www.1112.net/lastpage.html.*
Where do you also see this double ring of "high tech/high touch" coming together?

I is for Interreligious Dialogue

In February 1999, President Clinton brought Yasir Arafat to the Presidential Prayer Breakfast in Washington. Evangelical Christians wondered if this was just one more sin to be added to his list. Was it? Or was it an outcropping of the need for interreligious dialogue? Was it an acceptance of other religions as partners in the quest for truth and justice?

Poet Denise Levertov's "The Cutting Beam" asks us to imagine two neighbors:

> *your house, my house, looking across, friendly:*
> *imagine ourselves*
> *meeting each other*
> *bringing gifts, bringing news.*[16]

Interfaith connections in the 21st century will be like this—neighbors sharing gifts and finding fresh ways to explore the universe together.

We don't engage in adversarial relationships with non-Christians. Why should we espouse adversarial relationships with non-Christian religions? I don't have to compromise my faith in treating other faiths with respect and generosity any

16. Denise Levertov, "Cloud Poems III, The Cutting-beam," in her *The Freeing of the Dust* (New York: New Directions, 1975), 63.

more than I would compromise it by treating *people* of other faiths with respect and generosity.

In *The Good Heart*, the Dalai Lama recommends that Christians, if they learn anything from Buddhism, use what they learn to make them better Christians. He urges people not to try to blend different religious traditions into a least-common-denominator fruit salad.[17]

At the Asian Bishops Synod hosted by the Vatican in 1998, the bishops of Malaysia, Singapore, and Brunei listed what the church could learn from dialogue with other religions. Here are the "gifts" they suggest we could receive from our neighbors, if only we were humble and hospitable enough:

> From Muslims the Church can learn about prayer, fasting, and almsgiving.
>
> From Hindus the Church can learn about meditation and contemplation.
>
> From Buddhists the Church can learn about detachment from material goods and respect for life.
>
> From Confucianism the Church can learn about filial piety and respect for elders.
>
> From Taoism the Church can learn about simplicity and humility.
>
> From animists the Church can learn about reverence and respect for nature and gratitude for harvests.
>
> The Church can learn from the rich symbolism and rites existing in their diversity of worship.[18]

17. Dalai Lama, Robert Kiely, and Dom Laurence Freeman, *The Good Heart: A Buddhist Perspective on the Teachings of Jesus* (Somerville, MA: Wisdom Publications, 2000). This is a remarkable book, in which a Christian meditation society asked the leader of Tibetan Buddhism to read the teachings of Christ and comment on them from his religious perspective.

18. "Look at It Our Way: Asian Bishops Respond to Rome," *The Tablet* (2 May 1998), 571.

Paul believed in a revelation of God in creation (Rom. 1:19ff.; Acts 14:17; 17:24ff.), in culture, even in other religions. There is truth to be found in creation. There is truth to be found in other religions. God is present throughout creation, writes Welsh priest/poet R. S. Thomas:

> *Other incarnations, of course,*
> *consonant with the environment*
> *he finds himself in,*
> *animating the cells.*[19]

For biblical scholar N. T. Wright, the notion that there is no truth to be found in other religions is unbiblical. "Colossians 1:16 implies that all philosophies or religions which have some 'fit' with the created world will thereby reflect in some ways the truth of God. It does not, however, imply that they are therefore, as they stand, doorways into the *new* creation. That place, according to 1:18, is Christ's alone."[20]

> The Orthodox Christian has no reason to think that all the truth claims made by other world religions are false, but only those that are incompatible with Christian truth claims.
>
> —PHILOSOPHER/THEOLOGIAN WILLIAM LANE CRAIG[21]

Interreligious dialogue does not exclude evangelism, of course. No, it makes evangelism possible in a spirit of "gentleness and respect" (1 Peter 3:15). In dialogue, all conversants

---

19. R. S. Thomas, "Other Incarnations," in "Incarnation," the second section of his unified theme collection of poems, *Counterpoint* (Newcastle upon Tyne: Bloodaxe Books, 1990), 33.

20. N. T. Wright, *The Epistles of Paul to the Colossians and to Philemon,* Tyndale New Testament Commentaries (Grand Rapids: Eerdmans, 1986), 79.

21. William Lane Craig, "Politically Incorrect Salvation," in *Christian Apologetics in the Postmodern World,* ed. Timothy Phillips and Dennis Okholm (Downers Grove, IL: InterVarsity Press, 1995), 77.

bring their commitments to the table while respecting one another's commitments too. Without maintaining our comments, what is there to talk about.

Perhaps someone says, "But I have Hindu neighbors and they're 'not so bad.'" Or even better, "They're good people." That doesn't mean dialogue excludes evangelism, because "good people" need Christ. We don't always need to tell "good people" how bad they are. We can tell "good people" how great Christ is and how much better they can be with Jesus living in them.

If you treat people of other religions with anything less than gentleness and respect, if you refuse to receive gifts from them, don't think you are honoring either your neighbors or Christ. You are doing the opposite. And if you think that interreligious dialogue means you can't offer gifts to others, including an invitation to join you as a follower of Christ, then please, think again.

I is for Intersubjectivity

Objectivism is an Enlightenment fashion but epistemological fantasy. The objectivist assumption—that "empirical knowledge, acquired in the scientific format, represents the world independent of the knower and his values, or in a way that only implicates him peripherally"[22]—is a relatively recent approach to knowledge. It is based on a concept of logic successively disproved by the likes of mathematician Gottlob Frege, physicist Werner Heisenberg, philosophers Bertrand Russell and Ludwig Wittgenstein, metaphysician Alfred North Whitehead, among others, and even in the writings of Zeno of Elea, the ancient Greek philosopher (Zeno's paradox). For all of them, what proves the objectivist argument's undoing is the disabling realization that one can be objective about anything, but only from a subjective point of view.[23]

22. This is the objectivist understanding of science, as defined by Francisco J. Varela, *Principles of Biological Autonomy* (New York: North Holland, 1979), 276–77.
23. This is a paraphrase of Richard E. Cytowie, *The Man Who Tasted Shapes* (New York: G. P. Putnam's Sons, 1993), 226.

If you doubt that many Christians were brainwashed by Enlightenment modernity, just ask them how they feel about "objective truth." They will defend the concept of objective truth as if it were the gospel itself, and they will most often see any assault on objective truth as a surrender to what they call "subjectivity." In this way they show themselves to have been entrapped by modernity in the very way they see reality.[24] For them, reality falls into two categories, the impersonal objective category (which is good, true, and trustworthy) and the subjective category (which is shaky, biased, false, and dangerous). Unfortunately for defenders of objectivity, this reality isn't real. It is a figment of the Enlightenment, and it never really existed, even though Enlightenment rationalists were sure it did.

For Christians, objectivity is never the last word, because behind all objects there is always a Subject, God, who is not only the ultimate Subject, but is also the Personal Subject. If this is true, then nothing in the universe is purely objective; nothing in the universe has no subjective value associated with it, because God has subjective values for everything (including sparrows that fall, and one would assume, the carbon and hydrogen atoms that yield the sparrow and the gravity that causes the sparrow to fall). The very concepts "subjective" and "objective" are unbiblical categories, for in the Scriptures there is always subject-object interaction.[25]

24. To demonstrate the truth is mediated through language, Frank T. Birtel gives the example of Christopher Columbus. "A speaker who says Columbus was a man who discovered America and proved the world was round clearly refers to Columbus even though Columbus did neither of these things. Upon what does the reality of the reference hinge?" Birtel goes on to ask: "When theology is proclaimed in the language and metaphors of another linguistic and cultural community, valid reference is lost. The community of the faithful live in one community, and Rome is another" (Frank T. Birtel, ed., *Reasoned Faith: Essays on the Interplay of Faith and Reason* [New York: Crossroad, 1993], 166–67).

25. The best definition of "objectivity" comes from Stanley Grenz, who explains objectivity, not in terms of what we can hear, see, taste, touch, smell, but the world as God wills it. See his essay, "Articulating the Christian Belief-Mosaic: Theological Method after the Demise of Foundationalism," in *Evangelical Futures: A Conversation on Theological Method*, ed. John G. Stackhouse Jr. (Grand Rapids: Baker, 2001), 104–36.

In this universe—the one Christians really should believe in rather than the objective Enlightenment figment—we as personal subjects interact with other personal subjects and the ultimate Personal Subject, and we interact with objects that human personal subjects and the ultimate Personal Subject value in varying ways and degrees.

True, Christians who wave the "objective truth" flag are against something worth being against: an arrogant human subjectivity that ignores the greatest Subject—God. That's worth being against! But we would do better to move out of the Enlightenment universe and back into God's universe, which is neither objective nor subjective, but rather intersubjective—a universe where created subjects and the uncreated Subject all interact in wonderful ways.

When our theology regains this personal, intersubjective (and biblical!) feel again, it won't sound so mechanistic and outdated (i.e., "modern") to postmodern people.

I is for Irony

Find it hard to tell whether it's praise or parody?

Professional football coach John Madden had a saying he gave to his players: "Don't worry about the mules going blind, just load the wagons." Madden says he never really knew what it meant, but it always seemed to work, so he kept saying it.

Here is a question comedian George Carlin asks his audiences: "If you try to fail and succeed, which have you done?"

Wherever postmoderns turn, they bump into parody, satire, and irony. Postmoderns are superb carpenters of conundrums.

Postmoderns enjoy, if anything, an overdeveloped sense of irony and a treacherous knack for slipping playfully in and out of clichés. Through its variety of shifting angles of perspective and illusion, irony is how postmoderns subvert. In one of Douglas Coupland's stories, an old friend tells Scout: "I'm trying to escape from ironic hell: Cynicism into faith; randomness into clarity; worry into devotion. But it's hard because I try to be sincere about life, and then I turn on the TV and see a game show host and have to throw up my hands and give up." Scout says at one point: "I think there was a trade-off somewhere along the line. I think the price we paid for our golden life was an inability to fully believe in love; instead, we gained an irony that scorched everything it touched. And I wonder if this irony is the price we paid for the loss of God."[26]

> As ironic modern worshipers we congregate at the cinematic temple. We pay our votive offerings at the box office. We buy our ritual corn. We hush in reverent anticipation as the lights go down and the celluloid magic begins. Throughout the filmic narrative we identify with the hero.... We vicariously exult in the victories of the drama. And we are spiritually inspired by the moral of the story, all the while believing we are modern techno-secular people, devoid of religion. Yet the depth and intensity of our participation reveal a religious fervor that is not much different from that of religious zealots.
>
> —GEOFFREY HILL[27]

It is for this reason that Reinhold Niebuhr has been called "that prepostmodernist lover of American ironies."[28] It is also for this reason that Christian fiction, some of which is best-seller status, is so widely shunned and panned by postmoderns. In the words of one reviewer, "There are no curses or smut, of course, but also no plain-spoken nouns

26. See Douglas Coupland, *Life After God* (New York: Pocket Books, 1994), 287, 273.

27. Geoffrey Hill, *Illuminating Shadows: The Mythic Power of Film* (Boston: Shambhala, 1992), 3.

28. David Tracy, "Modernity, Antimodernity, and Postmodernity in the American Setting," in *Knowledge and Belief in America: Enlightenment Traditions and Modern Religious Thought*, ed. William M. Shea and Peter A. Huff (New York: Cambridge University Press, 1995), 329.

and verbs denoting body parts or functions. Above all, no humor. No jokes, no kidding, no double meanings, no quirks, and certainly no irony."[29]

> The world is comedy to those that think, a tragedy to those that feel.
>
> —ENGLISH AUTHOR HORACE WALPOLE, IN A LETTER, 16 AUGUST 1776

If you dislike irony, brace yourself, because when you start listening to postmodern scholars in biblical studies (like Walter Brueggemann at Columbia Theological Seminary, Richard Hays at Duke, businessman and lecturer Mark D. Nanos, or Jo-Ann Badley at Newman Theological College), you will discover layer upon layer of highly sophisticated ironic readings in the Bible itself.[30] For example, they will lead you to start noticing the ironic attitude toward the monarchy in the Old Testament, or the ironic attitude toward "good Gentiles" (Melchizedek and Jethro, Uriah the Hittite, the nameless Roman centurion in the Gospels, Cornelius)—and especially Gentile women (Rahab and Ruth in the Old Testament, the Syrophoenecian and Samaritan in the New).

In fact, once you begin to savor the delicious, subversive, clever, brilliant, and pervasive levels of irony being surfaced and celebrated by these new post-liberal, post-conservative, post-critical biblical scholars, you will blush over the naïve readings that you have endorsed and preached in the past. Once you get over the shock and embarrassment, don't fear: You will love the

---

29. *Time* reporter Martha Duffy in a review of Christian fiction, "The Almighty to the Rescue," *Time,* 13 November 1995, 107.

30. Walter Brueggemann, *The Bible Makes Sense* (Louisville: Westminster John Knox, 2001) and *Texts That Linger, Words That Explode: Listening to Prophetic Voices* (Minneapolis: Fortress Press, 2000); Richard Hays, *Complete Interpretation of the New Testament* (Louisville: Westminster John Knox, 1998); Mark D. Nanos, *The Irony of Galatians: Paul's Letter in First-Century Context* (Minneapolis: Fortress, 2001).

I is for Irony

Bible and revere its inspiration more than ever, and your post-modern hearers will find in the Bible a book that resonates powerfully with the complex ironies of life.

These resonant readings of the Scriptures are a thousand times more precious to postmodern people than the simple, univocal, "clear," black-and-white, nearly mathematical readings of modern scholars and preachers.

> My belief is completely separate from the culture of Christianity. I see some flaws in it but I'm committed to Christ, not Christianity.
>
> —Techno artist Moby[31]

---

31. Moby continues: "But to me looking at the universe speaks of the existence of God; the existence of an architect at least and if you want to understand the character of the architect you've got to look at the character of the universe. If you want to learn about God, look at a forest." See "Moby: Animal-Right?: Tony and Dave Talk to Moby," *Retroactivebaggage* 14 (October 1996). See *www.baggage.co.uk*. Accessed 19 April 2001.

J is for J-Factor

● As Tarzan said to Jane, and then Jane fed back to Tarzan, "Don't forget to hang on to the Vine."[1]

● The Archimedean point, that outside objective point without which everything becomes subjective. Jesus is Absolute Truth, the Subject/Object, the objective referent that relativizes everything else. Jesus is the infallible, inerrant image of God. Everything we have said in this A-to-Z primer that seeks to adjudicate the imperative of postmodernity and the claims of Christ can be reduced to one word: Jesus.

Jesus is our Meridian. In Christ, Genesis begins again.

> By blood and origin, I am Albanian. My citizenship is Indian. I am a Catholic nun. As to my calling, I belong to the whole world. As to my heart, I belong entirely to Jesus.
>
> —MOTHER TERESA

Jesus is the answer. Literally. Jesus is the answer to every question. (Well, not *every* question. Sometimes a bushy-tailed creature that eats nuts, as the child responding to a question during "Children's Sermon" realized, is really a squirrel.) Jesus doesn't help us find the answers. Jesus doesn't show us what the answers are. Jesus *is* the answer.

What is the most important thing that could happen to that person in front of you? He or she meets Jesus, the Bread of Life. Every person you have ever met would be better off if he or she would follow Jesus better. What the postmodern soul hungers for "is ultimately not a variety of interesting and moving insights but a single universal truth."[2]

1. Thanks to Jenny Jackson-Adams for this quote.
2. Richard Rory, quoted by David Brooks, *Bobos in Paradise: The New Upper Class and How They Got There* (New York: Simon & Schuster, 2000), 237.

I know that my Redeemer liveth, and that he shall stand at the latter day upon the earth; and though this body be destroyed, yet shall I see God; whom I shall see for myself and mine eyes shall behold, and not as a stranger.[3]

But the Bread of Life needs to become fresh manna for every tribe and culture to pick up. In the era of Christendom, when people said "no" to Jesus, they knew what they were missing. In this new world, we must present a Jesus that the world doesn't know it is missing. In the same way that some biographies need to be rewritten for each generation,[4] the story of the Incarnation needs to be incarnated—in this case, Jesus as the first premodern postmodern—so that people can, *not* just make Christ the center of their lives, but bring their lives into the center of Christ's life.

> Let us fix our eyes on Jesus, the author and perfecter of our faith.
> —HEBREWS 12:2 NIV

The three most significant remarks in intellectual history, according to essayist/novelist David Lodge, are these:

1. Descartes' "I think therefore I am"
2. Nietzsche's "God is dead"
3. Darwin's "Crying is a puzzler"[5]

---

3. Job 19:25, 27 as found in the "The Order for the Burial of the Dead," *The Book of Common Prayer,* 1979 edition.

4. Virginia Woolf argued that "there are some stories which have to be retold by each generation." See Virginia Woolf, "Not One of Us" (October 1927), in her *Collected Essays*, ed. Leonard Woolf (London: Chatto & Windus, 1966–67), 4:20: quoted in Hermione Lee, *Virginia Woolf* (New York: Alfred A. Knopf, 1997), 11.

5. As stated by one of the main characters, Ralph Messenger, in David Lodge, *Thinks: A Novel* (New York: Viking, 2001), and quoted in Joyce Carol Oates, "Hot-Blooded Brits," *TLS: Times Literary Supplement* (23 February 2001), 21.

Lodge forgot the fourth and most significant remark in intellectual history: Jesus' definition of God—"God is Love"—and Jesus' replacement of the Golden Rule with the Titanium Rule, or what he called the New Commandment: "Love others as I have loved you."

For radically orthodox Christians in the emerging culture, then, even though "J is for Jesus," Jesus should also be the Alpha and Omega, the A and the Z, the first word and the last in this primer.

Or in the words of Scripture, "Then he said, '... I'm A to Z. I'm the Beginning, I'm the Conclusion'" (Rev. 21:6 THE MESSAGE).

EPICtivity J: J-Factor

Gather your team together and bake or buy a birthday cake. Assemble candles, balloons, and other party materials. Go to a section of town you normally avoid and knock on doors or talk to people on the street until you find someone who has a birthday coming up soon, adult or child. Deliver the party materials, light the candles, sing "Happy Birthday," and then leave.

- Have each person describe his or her experience.
- What does it mean when Jesus says, "When you do it for the least of these, my brothers, you're doing it personally for me" (see Matt. 25:40)?
- Why do we need the poorer as much as they need us? Why do the richer need us as much as we need them?
- Describe what a Christlike church looks like, based on this shared experience.

J is for Judas

Judas' main problem was his inability to escape self-reflexivity, which ultimately leads to death. For the self-reflexive person, everything is always "about me."

Two prime examples of self-reflexivity from the emerging culture:

1. TV shows about TV.[6]
2. All discussions of postmodernity, which must make use of the concept of modernity to talk about postmodernity.[7]

Another name for every one of us: Judas. And Peter and Andrew and John and Matthew and . . . "more like DUH-sciples than di-sciples!"[8]

To be human is to betray Jesus. Notwithstanding all our efforts to the contrary, no doubt we have betrayed him in this book as many times as Peter did in a Judean courtyard.

> Christ, have mercy.
> Lord, have mercy.
> Christ, have mercy upon us,

. . . "DUH-sciples" all.

---

6. There is *The Larry Sanders Show,* HBO's brilliant "behind-the-scenes" deconstruction of the talk show. Before that there was *Murphy Brown, Sports Night, Frasier,* and MTV's *Real World.* With *Mystery Science Theater 3000* and *Beavis and Butt-head,* we can watch comedians, aliens, and even cartoons watching TV.

7. For more on this reflexivity, see Gustavo Benavides, "Modernity" in *Critical Terms for Religious Studies,* ed. Mark C. Taylor (Chicago: University of Chicago Press, 1998), 186–201.

8. As quoted by Deborah Krause, "School's in Session: The Making and Unmaking of Docile Disciple Bodies in Mark" in *Postmodern Interpretations of the Bible—A Reader,* ed. A. K. M. Adam (St. Louis: Chalice Press, 2001), 177.

K is for Kaleido-
scopic Change

Culture is like a kaleidoscope. Every time someone shakes it or even gives it a tiny twist, the images change . . . never to return to the shape they were in.

Postmodern culture is a hall of refracting mirrors. From whatever angle on whatever day, there is new beauty and fresh perfection.

The velocity of change is fierce. Some change is still incremental, but most of it now is exponential—discontinuous, disruptive, and destabilizing. The half-life of everything has shortened. Impermanence rules in every discipline. Scientist Murray Gell-Mann admits that "when I go three orders of magnitude I go to a new science."[1] The scientific community has arguably gone through three new sciences since the Newtonian paradigm that built the modern world.

One of the key laws of ecology for postmodern leaders is L > C.

L > C means that for an organism to survive, its rate of learning (L) must be equal to (=) or greater than (>) the rate of change (C) in the environment. Everything that is alive is a learning organism.[2]

The distinctions of "learned" and "unlearned" no longer apply in this new world. There are only learners and non-learners.

1. As quoted by John Holland in "Spiritual Robots: John Holland Presentation: Conscious Machines, Complexity," at the "Will Spiritual Robots Replace Humanity by 2100?" symposium, Stanford University (1 April 2000); *www.technetcast.com/tnc_program.html?program_id=82*. Accessed 5 August 2001.

2. Leonard Sweet, *Eleven Genetic Gateways to Spiritual Awakening* (Nashville: Abingdon, 1998), 48.

> We are not what we know.
> We are what we are willing to learn.
>

Parable #1 of Exponential Change: The Pentium processors on which this book is being written handle data at a rate of 1.6 gigabytes per second. The chip that powers the new PlayStation 2 (PS2) moves data at about 48 gigabytes a second. In other words, a single upgrade in video technology can bring a 50-to-100-fold increase in processing power. Pac Man is to Sony PlayStation 2 what a Roman candle is to an IBM missile.

Parable #2 of Exponential Change: If one person told only two people about the *secret*—the love of Jesus—and if those two kept "faith" and kept the promise and told two more the next day, and so on and so on, in twenty days more than a million people could be sharing the *secret*. Within thirty days more than a billion people could be involved. Within thirty-two days, the entire population of the earth could be "in" on our "*secret*."

The church in modernity was off-balance, reeling from a culture that once revered it and now rejected it. As a result, it simply tried to keep standing, to stand firm, to not collapse—to not change, because change felt like defeat or decay. While this resolute firmness is admirable, it can't be the final word for the church in the emerging postmodern world, because standing firm can too easily be an excuse for going stale.

Ultimately, the church is called to do far more than either standing firm or being willing to change itself. Like a candle in darkness, salt in meat, yeast in bread, or seeds in a field, the church is called to be a change agent, bringing positive change

---

3. Every two years the Gihon Foundation brings together world-class thinkers and asks each leader to identify the single issue that should be elevated in everyone's mind. They then publish their reflections (called "the world's most expensive fortune cookies") on their website, *www.gihon.com.* This was one of them. Accessed 17 July 2001.

to God's world. The world is changing. The church is changing. Change is changing. The only question is whether we will change in ways that result in changes for the better.

If you dislike change, this talk about kaleidoscopic change is bad news. Here (again) is some worse news. If you resist change, you will change. Your act of resistance to change will change you—into an increasingly resistant person, a tenser person, an angrier or sadder or more combative person. The change you were resisting may have been bad. But the change in you may be worse. This holds true not only for individuals, but also for organizations. To avoid changing in destructive and unintended ways, it makes sense to choose change in constructive, intentional ways. (See **Blur.**)

A change-resistant deacon board once said to their pastor, "The reason we don't want our church to change is that everywhere else in our lives, we are assaulted by change—at work, at home, in the culture at large. We want the church to be the one stable place in our world." The pastor resigned. Who won?

There was a big educational debate in the last third of the 19th century about a new technology that some believed threatened the very foundations of the educational experience. For decades students had used pencils when taking notes and taking exams. But in 1880 a new kind of pencil was introduced: one with an eraser at one end.

This had never been offered before, and many educators rose up in arms. Why? It encouraged students to make mistakes. It made it possible to hide mistakes.

"Let students avoid errors in the first place and they won't need an eraser."

EPICtivity K: Kaleidoscopic Change

Attach the name of your church to the following items with a paper and rubber band:

A plastic bottle half-filled with water (keep the cap on)
A can of pop
A plastic bottle filled to the top with the cap removed
An unopened glass bottle of SoBe drink
Create your own variation

Place these items in the freezer two days prior to your team meeting. *Be sure to place containers in zip-closing bags to avoid spillage!* Also, be careful when taking damaged containers out of the freezer—you may want to use gloves.

Display on a table all the frozen containers. Read Charles Darwin's quote on change:

It's not the strongest of the species that survive, nor the most intelligent, but the one most responsive to change.

Hand out 3 x 5 cards and have participants comment on each of the displays.

- Which of the containers were more adaptable to change?
- Which of the containers were the least adaptive?
- Where do you think our church or ministry needs to experience the most change?
- What hurdles exist that hinder change?
- What are the implications if we choose not to change?
- What is the potential benefit for God's kingdom if we do change?

> • How can we help the people God has entrusted to us to walk the walk of change?
> • Where do I need to change?

K is for Karaokees

The emerging culture is a karaoke culture. People want to hold the mike themselves, or at least feel that they could take it if they wanted it. Leaders must provide people with karaokees in whatever they are doing.

Bob Woodward, reporter for the *Washington Post*, boasts that he tried the first interactive Landon Lecture series at Kansas State University on 30 March 2000, where his remarks were shaped around a series of questions he asked his audience.[4] But the truth is that our last three presidents inserted karaokees into their speeches. Reagan started the tradition of bringing people to his speeches and telling their stories. Bill Clinton further developed the tradition. But George W. Bush, in his first big speech after his inaugural address, upped the size of the karaokee by not just pointing to those in the audience and telling their story, but handing them the mike and inviting them to tell their stories: the story of how without a tax reduction they would be forced to go on welfare; the story of how a faith-based initiative made a life-or-death difference; and so on.

The postmodern "Dear Abby" is found on the Internet, at sites like *Allexperts.com*, *Askme.com*, *Epinions.com*, *Exp.com*, *Keen.com*, *Experts-Exchange.com*, *ExpertCentral.com*, where everyday people become experts—and receive honor for it.

Why are there breaks in the text of this book? It's a karaokee. They give the reader little intermissions and slight pauses and

4. See Bob Woodward, "Honest Communication: Finding Out What Really Happened," *Vital Speeches of the Day* 61 (1 June 2000), 484–88. See *pqasb.pqarchiver.com/votd*. Accessed 4 October 2000.

encourage your response in the form of talk-backs, note-making, questioning, or hesitancy.[5] They are an acknowledgment that you may have a different or even opposing point of view.

Why do we try to finish as few sentences as we can when speaking? It's a karaokee. If you finish my sentence before I do, it's your sentence. You got there before I did.

Why the use of what linguists now call "the rising inflection" among postmoderns?[6] This hesitancy ("Are you with me?" or "You may not agree with this, but hear me out, okay?") is not an admission of uncertainty or a need for help but a heightening of audience participation.

Karaokees are postmodern forms of "performance art"—or better yet, participatory art.

K is for Kitsch

Everything that exists can be a means of worship and prayer. Even material culture. Even the cheap, the schmoltz, the fantastical, the funky of material culture. Even kitsch.

Kitsch is found in the two levels of culture the modern church was least prepared to embrace. In the modern world there were three (some say four)[7] levels of art: (1) high culture (or high-falutin' art), (2) popular culture, and (3) folk culture. The modern church loved high culture as long as it was 200

---

5. See Eric Sanborn's essay, "Publishing for Postmoderns." It can be ordered from *www.pcisys.net/~stanford/pubpomos.htm*. Accessed 11 June 2002.

6. Karen Ritchie, "Marketing to Generation X," *American Demographics* (April 1995), 36.

7. Michael Kammen argues that there is a difference between popular and mass culture, or at least there was until the advent of electronic culture. By "popular culture" he means traditional culture; by nature, traditional culture is participatory, and people themselves interact with each other and create their own customs and mores. Mass culture is the product of mass communications technology; in this the people are passive recipients of others' creativity. "Popular culture reached its prime in the half-century from about 1885 to 1935, when it came increasingly to be supplanted by mass culture, which emerged fully in the decades following the Second World War. It produced 'spectatoritis,' the disease of the couch potato, all eyes and indolence." See Michael Kammen, *American Culture, American Tastes: Social Change and the 20th Century* (New York: Alfred A.

years old; it eventually embraced some forms of folk culture (Southern gospel, black gospel) while resisting others (Latino/a salsa, Javanese gamelan, Jamaican reggae, Congo Ashanti chants, the sound world of Indian sitars).

But the modern church would make no concessions to popular culture.[8] It was the Devil's planet, and the only way the church would touch pop culture was with asbestos gloves or ice tongs.

You come across the kitsch in popular culture and folk culture—the two arenas in which the modern church struggled the most. What is more, in the emerging culture all three forms of art are conflating into one, and the "one" they're coalescing around is pop culture. The only thing keeping many symphonies (high culture) alive for people today is that the orchestras are now performing numbers from both pop culture (Beatles, Broadway shows, etc.) as well as folk culture.

Kitsch evidences postmodern subscription to incarnational theology: God is to be found in both spirit and matter (no matter how strange). Postmoderns revel in the revelation of the Eternal hidden in the earthly. Nothing is so humble or freakish that it can't be a worship aid and prayer relief. The power of God's Spirit can do more than General Electric, which "brings good things to life"; it can also bring little, odd, and kitsch "things" to life.

The typical Protestant view of matter as devoid of meaning will prove to be a theologically vagrant notion in the history of Christianity. The Catholic Christian and Orthodox Christian view of matter, in which meaning is immanent and ingrained, is better at withstanding the test of tradition and theology.

Knopf, 1999), 22–23, 70, 76–83, 89, 186. For the quote see, Harold Perkin, "The People and the Mass," *TLS: Times Literary Supplement* (25 February 2000), 10.

    8. For some postmodern approaches to popular culture, see Damaris Trust: Relating Christian Faith and Contemporary Culture at *www.Damaris.org,* a UK-based site that provides Bible studies around key elements in pop culture (bands, movies, TV shows, etc.), and Dick Staub's Seattle Center for Faith and Culture website, *www.culturewatch.net.* Accessed 17 July 2001.

Beware: Postmoderns are as much if not more susceptible to dejà lu as dejà vu. If moderns had the tendency to state the obvious, postmoderns have a tendency to state the odd. Put the odd, the kitsch, the quirky, the high jinks, and the campy together (see the EPIC performance artists Blue Man Group, or attend one of Atlanta's Red Baron's Auctions), and postmoderns are smitten as much as a cat sniffing nepetalactone (alias catnip).

L is for Laughter

⬤ What God indulges in when we set "plans."

Children laugh about 400 times every day, while adults on average laugh about 15 times. Some adults laugh annually . . . or less. Shipping executive Aristotle Onassis engendered the only known joke of Chinese leader Mao Zedong's life. "If Mr. Khrushchev had died," said Mao, "I doubt if Mr. Onassis would have married Mrs. Khrushchev."

For health purposes, three belly laughs a day are required.

A pastor was telling the congregation about the little girl who came home from choir rehearsal one night and told her mother, "We learned a new Easter hymn tonight, Mommy."

"Really, dear? What's that?" her mother inquired.

The little girl said, "Christ Has Rhythm!"

No sooner had those words left the preacher's lips than one of the young adult men in the congregation responded, "He has rhythm indeed!"

Four-year-old Soren Coventry Sweet had a favorite praise anthem: "He is exalted." Except that to her non-reading brain, the words reverberated differently. So every time the Sweet family sings that one praise song, we laugh together and follow a child's lead into unexpected reveries of theological insight into what it must be like to be God with creatures like us: "He is the Lord, forever his truth shall reign; . . . He is exhausted for he is exhausted on high."

Modern churches became sick because they were afraid of too much laughter or rhythm. Singer Jerry Lee Lewis tells how his life as a preacher came to an abrupt end. While playing a hymn to students, "I kinda put a little feeling into it, a little Louisiana boogie-woogie. The students loved it, they stamped and hollered. I felt the spirit move me so I kept going on the

> The sorrows of the mind
> Be banished from this place.
> Religion never was designed
> To make our pleasure less.
>
> —OMITTED SECOND VERSE OF ISAAC WATTS'S
> HYMN "COME, WE THAT LOVE THE LORD"

piano, singing as powerful as I could. The students all clapped and rose to their feet in joyous rapture. The Dean expelled me, so I came home."[1]

The value of laughter in learning is grossly underappreciated. When people are not either crying or laughing, it is hard to believe they are learning much.

The shortest verse in the Bible is not "Jesus wept" (three words in Greek). It is "Rejoice evermore"[2] (only two words in Greek). Think how much more of God's truth the laughter-hating Hildegard of Bingen and St. John Chrysostom could have revealed if they had not banned laughter from faith.

EPICtivity L: Laughter

Rent or purchase a mixture of the following videos: *Candid Camera Classics*, *Best of Saturday Night Live*, *Sports Bloopers*. Preview and select about 30 minutes of video clips. Show the videos without explanation. Then ask the group these questions:

- How many of you thought we were wasting productive time watching the videos? If so, explain to the group why you felt this way.

1. Quoted in Peter Doggett, *Are You Ready for Country?* (London: Viking, 2000), 259–60.
2. John 11:35 KJV and 1 Thessalonians 5:16 KJV.

- What does stress look like for you? How do you seek relief (good ways and bad ways)?
- What does stress look like for us as a group or church? How do we seek relief (constructively and destructively)?
- Which is your favorite video clip? Why?
- Why do you think God created laughter?
- Are you personally experiencing enough laughter?
- Is our team having enough fun and laughter?
- Is our ministry/church/group laughing enough?
- How can we bring more laughter into our ministries?

L is for Liberation

Lay liberation: While academics have broadened the Reformation idea of vocation to "the prophethood of all believers" and "the public theological responsibilities of all believers,"[3] Luther's dream of the "priesthood of all believers" remains to be fulfilled. To distrust the people is to distrust the Spirit

Lay liberation can be an adventure in missing the point. When we speak of lay liberation, we generally focus on allowing a nonpaid-professional-clergy share in the sacerdotal/clerical/churchly functions—preaching, administering sacraments, and so on. In other words, we want to liberate the laity to serve God in church buildings during meetings.

Real liberation would be this: To see every believer as a minister commissioned to serve God in his or her neighborhood, workplace, classroom, and circle of friends. The action is not merely "in here" in the worlds of prayer, worship, teaching, and altar calls. No, the most important lay liberation is for

---

3. An illuminating discussion of these expansions can be found in Max L. Stackhouse, "If Globalization Is True, What Then Shall We Do? Toward a Theology of Ministry," *Theological Education* 35 (Spring 1999), 155–66.

ministry "out there," in the world God loves, where the Spirit of God is alive and well. (See **Outside-the-Box/Boat Thinking.**)

Clergy liberation: What we have learned about power brokers being in their own kind of bondage applies here. Lay liberation is also a clergy liberation—from control to release, from bottom-line responsibility to interdependence and synergy.

L is for Loopy

True postmoderns struggle with PowerPoint. It's too uniform, too monotonous, too noninteractive, too stock, too uncomplicated, too linear.[4]

Want to do ministry in the modern world? Get linear. Think straight.

Want to do ministry in this emerging culture? Get nonlinear. Think looped. Climb through Escher circles of surprise and unsettlement.

The vast bulk of life is nonlinear. Even God doesn't think straight: Look at nature. How many sharp angles, hard edges, and straight lines can you find? It's brimming with zigzags and oxbows, razorbacks and curves—forms and shapes now being rediscovered by artists and architects living out of a postmodern genre. Canadian-born Frank Gehry's design of the Guggenheim Museum in Bilbao, Spain, and the Experience Music Project in Seattle are the death knell of box buildings and the cockcrow of curvaceous, nonlinear, shapely buildings with few right angles or edges. "Blobitecture" its critics call it.

Say that 90% of life is nonlinear and 10% is linear. Modernity tried to build and rig a world on that 10% straight, smooth line; it forgot about the 90%. Postmodernity tends to build a world on the 90% and forgets about the 10%. Consider the New Age

---

4. For what happens to the Gettysburg Address when it becomes a PowerPoint Presentation, see *www.norvig.com/Gettysburg*. Accessed 17 July 2001. With a hearty "amen" to Thomas A. Stewart, "Ban It Now! Friends Don't Let Friends Use PowerPoint," *Fortune* (5 February 2001), 210.

movement. Or watch television, where plots resemble more a live-action CD-Rom adventure than old TV shows. All TV producers and filmmakers are now looped.[5]

God didn't put us through 500 years of linearity for us not to learn something. God didn't leave us in an Age of Reason for no reason. Forget linear? You might as well say, "Forget truth." The statement that "Martin Luther 'posted' his 95-point sermon in 1515" is quite different from the statement that "Martin Luther posted his 95-point sermon on All Saints' Day 1517."

Put the linear and the loop together (combine linear time and circular time), and you get a spiral, the biological symbol of life, the mathematical symbol of the infinite. (See **Helix.**)

Modern discipleship was as linear as an assembly line: Insert non-Christian raw material here, start conveyor belt, pass raw material through evangelism chute, progress through follow-up treatment, insert knowledge in linear fashion modeled after modern education systems (which were themselves modeled after linear manufacturing processes), fine-polish with books 1 through 7 in discipleship series, add optional leadership development features, and plop! Off the conveyer belt falls a mature Christian.

It would be nice if it worked that way (maybe). It doesn't. Spiritual growth reflects organic growth more than mechanized processes. Think of a tree. Does it go through a straight linear growth process? Well, yes—it grows from one year to the next, straight ahead through time. But no—because that time is a cyclical experience of seasons: winter, summer; latency, activity.

---

5. For example, Orthodox Christian/Ukrainian Yury Miloslavsky's *Urban Romances* (1994) and Quentin Tarantino's work on some of the best and worst films of the 1990s— *Natural Born Killers* (worst) and *Pulp Fiction* (best). Tarantino has been acclaimed as "the first post-postmodernist." *Pulp Fiction* (1994) is subtitled "Three Stories about One Story." It is put together as a novel: the circular form, the dislocated time sequence, the nonlinear narrative, the weaving together of several disparate stories. You start with one character and then jump to another, seemingly unrelated by either blood or history, and end by making an unexpected connection. This is like what we watch each night on television—e.g., *ER*.

1

For animals and humans, it's sleep, waking, work, rest, morning, night. Life is a kind of loopy linear cycle: progress, set-back, breakthrough, slowdown, growth, pruning, same thing, cyclically but different too, year after year.

What would a loopy, spiraling, helical discipleship process look like? What would a spiral sermon structure feel like to hear or prepare? Do you feel your creative juices stirring?

L is for Lost

Lost has become something of a technical term in recent years to refer to unsaved, unbelieving, unconverted, and otherwise non-Christian people. True and helpful phrases like "lost people matter to God" have popularized this usage.

The term is largely derived from three parables Jesus told in Luke 15 about a lost sheep, a lost coin, and two lost sons (though they were lost in different ways). Unfortunately, the term can easily and inadvertently reinforce an us/them or in-group/out-group attitude in Christians, whereby we think of ourselves as "the found" insiders and of others as "the lost" out-siders—with the outsider term developing a pejorative feel, and the insider term an elitist feel.

The fact is, few people would appreciate it if they knew we referred to them as "the lost."

Meanwhile, there is reason to ask, Who is really lost, them or us? Consider an analogy to mail. When a letter is sent, and it never arrives at its intended destination, we say it is lost. Similarly, Christians have been sent into the world, "as the Father has sent Me," according to Jesus (John 20:21), as a kind of love letter from God to all. Yet few of us have actually arrived with our message in the world to which we have been sent. Per-haps we would be wiser to refer to *ourselves* as the lost.

Additionally, what is striking in the three parables of Luke 15 is not actually that the sheep, coin, and sons are lost. Rather, it is that they are treasured and *missed*. The shepherd misses one out of 99 sheep, the woman misses one out of 10 coins, and the father misses a son who has rebelled, acted disgracefully and foolishly, even wasting half of the father's wealth. In all three cases, what was lost was sincerely, intensely missed.

Until further notice (that is, until we actually arrive at the destination to which we were sent), perhaps we should refer to ourselves as "the lost," and the people formerly known as "lost" should be referred to as "people God treasures." Just a suggestion.

L is for Love

● An undervalued word in recent Christian communication, having been replaced by "community."

Community is a good and useful word, but it is also dangerous. Why? Because community can become a commodity one seeks to acquire or experience by attending a church that talks a lot about it. And talking about community and promising community are almost guaranteed to hinder the community gathered around the talk and promise from experiencing true "community."

An analogy will make the reason clear. If a sign were put up along a busy street saying, "Self-Image Group meets here at 7:30 p.m." or "Acceptance Group meets here at 8:30 p.m.," what kind of people would show up? You can almost guarantee that no people with a high self-image or a high acceptance of others would show up for either; rather, people struggling with self-esteem would crowd the room at 7:30, and shy, lonely souls needing acceptance would show up at 8:30. One could just about guarantee that a roomful of people struggling with insecurity and inferiority would do little in their hour to encourage one another; nor would lonely and shy people go far to show one another acceptance.

> Hell is not to love anymore.
>
> —FRENCH NOVELIST GEORGES BERNANOS

Similarly, when we advertise community as our "product," we will attract people who want to consume it, and thus we will soon dissipate whatever capacity we had to produce it.

Instead, if we take Jesus' cue and put up a sign that says, "Learn How to Love, tonight at 8:00 p.m.," whoever shows up can be challenged and encouraged to serve, forgive, reconcile with, give to, speak the truth to, not judge, and be merciful to one another. In this way, by focusing on learning to love, people will hardly be able to leave that hour without experiencing some increasing measure of community. (See **Holiness.**)

M is for Mainline Church

● A synonym for "modern church." Also a pseudonym for the fastest-dying churches in the world (Presbyterians, United Methodists, UCCs, Lutherans, American Baptists), churches that do many good things— except grow. Too often, mainliners are either antigrowth, suspecting churches that are growing of having "sold out," or they don't care whether they grow or not.

One thinks of the tragic story of the Carolina parakeet. It was one of the most ubiquitous birds of early American history— and the only parakeet native to the U.S.—but its population and high-flying success collapsed because of deforestation as the species plummeted to extinction in a matter of decades. One recalls Paul's words about those who think they stand firm and tall taking heed lest they fall (1 Cor. 10:12).

Mainline churches traveled at breakneck speed since the 1950s from "mainline" tracks to "oldline" then "sideline" now "offline" status. It was predictable: Those who invested the most in the previous model (print culture) are the most likely to resist the new model (the postanalog age). Mainliners are hardliners in their digiphobia.[1]

But this is not the most immediate and pressing crisis of the "mainline." Almost no one wants to talk about this (except David J. Wood of the Louisville Institute), but the fact remains that there are very few clergy under 35. Leaders from the emerging culture are simply not joining the ranks of ordained clergy in the mainline denominations. In the Presbyterian church, the number of clergy under 36 fell to 7%, a drop of 71.4% in 25

1. Clayton M. Christensen, *The Innovator's Dilemma: When New Technologies Cause Great Firms to Fail* (Cambridge, MA: Harvard Business School Press, 1997).

years.[2] In United Methodism, 25 years ago about 80% of semi-nary graduates were under 35. Today it's just the opposite. In 1997, the General Convention of the Episcopal Church reported that of the 8000 ordained clergy in the church, fewer than 300 were under the age of 35.[3]

But maybe, just maybe, there will arise from the mainline embers some new sparks. Maybe decades of numerical decline (especially as it constricts operating budgets) will awaken the emperor to his naked condition. Maybe not. But believers in resurrection shouldn't call anything impossible.

> I thought my fireplace cold.
> And stirred up the ashes;
> My fingers got burnt.
>
> —SPANISH POET ANTONIO MACHADO[4]

Even so, there is a danger in holding this hope. Aside from the "righteous remnant" mentality of many rip-roaring denom-inationalists, what if Jesus doesn't want to save the den-ominational structures as they exist? What if trying to save our denominations becomes a distraction from what Jesus really wants to save—namely, the world, our neighbors, people? Could it be that the only way to save mainline denominations is for the denominations to stop trying to save themselves and instead join Jesus in trying "to save that which was lost" (Matt. 18:11 KJV)? Could it be true of mainline denominations that if they try to save their lives, they will lose them, and that only by losing their lives for Christ's sake will they find them?

2. Hilary Wicai, "Clergy by the Numbers," *Congregations* (March/April 2001), 6.

3. At a gathering of some of those 300, the papers were collected as *Gathering the NeXt Generation: Essays on the Formation and Ministry of GenX Priests*, ed. Nathan Humphrey (Harrisburg, PA: Morehouse, 2000).

4. Antonio Machado, "Proverbs and Song-verse, lviii," in his *Selected Poems,* trans. Alan S. Trueblood (Cambridge, MA: Harvard University Press, 1982), 191.

Meanwhile, the more conservative evangelical and charismatic churches, which grew while (and maybe because?) the mainlines declined, should not be smug as we move into the new world. Along with the Carolina parakeet, the passenger pigeon (which was even more common than its more colorful cousin) also went extinct.

Nobody stands secure for very long in any world—ancient, modern, or postmodern.

M is for Margins

To be at the center in the future, you have to go to the margins today.

In modernity, power was concentrated in centers and size. In the postmodern world, margins, regardless of their size, become centers of a different kind of power. Centered power dominates, and that's about it. Marginal power is far more interesting. It bothers, bedazzles, fascinates, mystifies, attracts, entices, inspires.

In modernity, the megashopping mall along the superhighway dominated our attention, as did the megachurch. By contrast, postmodern Christians will be as attracted to the creative, innovative, and probably smaller marginal church as postmodern shoppers will be to the small boutique or gallery or café hidden around the corner or on the edge of town. Why? Because mass-produced mega-institutional products are fast and convenient and cheap, but not nearly as interesting and fresh as unique home-cooked, homegrown, homemade creations from the margins.

> Not everything that counts can be counted, and not everything that can be counted counts.
>
> —ALBERT EINSTEIN

There is no great virtue to smallness. As the saying goes, "Bigger is not better, and smaller is not better, but better is better." At the margins, better often becomes the focus.

In every situation there are many margins while there is only one center. Do not ignore the center, agents of emergence. But at the same time, look to the margins for a different kind of empowerment.[5]

If you are on the margin, do not feel inferior or unimportant. Remember Nazareth, Bethlehem, and Golgotha—all marginal places.[6]

M is for Matrix Moment

Named after the movie *Matrix*, a multimedial commentary on one verse of Scripture, 2 Corinthians 4:18: "So we fix our eyes not on what is seen, but on what is unseen. For what is seen is temporary, but what is unseen is eternal."

The main character in the movie had to decide whether to pledge allegiance to the world that was familiar and safe—a digitally simulated dream world called the matrix—or a scary, nonillusory real world that could only be met with courage and saving love.[7]

This is a matrix moment for the church. Which pill will it take: the blue pill or the red pill? Which power is your life and your church living out of—the power of the invisible, or the power of the visible?

5. Michael Slaughter, *Out on the Edge: A Wake-up Call for Church Leaders on the Edge of the Media Reformation* (Nashville: Abingdon Press, 1998).

6. For more, see Cheryl J. Sanders, *Ministry at the Margins: The Prophetic Mission of Women, Youth, and the Poor* (Downers Grove, IL: InterVarsity, 1997); Amy L. Sherman, *Restorers of Hope: Reaching the Poor in Your Community with Church-based Ministries That Work* (Wheaton, IL: Crossway, 1997).

7. The resurrection of the ancient gnostic heresy from our immersion in information technology is dealt with sensitively by Erik Davis, *Techgnosis: Myth, Magic, and Mysticism in the Age of Information* (New York: Three Rivers Press, 1998).

M is for Metanarrative

● Any founding or overarching story that gives rationale and legitimation for a particular worldview, perspective, or value system.

The Enlightenment metanarrative of progress and perfectability through reason and science has been undermined by what French cultural theorist Jean-François Lyotard announced as postmodernity's "incredulity toward metanarratives."[8] (Lyotard's now-famous work, published in France in 1979, began the postmodern discussion in academic circles.)

The postmodern critique of metanarratives is but an echo of the biblical warning against idolatry and, by implication, the totalizing of any theory or narrative other than God's story.

Many concerned Christians respond to this postmodern suspicion regarding metanarratives with angst: "But don't we have the only true metanarrative?" we say. "Isn't the gospel the true metanarrative?"

These questions are best answered with a question: Which version of the gospel?

- The prosperity (name-it-and-claim-it) gospel?
- The so-called full gospel that too often seems to focus more on the relief of Aunt Minnie's sinus problems than on the relief of the poor in our megacities?
- The fundamentalist gospel that restricts grace to those who have said a prescribed prayer or walked a prescribed aisle—two practices that have little biblical basis and are generally linked to actual discipleship by the thinnest of threads, if at all?

8. Jean-François Lyotard, *The Postmodern Condition: A Report on Knowledge*, trans. Geoff Bennington and Brian Massumi (Minneapolis: University of Minnesota Press, 1984), xxiv. Published in its original French edition as *La Condition Postmoderne: Rapport sur le Savoir* (Paris: Les Editions de Minuit, 1979).

- The Reformed gospel that says that if you're the elect, you're blessed, and if you're not, too bad?
- The polite mainline gospel that says—actually, no one is quite sure what it says?

"No," we'll say, "it's not these contorted or distorted versions of the gospel; it's the gospel as *we* understand it." To this, the postmodern will smile, almost say something, and then just walk away, whistling.

This is precisely the danger of metanarratives that postmodern folk wish to alert us to: whoever the "we" is, that "we" is sure that their version of the gospel is the true one that should correct all the others (and thus "totalize"). Do you think the Islamic fundamentalist is any less confident of his metanarrative than the radical relativist is of hers, or you are of yours?

So what is a Christian to do?

First, we do not recommend that we claim to have the true metanarrative. The word carries a lot of freight, connotations that few of us understand, so we believe it is wiser to work with simpler words to describe our message—words like "gospel" and "Good News."

Second, we should be confident and humble at the same time. We assert that the only narrative that really counts is God's. God is the only one who really understands what's going on. God is our only confidence. All our narratives are contingent and corrigible, not totalizing. We hold them gently, always knowing most strongly that only God knows totally and we are just human beings, just beginner disciples, with a lot to learn and unlearn.[9]

9. For an example of how this looks and feels, see Leonard Sweet's foreword ("Don't Take It from Mike") to Michael Slaughter with Warren Bird, *The unLearning Church: Just When You Thought You Had Leadership All Figured Out* (Loveland, CO: Group Publishing, 2002).

Third, if "actions are in effect lived narrativizations,"[10] as Hayden White puts it, then we should see our lives, our narratives, as part of God's master narrative, and telling stories without words as the chief form of moral and religious education.

M is for Metcalfe's Law

Moore's Law: Micro-processing power doubles every 18 months.

Moore's Law Revised: Processor power doubles every 18 months and halves in price. In other words, technology is getting smaller and faster and smarter and cheaper.

Everyone knows about Moore's Law. It was propounded by Gordon Moore, cofounder of computer-chip giant Intel. The number of transistors on chips would double every 18 months or so. Software is not following Moore's Law; hardware is. Moore's Law is linear. How long will it hold? By 12 to 15 years the law runs out of steam, experts predict.

Metcalfe's Law: Propounded by Robert Metcalfe, founder of 3Com Corporation; it states that a network's value increases exponentially as the number of users on the network increases geometrically.[11] Therefore: Utility = Users^2. That is, the exponential value of a network equals the number of nodes connected to it, squared.

Metcalfe's Law is winning out over Moore's Law.

Moore's and Metcalfe's laws compound the rate of change: As pace of information and innovation increases, lifespans of products and lifecycles of services shorten, human knowledge is increasing exponentially, change is changing exponentially; technological developments are cumulative and transformative.

10. White stresses the critical role of the narrative imagination in history—and the complexity of interaction between the narrative representation and what is being represented. For more, see Hayden White, *The Content of the Form: Narrative Discourse and Historical Representation* (Baltimore: Johns Hopkins University Press, 1987), 54.

11. "A Network Becomes More Valuable as It Reaches More Users," *InfoWorld Magazine* (2 October 1995), 53.

Whether they should be stoppable is the ethical and moral issue of the 21st century.

M is for Misery

Misery is in. Martha Stewart is out. Not because of what she does (or might have done—with her stock), but the way she does it—it's too perfect, too saccharine sweet. Where's the struggle? Where's the pain? Where's the messed-up hair in the kitchen? "Get real."

Find a hymn or song with the word "doubt" or "pain," "desire" or "disappointment." Sing it in church, and watch your postmodern people almost rise out of their seats, so grateful to acknowledge in public worship the darker realities of their lives and the muddle of "life's two most important horizontals" (A. L. Kennedy's phrase for sex and death).[12]

This honesty about failure, fakery, doubt, discouragement, desire, and pain trembles on every page of the Bible. When postmoderns read the Bible, they find no heroes other than God. No knights, all knaves. All villains. Everyone is messed up and deserves nothing. Abraham is not a hero. Noah is not a hero. David is not a hero. Moses is not a hero. The "communion of saints" in Hebrews 11 is more a rogues' gallery than a saint reliquary.

This emerging culture may identify more with the suffering Jesus than the glorified Jesus—the Jesus who was part of a single-parent household, the Jesus who was single long past what was normal, the Jesus who shunned the fast-track of building a mega-following for the slow lane of investing in a small community of tremendous diversity, a Jesus who had no real place to call home but was always on the move, a Jesus who was accused of choosing the wrong friends and embraced his critics' charge ("a friend of sinners") as a badge of distinc-

12. A. L. Kennedy, in her introduction to *New Writing 9,* ed. John Fowles and A. L. Kennedy (London: Vintage, 2000), x.

tion, a Jesus who could not get along with the established authorities and hierarchies of his day.

When the disciples saw the risen Lord, "they worshiped him; but some doubted" (Matt. 28:17 NRSV). There is a whole—largely neglected—category of Psalms called psalms of lament; there are whole books in the biblical library like Ecclesiastes, Job, and Lamentations that twist and writhe in uncertainty and pain. In modernity, when we preached these (if we did so at all), we preached them as anomalies, problems that could easily be resolved. We preached Paul's agony in Romans 7 as something easily negated by the "victory" described at the end of the chapter. In so doing, we shortchanged the Good News, as if it were too fragile to handle the bad news of life.

The good news in the emerging culture will be that the bad news really stinks and is really strong, but the Good News can handle it because it is even stronger. We won't "protect" the good news by downplaying the bad, but we will accentuate the good news by showing respect to its opposition.

In the future, we won't perfume the misery so much. We will acknowledge it, share it, bring it into the light. Misery is where it's at because God meets us there.

M is for Mission

● What every church of every age tends to take for granted, and what we have conveniently forgotten in many creative ways. For example, we have made a fetish of mortar and brick and forgotten our mission.

What the church needs most is not more pastors or more worship leaders but more missionaries—postcolonial missionaries with a kingdom vista, not an empire visa. In fact, in post-Christendom culture there are no more pastors, only missionaries. In the words of one missiologist calling for a new missional theology for the church: "This is a time for a dramatically new vision. The current predicament of churches in North America requires more than a mere tinkering with long assumed notions about the identity and mission of the church."[13]

A church without a mission is not a church. Of course, what matters most is not whether your church has a mission. Here's the question: Will God's mission have your church?[14]

Sorry, golfers: When your big goal is to see how far you can bring down your handicap before you die, that is not a sufficient mission for your life.

EPICtivity M: Mission

Purchase a hologram picture. (If you look at it long enough, you can eventually see a three-dimensional picture behind the scribbles and symbols.) Track the time with a stopwatch to see how long it takes each member of the group to finally see the picture. Answer the following questions:

- For those who saw it quickly, how did you feel about those who couldn't see it?
- For those who couldn't see it, how did you feel about those who could?
- What did others say and do that hindered or helped you to see the picture?

Next, set up this scenario: Imagine that every minute it took for a person to finally see the picture represents three years during which the person doesn't "get" your ministry's mission.

13. Darrell L. Guder, ed., *Missional Church: A Vision for the Sending of the Church in North America* (Grand Rapids: Eerdmans 1998), 77. See also Darrell L. Guder, *The Continuing Conversion of the Church* (Grand Rapids: Eerdmans, 2000).

14. This is the theme of David J. Bosch, *Transforming Mission: Paradigm Shifts in Theology of Mission* (Maryknoll, NY: Orbis Books, 991).

- How would you feel if this were true?
- Would it make any difference whether a person in your church understood your mission or not? What difference?
- What would the potential impact be if you tried to force people to pretend they could see what they don't really see?
- What can you learn from the picture experience about helping your team to "see" your mission clearer and sooner?

M is for Modernity

Born: about 1500 A.D. in Europe.

Matured: About 1750 A.D. in "the Enlightenment."

Died: ? (It is probably too soon to pronounce its death, although modernity aged rapidly in the late 20th century.)

In the creation of print culture (think of it: Augustine never held, never read a Bible as we think of a Bible), the origins of modernity lay in the 15th and 16th centuries in the Reformation and Renaissance (and, of course, their roots go back farther still). Luther's words "Here I Stand" conveniently summarize the essential identity of modernity:

Here = Present: Modernity focused on the here and now. It understood itself as having moved beyond the past—the Roman Catholic medieval past, the past that trusted authorities, the past that revered kings as ruling by divine right, the past that understood the earth to be the center of the universe.

I = Individualism: Descartes' later dictum "I think therefore I am" doubled the emphasis on "I"—the individual thinker, the individual knower, the autonomous individual increasingly disconnected from both the human community and the Creator.

Stand = Static Propositions and Stable Physical Laws: The modern world was confident that, just as there were discernable laws that governed the physical universe, there were free-floating moral laws and spiritual standards upon which one could stand in certainty.

Modern: The world the culture is moving out of.

Modern: The world the church lives in. In fact, many "traditional Christians" may be more "modern" than they are "Christian."

Modernity as a broad cultural movement has pursued several key themes:

—*Conquest/control*: Of nature by technology; of mystery by research and analysis; of flaws in human nature by institutions; of the whole world by Western culture, religion, science, economics, media, and governmental ideals.

—*Mechanization*: Machines have become not only the tools of conquest, but also the metaphor by which we understand ourselves, our world, and even God (the Clock Maker or Machine Designer/Operator). Descartes said that a healthy human being is like "a well-made clock."

—*Rationalism/secular science*: Using empirical analysis and experimentation, all mysteries can be replaced with knowledge and all problems can be solved with technology.

—*Reductionism*: The belief that big things can be understood by breaking them down into smaller constituent parts, and that the ultimate truth of things is discovered in their analysis, dissection, or reduction.

—*Individualism*: A valuing of individual liberties and pursuits, and a suspicion of any reality that limits individual freedom and desire.

—*Consumerism/materialism*: A shared goal of both capitalism and communism (modernity's two primary economic systems), based on the belief that money will in fact buy the best happiness that is to be had.[15]

15. For substantial discussions of our orgy of consumerism, see Mike Feathersone, *Consumer Culture and Postmodernism* (London: Sage, 1991); Rodney Clapp, *The*

The benefits of modernity have been great: more individual freedom and choice, more material goods, greater physical health and comfort, the concept of love as we know it. The costs have been correspondingly high: more individual alienation, an erosion of family and community strength, poorer planetary health and increased psychological stress, and not least, spiritual impoverishment commensurate with material enhancement. Cost-benefit analysis has led many formerly modern people—including many Christians—to seek a new way of living beyond the themes of modernity. (See **Postmodernity.**)

> this need to dance,
> this need to kneel:
> this mystery.
>
> —POET DENISE LEVERTOV[16]

M is for Mysticism

Modernity, it has been said, killed one ghost too many (namely, the Holy Ghost). In destroying superstition, it also destroyed sacredness. Not surprisingly, the mystical dimensions of the world and soul that modernism tried to destroy are returning with a gentle vengeance. The disenchanted world is seeking radical reenchantment.

Rabbi Abraham Heschel defined God as "meaning that mystery alludes to." Postmoderns are more likely to define God as "mystery that meaning alludes to."[17] They carry within them a

Consuming Passion: Christianity and the Consumer Culture (Downers Grove, IL: InterVarsity Press, 1998); Jay McDaniel, *Living from the Center: Spirituality in an Age of Consumerism* (St. Louis: Chalice Press, 2000).

16. Denise Levertov, "Of Being," in her *Oblique Prayers* (New York: New Directions, 1984), 86.

17. Of course, in an ontological sense, Heschel is correct. But postmoderns are more likely to approach God from an epistemological sense. See Abraham Heschel, *Who Is Man?* (Stanford, CA: Stanford University Press, 1965), 77.

mystical consciousness. In their world, the inanimate becomes animate (Furby, LEGO Mindstorms), magic and mystery and miracle are everyday occurrences through nonconceptual thinking (intuition, aesthetic inclinations, spiritual enlightenment, emotions, images), through mystical enlightenment, through anomalous and peak experiences, and through soul journeys.

Moderns tended to trust theories rather than sensations, ideas rather than intuitions, conceptions rather than perceptions. Postmoderns reverse the order. Einstein is their patron scientist because he admitted that he came to his theory of relativity, not through objective, scientific pursuits of objective facts, but through leaps of the imagination (a word that we undoubtedly should have given a special entry)[18] and intuition starting at sixteen years of age.

MIT researcher Sherry Turkle asked children to classify Furby as living or dead: They simply refused. They would not fit these simulated pets into either established category, intuitively knowing that they would need to invent new categories for their playthings.[19] Mystical experiences of union with God are potent antidotes to postmodern feelings of loss of connection and cries for deep connection.

> We wake, if ever we wake at all, to mystery.
>
> —Writer Annie Dillard

18. Gary A. Phillips is a biblical scholar who specializes in postmodern methods of reading the text. Here is his estimation of the role of imagination in the life of the biblical scholar: "It is for this reason that the imagination plays such a strategic role in the postmodern effort to signify the presence of the other and to point to alternative ways of thinking and living. The postmodern imagination is the provision we have for dealing with the condition of modernity. Imagination is a propaedeutic that helps us to see and hear the ethical call to live in community. The imagination, postmodern critique announces, aids in drawing out transcendence and the other in the encounter with the biblical text." See "Drawing the Other: The Postmodern and Reading the Bible Imaginatively," in *In Good Company: Essays in Honor of Robert Detweiler*, ed. David Jasper and Mark Ledbetter (Atlanta: Scholars Press, 1994), 412.

19. Mark Pesce, "The Magical World," *Science and Spirit* (March/April 2001), 29.

Christian leaders (except those so won over by modernity as to have lost appreciation for the mystical) will generally celebrate this renewed thirst for transcendence. But still, seasoned pastors who have been around the ministry block more than a few times will wonder: What about the weirdos? They know that as soon as we say we are open to the mystical, we will find people having visions and receiving messages and offering prophecies that are as hard to swallow as they are to refute. So how do we handle the weirdos?

First of all, in fairness, there is no shortage of rational weirdos either. (We're just more used to them.) They offer the latest "church of the last detail" discovery from their biblical "research," often unfolding new and wild insights from a single phrase in the book of Revelation. (Just turn on a religious radio or cable TV station if you need data.) Mystical craziness isn't the only species in the genus. One would think that the "rules of logic" would provide a court of appeal to tone down some of the wild doctrinal speculations, but like popular radio, modern religious history keeps spinning out "hit" after "hit," with no end in sight.

Beyond that, probably the best way to inhibit crazy mysticism is by modeling a healthy mysticism. As the old bromide says, "The best antidote to misuse is not disuse but proper use." Those who maturely model an accountable, humble, non-power-tripping mysticism can help others to see spiritual experiences as an integral part of life.

By the way, it is worth noting that the rigid compartmentalization of the cosmos into "natural" and "supernatural" categories is not a biblical construct but a modern one. In the biblical world, our natural and supernatural categories are bound up in a bigger world of signs and wonders, where all manner of things can be significant and remarkable. In that world, rational and mystical are friends, not enemies, two wings on the same dove. By moving beyond our modern dichotomies, the rational doesn't need to try to extinguish the mystical, and

the mystical doesn't have to reassert its right to exist by claim-
ing superiority. Both find their place in God's world.

Moreover, the new brain science is affirming the reality of
mystical experience. It appears we are hard-wired for God. The
bio-neuro-mechanics of mystical unitary experiences are unde-
niable and fascinating. (See **Augmentation; Genetic Predestinationism; Neurological Pre-ReWirings.**)

> I am not a theologian. I am a Christian, a feminist and a writer: a fictionalizer, a liar in Plato's definition. I rather incline to the definition of theology as (1) the art of telling stories about the divine and (2) the art of listening to those stories.
>
> —Novelist Sara Maitland[1]

N is for Narratives

Postmoderns might not like metanarratives, but they love narratives. In the words of poet D. J. Enright, "many things are not worth doing, but almost everything is worth telling."[2] Two of the greatest storytellers of all time: Dante Alighieri of Florence, one of the most incomparable storytellers who ever set pen to paper; and Stephen Spielberg of Hollywood, probably the most mesmerizing storyteller who ever projected through a lens onto a screen.

The future belongs to the storytellers and the connectors.

Theologian Robert McAfee Brown said people live plural stories, some of which may conflict with the story God is authoring in their lives:

> I not only *am* many stories, but *have* many stories. . . . I am constantly balancing—or juggling—a number of ways of telling my own story: the masculine version, the American version, the human version, the Christian version. . . . Within

---

1. Sara Maitland, *A Big-Enough God* (New York: Henry Holt, 1995), 7.
2. D. J. Enright, "Another Anecdote from William IV Street," in *Under the Circumstances: Poems and Prose*s (New York: Oxford University Press, 1991), 51.

this multitude of stories, I accord one story, or several stories, a higher authority than others.... If things go well, my normative story is increasingly bolstered and authenticated.... But things may not go well.[3]

Jesus gives us a long and deep tradition, a home where we are surrounded by stories and ancestors and rituals and saints and martyrs. We have taken this much too much for granted. We have been dulled and desensitized to the splendor of the Christian story. Søren Kierkegaard was right when he said that it is easier for somebody who is not a Christian to become a Christian than it is for somebody who is a Christian to become a Christian.[4]

When you become a Christian, you become part of a tradition that has a priceless galleria of images, stories, metaphors, rituals, and hymns as well as historians, philosophers, dramatists, novelists, poets, scientists, and prophets.

We need to go out and come in again. Hence the enduring audience for Christian fantasy writers like James Hogg, George MacDonald, G. K. Chesterton, C. S. Lewis, J. R. R. Tolkien, Walker Percy, and Flannery O'Conner.

Christian leaders will celebrate this resurgence of the narrative, and it will affect their ministries in many ways. First, of course, they will rediscover that the whole Bible is in a real sense narrative. The Gospels and historical books have always been recognized as narrative, but we seemed to forget that the Psalms were poems that arose in the story of Israel, and the prophets expressed their inspired messages in that same story. Old Testament laws were given—and rescinded—at different points in the story, and they only make sense within their narrative situation. The New Testament epistles were letters that

---

3. Robert McAfee Brown, "My Story and 'The Story,'" *Theology Today* 32 (July 1975), 167.

4. Søren Kierkegaard, *Concluding Unscientific Postscript*, trans. David F. Swenson (Princeton, NJ: Princeton University Press, 1941), 327.

function for us much like an epistolary novel, embodying stories of relationships built and threatened, lessons learned and forgotten, dangers warned of and faced, discouragements expressed and encouragements exchanged. (See **Versus Verses.**)

What's more, the preacher will be less likely to use stories (true ones and fictional ones, contemporary and ancient, his or her own and others', funny ones and tear-jerkers) merely to illustrate points or add interest, humor, or poignancy. Rather, the preacher will use stories to make and carry the points, to in fact *be* the points, much as Jesus did with his mini-narratives we call Parables of the Kingdom. It's the difference between illustration and animation.

What's more, preachers will prepare, deliver, and leverage their sermons not just to add cupfuls of information to the mind-buckets of their hearers, but rather to intersect their narratives, their life-stories—as individuals and as communities—so those real-life stories will more harmoniously and energetically align with the trajectory of God's unfolding and ongoing story that begins, "In the beginning God created the heavens and the earth" (Gen. 1:1) and ends with a new beginning: "I am making everything thing new!" (Rev. 21:5).

EPICtivity N: Narratives

This is from master storyteller Garrison Keillor:

> These days I live in big foreign cities—NY and Copenhagen—but I think about America every day and imagine a town, an avenue of old frame houses, a boulevard of tall trees, a June night, lawn sprinklers swishing across the grass and popping the flower bushes by the porch. A dog on the porch. Lights behind the curtains. Rock 'n' roll in an upstairs window. Charcoal smoke in the air, a whiff of burgers. A gang of kids skidding around on the gravel, giggling. A screen door slaps, and a dad marches out to the garage.

Yard after yard, block after block, every sight and sound utterly familiar.

This is the American neighborhood of childhood comfort and fantasy, of teenage ambition, and of tenderness and misery and splendor and comedy of marriage. Movies and novels of brutality and greed may sell a zillion copies, but they're irrelevant to life on this avenue, which is based on faith, hope, humor, and love.[5]

Listen to one or two short stories from the audiotape series "Love" or from another collection series from Garrison Keillor's *Prairie Home Companion*. (Especially recommended for Christian leaders: "The Gospel Birds" and "Pastor Inqvist's Trip to Orlando," both from *Gospel Birds and Other Stories of Lake Wobegon*.)[6]

- What stood out to you in the story you just heard?
- What are some of the emotions you experienced while the story was being told?
- What makes storytelling so powerful?
- If this story had been boiled down to some points, moralisms, or propositions, what would they be? How would you compare the impact of explaining those points with the impact of hearing the story?
- How can you make God's story to mankind come more alive?

Ask each person on your team to create a timeline of their life showing their journey's highs and lows. Explain your time-lines, giving at least twenty minutes per person, plus another fifteen minutes for questions. (Or, over several meetings, share

5. Garrison Keillor, "Love" in *More News from Lake Wobegon*, cassette tape (St. Paul: Minnesota Public Radio, 1989).
6. Garrison Keillor, *Gospel Birds and Other Stories of Lake Wobegon*, cassette tape (St. Paul: Minnesota Public Radio, 1985).

a story from each decade of your lives, beginning with a story from your first ten years of life, etc.)

How can we "storify" our ministries?

N is for Neurological Pre-Rewirings

The architecture of the mind is changing. The postmodern consciousness involves a sea change in human cognition. Postmoderns are beginning to think in brand new ways that are creating new creative experiences. How we experience meaning and how we evaluate life are undergoing a cognitive metamorphosis.

> If I were again 25, with whatever talents I had at that age, I would write for the movies, on the principle that they communicate ideas with maximum effectiveness and in doing so reach a vast audience.
>
> —Novelist James A. Michener[7]

Postmoderns have multiple intelligences, even "multiple minds."[8] With a cognitive mind attached to reason and an emotional mind attached to experience,[9] postmoderns are "mosaic thinkers"[10] who process information in fields rather than furrowed lines.

Their minds work like multilane superhighways, as postmodern missionary Andrew Jones puts it, with traffic moving at

---

7. James A. Michener, as quoted in "Quotes and Facts #1," *Current Thoughts & Trends* (October 1994), 17.

8. The phrase is Richard E. Cytowic's in *The Man Who Tasted Shapes: A Bizarre Medical Mystery Offers Revolutionary Insights into Emotions, Reasoning, and Consciousness* (New York: Jeremy P. Tarcher/Putnam, 1993), 222.

9. Two books by Daniel Goldman that should be read simultaneously are *Emotional Intelligence* (New York: Bantam, 1995) and *I Felt God ... I Think: Authentic Passion in the 21st Century* (Odessa, TX: Damah Media, 2001).

10. With thanks to Karen Neudorf of *beyond* magazine for this phrase.

different speeds in various lanes. They are less likely to experience writer's block (can't think of anything to say or write) than writer's traffic jam (too much going on to distill into linear sentences).

It's not that natives of the emerging culture don't have an attention span. They have a different kind of attention span. What made shows like Hill Street Blues, L.A. Law, St. Elsewhere, ER, Law and Order, and The West Wing "breakthrough successes" was their multiple storylines and multiple characters that don't require you to follow one narrative from beginning to end, but invite you to check in on the proceedings at will. In all genres, narrative complexity is expanding to include character complexity.

In the emerging culture, the one-eyed lens is king. It behooves moderns to remember that the Word became flesh. Not print, but flesh. And that flesh was first a Person who became an oral story which became manuscript scroll which became manuscript parchment which became paper which became screen which became . . . hologram? But the ultimate ongoing embodiment of that Person and Story is in the stories of our lives, woven together in communities of faith, hope, love, and mission.

In a double-ring of pre- and re-, the same way culture rewires our neurobiology in the continuing evolution of human brain function, it also appears that our brains are prewired in ways that predispose us to transcendent yearnings and experiences.

Within the past fifteen years, studies of the neurobiological wirings of human beings have revealed a bioneuromechanical chain of events that lead to "unitary experiences" (oneness with Christ as experienced in worship, ritual, nature, and service) in which the brain's boundary settings (space, time, self) are loosened as the person becomes lost in "absolute unitary being" (the ultimate transcendent experience).

The documentable "realness" of mystical experiences, which can be seen by the naked eye in brain scans and charted on graphs, "is not conclusive proof that a higher God exists," argue these scientists, "but it makes a strong case that there is more to human existence than sheer material existence."[11] This science also makes a strong case for the effectiveness of the EPIC model and all "abductive" processes.

New Learning Styles: From Literacy to Graphicacy

Our neurological rewiring will require many adjustments. The impact of new learning styles on Christian education (from literacy to graphicacy) can only be described as revolutionary. It will require a new breed of architects and interior re-designers and landscape architects to help us re-vision what our worship and gathering spaces can be. In modernity, where learning was a one-lane road, focus was everything, so many of our buildings tended toward the boring. Why add color, art, interest, all of which would distract from the main point: the rational sermon consisting of abstractions?

For mosaic thinkers with multiple intelligences, the architecture, interior design, landscape design, art, and colors will all preach along with the sermon (which, as we have seen, will not be exclusively rational/analytical either). (See **Abductive Method; Mysticism; Narratives.**)

The sermon itself will need to be rewired to match the circuitry of mosaic, multilane thinkers. Ditto the book. (Can you imagine e-books with clickable links so we don't have to say, "See Abductive Method; Mysticism; Narratives"?)

11. Andrew Newberg, Eugene D'Aquili, and Vince Rouse, *Why God Won't Go Away* (New York: Ballantine Books, 2001), 172.

N is for New Science and Faith

Formerly science and faith were considered enemies, but they are now considering becoming friends again.

The modern era's warfare between science and religion is ending. A truce has been called, and some like those in the Society of Ordained Scientists, which was started by British biologist and Anglican priest Arthur Peacocke, are even talking of a conjunction. The new science has pulled the plug on anti-faith scientism, and what Kevin Sharpe calls the "mutual relevance"[12] of the spiritual and scientific worlds is being explored.

Just to explore the members of the board of the Center for Theology and the Natural Sciences, founded in 1981 and located at the Graduate Theological Union in Berkeley, California, is to make this point. It boasts such distinguished scientists as its founder, Robert Russell, a physicist and theologian; Nobel Prize-winning physicist Charles Townes; particle physicist Carl York; mathematician and space-time expert George Elis; and William Stoeger, an astrophysicist and Jesuit priest.[13]

So beware, preachers trained by modernity to insert a *versus* between faith and science! That war is ending, and your scientific neighbors, whom you have long seen as enemies, lie savaged by the road, needing your friendship. And beware, so-called creation scientists! You were dead right that something was wrong with modern science, but you have been barking up the wrong tree. Your enemy was neither Darwin nor evolution nor the Big Bang theory nor an "old earth" theory. It was rather the "orthodox choice" scientists made for the objective, mechanistic, value-free, third-person, mind-independent, God-less world of a now discredited "scientific method."

12. Kevin Sharpe develops his theory of "mutual relevance" in *Sleuthing the Divine: The Nexus of Science and Spirit* (Minneapolis: Fortress Press, 2001).
13. For more on the compatiblity of physics and faith, see Margaret Wertheim's *Pythagoras' Trousers: God, Physics, and the Gender Wars* (New York: Random House/Times Books, 1995).

Can we be open to this possibility: What if you and the evolutionists were both wrong? What if God used evolution as one of the divine's many fascinating creative processes, and what if the full range of God's creative processes also includes mysteries and wonders beyond those so far imagined by the most advanced evolutionist? Can you handle the possibility that you were both fully right about your opponent being partly wrong, and you were both completely wrong about yourselves being fully right?

Elsewhere, beyond these areas of tension, representatives of both the science and faith communities see plenty of challenges that will require them to work together for the good of the world.

Partly through the largesse of Sir John Templeton, science and spirit are finding common ground in "new consciousness" and "new science."[14] The more each side talks, the more each side seems to be, in small ways, repenting of its modern independence and arrogance.

Nobel Laureate Arno A. Penzins, an orthodox Jew who was co-discoverer in 1965 of the 2.7°K cosmic background radiation,[15] told the New York Times, "The anomaly of the existence of the universe is abhorrent to physicists, and I can understand why: the universe should not have happened. But it did."[16]

There are only two choices: Creation by God or Creation by Fluke. An increasing number of scientists are open to the former.

14. See, for example, Russell Stannard, ed., God for the 21st Century (Radnor, PA: Templeton Foundation Press, 2000). An excellent video resource and discussion guide of science and theology issues is The Question Is . . . (Radnor, PA: Templeton Foundation Press, 1995).

15. A discovery that "turned the science of cosmology into the most avidly investigated branch of modern physics," as quoted in Stanley L. Jaki, Universe and Creed (Milwaukee: Marquette University Press, 1992), 36.

16. Joseph Deitch, "Dr. Arno A. Penzias Tackling a Question: Why the Universe," New York Times (1 December 1991), Sec. 12NJ, p. 3.

N is for NGO

● Literally, a "non-governmental organization" that is without official political status but has tremendous political clout.

● One component of a grassroots citizens' movement that is growing in power and numbers. In the U.S. alone, there are about 30,000 citizens' groups, NGOs, and foundations. World-wide, the number exceeds 100,000. Their issues are broad: conservation, population growth, labor rights, women's rights, public policy, environmental justice, corporate reform, climate change, and more.[17]

The "Battle for Seattle" (the protests against the World Trade Organization in late 2000) is but a prelude of what is to come from NGOs protesting the oozing, dozing wealth of the world that is being hoarded and not invested in those who need help. Perhaps the best thing media tycoon Ted Turner ever said was this: "What good is wealth sitting in the bank? It's a pretty pathetic thing to do with your money."

In the next thirty years, we can expect NGOs to increasingly focus on biopolitics and the threat of genocide or extinction coming from three technologies: nanotechnology, robotics (especially the merging of biology and robotics dubbed "algeny"),[18] and genetic engineering.[19]

Bill Joy, the chief scientist and cofounder of Sun Microsystems, has written the most important article of the 21st century to date. In this article he argues that these three technologies, each one of which has huge commercial and military value, can end disease, end poverty, even end "work"

---

17. For a more generous assessment, see "The Non-Government Order," *The Economist* (11 December 1999), 21. It claims that there were more than two million NGOs in the U.S. and only 26,000 in the rest of the world at that time.

18. *Algeny* is a word invented by Joshua Lederberg for the mixing of biology and robotics. See Jeremy Rifkin and Nicanor Perlas, *Algeny* (New York: Viking Press, 1983), 17.

19. For a positive assessment of what these technologies might bring, see Ray Kurzweil, *The Age of Spiritual Machines: When Computers Exceed Human Intelligence* (New York: Viking, 1999).

as we know it. But the holocaust potential of these three tech-nologies, especially their "democratizing the ability of individ-uals to do great harm," has caused Joy to advocate among the scientific community the temporary relinquishment of them.[20]

No one is doubting Joy's picture of a future world of designer drugs, self-replicating nanobots, transgenic technologies, DNA computers (which started in 1995: one milligram of DNA can hold as much information as one million compact discs), better biological models of intelligence, molecular computing with materials so small that they can be integrated into living cells, and more.

The deeper debate revolves around whether or not scientists can or should stop being scientists or whether a better approach would be to "manage the dangers" and train the technology as good trustees. There is widespread scientific skepticism that faith communities can contribute anything of significance to their ethical conundrums and plight.[21] Joy sees a moral universe with about as much strength and protection against these ethical tsunamis as a stilt house with a thatched roof.

Is he right? Are we totally unprepared for what is coming—no, what is already here? Can you name one religious leader who understands the issues? What is your church doing to contribute to the conversation?

N is for Nonlocalism

● A revolutionary new understanding of space-time that seeks to explain the separateness and yet the connectedness of all that exists.

---

20. Bill Joy, "Why the Future Doesn't Need Us," *Wired* (April 2000), 238–46. *www.wired.com/wired/archive/8.04/joy.html*. Accessed 5 July 2001.

21. For a probing of life and death bioethical pastoral problems, see Sondra Ely Wheeler, *Stewards of Life: Bioethics and Pastoral Care* (Nashville: Abingdon, 1996). You may want to check out the "Genetic Bill of Rights" at *www.ipcb.org*.

The journey from classical physics to quantum physics moves from a cause-and-effect, divide-and-conquer Newtonian world to a world of wholeness where objects affect each other and communicate with each other instantaneously over immense distances even though nothing physically links them and no known information passes between them.

Nonlocalism was first proposed in the famous EPR thought experiment conducted by Einstein-Podolsky-Rosen in 1935, reinforced by Bell's nonlocality theory in 1964, and finally proven under laboratory conditions by Alain Aspect and a team of researchers in 1982.

It is weird. It is mysterious. Some say it is the greatest discovery in the history of science.

Jesus introduced the concept of nonlocal correlations: "Just as you did it to one of the least of these . . . , you did it to me" (Matt. 25:40).

O is for Open-Endedness

● A key component of the post-modern mentality, where boundaries have been replaced by frontiers and where content wants to be free.

Although a few moderns saw that "stupidity consists in a desire to conclude" (Gustave Flaubert), the vast majority would bring things to a conclusion with neat and tidy endings, then tie a bow around it and seal it in shrink-wrap.

By contrast, natives of the emerging culture love the "never-ending story" where the plot is always thickening and the story keeps pumping out new meanings. Jazz trumpeter Miles Davis offered the postmodern credo: "I never end songs; they just keep going on."[1]

In a world of open source software and free agents, of "community without propinquity"[2] where old political borders are being annulled by global information flows, the future belongs to those who give away content. MIT, the global center of high-tech innovation, has announced that all of its online courses are available free. It is opening the doors to its most prized possession—content, including lectures, streaming video, and other course materials.

Of course, closed competition will grow alongside close cooperation. (See **Double Ring.**) But the implementation of the "copyleft" (as opposed to the copyright)—an idea invented by Richard Stallman, the founder of the Free Software Foundation in 1983—means that open-source projects will resource much of the innovation of the 21st century.

1. Miles Davis and Quincy Troupe, *Miles: The Autobiography* (New York: Simon & Schuster, 1989), 329.
2. As iconoclastic urbanist Melvin Webber said famously.

A concept best expressed in Jesus' parable of the weeds and the wheat in Mark 4. A farmer instructs his hired hands that they need not labor in plucking out the weeds. Let the weeds grow with the wheat. If you try to uproot them, he warned, you will uproot the wheat as well.

"The kingdom of heaven," Jesus said, "is like that." Don't squander your precious time and energy getting rid of those things you don't like. Devote yourself to making the good seed, the healthy wheat, grow. Let them all grow together, wheat and weeds. God will sort things out when the time is right, at harvest time.

O is for Ordinary Attempts

"Evangelism is too darn hard," says church planter/leadership developer Jim Hendersen. "That's why ordinary Christians don't do it." He continues,

> In 1996 a group of Christians decided to resign from this approach and find another way to do what we felt was our most important work. We decided to stop trying to be something we weren't and start being our ordinary selves. We decided that the reason traditional evangelism didn't attract us was because it was designed for extraordinary and unusual people. We quit doing more of what didn't work and started doing ordinary things we could do. Rather than trying to escape the ordinary, we decided to exploit it. Instead of discounting the things we were already doing, we started counting them. These evangelism activities were so unremarkable we decided to call them *ordinary attempts.*"[3]

3. See Jim Henderson, "Ordinary Attempts: Evangelism for the Rest of Us: Why Didn't the Right People Try?" *Next-Wave* (July 2000). See *www.next-wave.org/jul00/Ordinary_Attempts.htm.* Accessed 23 August 2001. See also the website *off-the-map.org.*

In the emerging culture, the more you have been indoctrinated in modern evangelism training, the more adroit you are at memorizing the lead-ins and lines and arguments and closings, the less effective you will be in helping the people God loves and misses to come home to him. Why?

Because they don't want a sales pitch, and they don't want their conversations to be steered, and they don't want to be preached to or "closed" or "handled." Postmoderns don't believe in hype and won't believe the hype. Fed up with commercials, they hunger for real communication. They want to be listened to, loved, befriended, and shown the love of God incarnated in the lives of ordinary people, so that when their curiosity bubbles over into sincere spiritual questions, the telling of the Good News flows naturally and authentically—as Peter said, "with gentleness and respect" (1 Peter 3:15).

More and more Christian leaders are training people to be good neighbors, not marketing reps. They are encouraging Christians to do ordinary things: smile, help someone whose car has broken down along the highway, be kind to children, ask questions and listen (sincerely, not just waiting for a good opening to insert a message), give others the rare gift of sustained and sincere attention, offer to stop for some groceries, be thoughtful, be interested, be friendly and downright neighborly.

In reality, they are returning what we often call "the Great Commission" to being a facet of what we often call "the Great Commandment." They are reintegrating the words of the gospel with the deeds of the gospel, two things God joined together that never should have been put asunder. And the results are encouraging. (See **Dedicated Server.**)

O is for Organic

The Cell Church and House Church movements are teaching us the power of decentralization, smallness, mobility, pilgrim mentality, and organic and relational understandings of the church. House Church Christianity especially is exploding all over the globe[4] and making us more sensitive to the church as an organic life-force not an organized mechanism.

One emerging theologian of the organic church movement is Christian A. Schwarz, whose "biotic principle" governing organic forms of life is directly opposed to "technocratic principles" that govern machines and mechanisms.[5] Schwartz's biotic principle becomes even richer when we remember that in God's creation, nothing grows in isolation. All living things are parts of communities.

Next time you're reaching for a metaphor to describe the process of spiritual growth, why not bypass machines, formulas, and assembly instructions and reach for forests, families, and ecosystems instead?[6]

O is for Other

● The favorite word of postmodern academics. Another way of saying that the marginalized become the center, that fault lines become front lines of ministry and mission.

4. For more exegetical treatments of the House Church movement see Robert Fitts, *The Church in the House: A Return to Simplicity* (Salem, OR: Preparing the Way Publishers, 2001); Met Castillo, *The Church in Thy House* (Manila: Alliance Publishers, 1982); Gene Edwards, *Overlooked Christianity* (Sargent, GA: SeedSowers, 1997); Frank A. Viola, *Rethinking the Wineskin: The Practice of the New Testament Church*, rev. ed. (Brandon, FL: Present Testimony Ministry, 1998); Larry Kreider and Ralph W. Neighbor, *House to House: Spiritual Insights for the 21st Century Church*, 2d ed. (Ephrata, PA: House to House Publishing, 1998); Robert Banks and Julia Banks, *The Church Comes Home* (Peabody, MA: Hendrickson Publishing, 1998). For more theological and cultural aspects, see Wolfgang Simson, *HousesThat Change the World: The Return of the House Churches* (Waynesboro, GA: OM Publishing, 2001); Steve Atkerson, *Toward a House Church Theology* (Atlanta: New Testament Restoration Foundation, 1996).

5. Christian A. Schwarz, *Natural Church Development: A Guide to Eight Essential Qualities of Healthy Churches*, 3d ed. (Carol Stream, IL: ChurchSmart Resources, 1998), and *Paradigm Shift in the Church: How Natural Church Development Can Transform Theological Thinking* (Carol Stream, IL: ChurchSmart Resources, 1999).

6. This is what William M. Easum and Thomas G. Bandy did in *Growing Spiritual Redwoods* (Nashville: Abingdon, 1997).

Or, to let the academics speak for themselves, to celebrate "the other" is "to open up spaces in culture and consciousness where we can speak, hear and recognize other and heretofore subordinated histories, realities, reasons, subjectivities, knowledges, and values which have been silenced and suppressed and certainly excluded from the formulations and determinations of the old modernist project."[7]

O is for Outed Church

Not enough Christians are "helping *out*" the church. Too many Christians are "helping *in*" the church.

Just about all of us have participated in a prayer circle where we stand, hold hands, and pray. Naturally, we form these circles facing inward, because then we can better hear and share in one another's prayers. Next time you are in one of these prayer circles, suggest to your circle that you face outward, in spite of the downside of acoustic dispersion. See if this "outing of the church" affects the content and thrust of your prayers.

The Scriptures "out" the church big-time. It starts in Genesis, when we are told to "fill the earth." The centralizing tendency of Babel is thwarted, and again people are told to disperse. Abraham is given a vision of blessing "all the nations," even though he is also given a Promised Land to inhabit. The prophets tell the people of God again and again that they are to be "a light to the nations," and they are stirred from their tendencies to stagnate and become a closed, ingrown, elite, hunkered-down community, barricaded in their own familiar territory.

Then Jesus comes and sends his disciples to "all the nations"—a strong resonance with Abraham's ancient promise

7. Arthur Marwick, "All Quiet on the Postmodern Front," *TLS: Times Literary Supplement* (23 February 2001), 13.

of global blessing. The church is dispersed from Jerusalem, and twenty centuries of church history bear out the church's vibrancy when it is looking outward and living out of the "out" words: outdoors, outreach, outshine, outlive, outlove.

When the church is in defensive mode, when it becomes what one writer aptly dubs a "navel academy," it creates boundaries, bars of exclusion, zones of isolation.[8]

But when the circle turns outward, boundaries are replaced by frontiers, walls by open doors, isolation by engagement.[9] St. Augustine warned us that the worst sin is to curve in on oneself. "Kingdom IN-Kingdom OUT" is Bob Roberts's phrase for it.[10]

One unfortunate "adventure in missing the point" (see **Out-of-Control Discipleship**) that preoccupied modern Christians was thinking that God is most concerned about who "gets in"—who gets into heaven, who gets into God's family, who gets into salvation. From all gospel indications, God is at least as concerned about who gets out—who gets out into the world with divine love and power, who gets out of bondage and into freedom, who gets out of death and into life. We made it sound as if "good" is the smaller place and "evil" the bigger—one needs to get out of the bigger and into the smaller.

What if the reverse is true? What if earth and evil and selfishness and privilege are small, cramped, and confining from God's higher perspective? What if good and sacrifice and service are the vast frontier, the wide-open spaces, where true freedom is found? What if all the "do-nots" of the Law are not confining, but rather are like dead-end signs, warning us that going this way will lock us into a small place? And what if all the "do's" of Scripture are

8. "Navel academy" is a phrase for the church coined by Francis Anfuso, *We've Got a Future: The 21st Century Church* (Sierra Madre, CA: 21st Century Ministries, 1989).

9. To turn your church outward, try using the book by radio broadcaster Dick Staub, *Too Christian Too Pagan: How to Love the World without Falling for It* (Grand Rapids: Zondervan, 2000).

10. Roberts uses this concept as the key training vehicle for the dozens of church planters sent out by his church (Northwood) every year in Keller, Texas.

invitations to the exhilarating, expansive spaces of life and joy to the uttermost in the expanding kingdom of heaven?

> The spiritual world … cannot be made suburban. It is always frontier; and if we would live in it, we must accept and even rejoice that it remains untamed.
>
> —HOWARD R. MACY[11]

The Good Shepherd, Jesus said, leads his sheep in and out so they find pasture. Yes, there is a time to be led into the sheepfold: at night, when wolves and thieves maraud. The pen is a place of protection. But leave the sheep in the pen for very long, and they will become smelly, dirty, hungry, and sick. Health isn't in the sheepfold. Health and life await us in the open pasture. How many of our modern shepherds lead the flock in and in, not in and out? How many of us worry almost exclusively about safety and protection and very little about playing, feeding, exercising, and reproducing out in the field?

What would happen to our churches if we focused less on keeping the sheep behind the boundary of the pen, and more on getting the sheep out into the frontier territory where the grass is truly greener?[12] We must, at this transitional time, recapture our core identity as disciples and apostles—two sides of one coin really: disciples who come together to learn so they can be sent out to teach, who are gathered to be blessed so they can be sent out to be a blessing, who withdraw from the world to be empowered by the Spirit of Jesus so they can be sent back out into the world as his kind voice, loving hands, smiling eyes, and healing touch.

11. Howard R. Macy, *Rhythms of the Inner Life* (Old Tappan, NJ: Fleming H. Revell, 1988), 39.

12. For a look at what an outward-focused church life might be like, see Steve Sjogren, *Conspiracy of Kindness: A Refreshing New Approach to Sharing the Love of Jesus with Others* (Ann Arbor, MI: Vine Books, 1993).

The rhythm must be maintained: "out" always follows "in." Our invocations gather us in a circle that tilts inward, shoulder-to-shoulder, but our benedictions focus the circle outward, pointing people out toward the world in the power of the Spirit, with a song on their lips and good news echoing in their hearts. When constructed this way that is both inward and outward at the same time, the circle becomes a wheel (and every person a spoke) that takes the church somewhere.

Imagine for a moment that you are God (and if this is too easy, beware!).

Imagine that you love the whole world (something that more than a few Christians seem to doubt about God).

Imagine that you also love the church, and you have commissioned the church to express your love to the world in word and deed.

Imagine that you have two churches in a certain town, one preoccupied with gathering to learn more and more of your love but consistently avoiding any outward focus, while the other rejoices to gather in celebration and rejoices even more to scatter in service and get beyond its four-walled world.

Which church would bring more joy to your heart? Now, returning to your real identity, ask which imaginary church is more like your own, and what you want to do about it. (See **Mission**.)

EPICtivity O: Outed Church

Ask your team to each tear out a residential page in the phone book. Attach each page on a dartboard and have each person in your group throw a dart at the page. Write down the name and telephone numbers where the dart landed. Take turns in the role of a polite and friendly survey-taker, using or adapting the script below:

Hi, I am _____ [your name], and I am part of _____ [name of church or group]. I'd like to ask for your help in a 90-second, five-question anonymous survey. Your answers will help us better understand how to serve our community. Would that be okay?

—What word comes to your mind when you hear the word *Christian?*

—One thing I like about church is . . . ?

—One thing that drives me crazy about church is . . . ?

—One piece of advice I would give a pastor or priest would be . . . ?

—If you could get a good answer to one question about God, faith, or spirituality, what would that question be?

After completing your calls, dialogue about your reflections. If you have time, compare what your survey tells you with what you hear from your friends and associates. When you complete your time together, form an outward-facing circle and pray for your community, and even more, pray that God will turn your congregation outward to be an expression of the Good News to your community.

O is for Out-of-Control Discipleship

To be always "in control" was the mark of great leadership in the modern world. Leaders in the postmodern world are out of control.[13]

Herb Kellerherm, CEO of Southwest Airlines, puts it like this:

I've never had any control and I never wanted it. If you create an environment where people truly participate, you

13. For an out-of-control manifesto, see Leonard Sweet, "A Magna Carta of Trust by an Out-of-Control Disciple," *www.leonardsweet.com.* Also Kevin Kelly, *Out of Control: The New Biology of Machines, Social Systems, and the Economic World* (Reading, MA: Addison-Wesley, 1995).

don't need control. They know what needs to be done and they do it. And the more that people will devote to your cause on a voluntary basis, a willing basis, the fewer hierarchies and control mechanisms you need. We're not looking for blind obedience. We're looking for people who, on their own initiative, want to be doing what they're doing because they consider it to be a worthy objective.[14]

> No person can write his[/her] autobiography in advance.
> —JEWISH THEOLOGIAN ABRAHAM HESCHEL[15]

O is for Outside-the-Box/Boat Thinking

"Out of the Box": A favorite Disney show for kids. It is also a favorite way for innovative Christian leaders to describe an approach that's new, creative, daring, bold. Ministry in the emerging culture will require leaders willing to venture out of the modern box.

Out of the boat: An allusion to Peter's water-walking, faith-stretching experience, about which he is often criticized (because he eventually sank), even though he should more properly be high-fived, back-slapped, and otherwise celebrated (because at least he tried!).

Postmodern ministry will require faith that is willing to get soaked in the process of doing something risky, unprecedented, and downright miraculous.

Out of the box/out of the boat thinking is especially important these days because it appears that God may be more active

14. As quoted in Kirk Hadaway, *Behold I Do a New Thing: Transforming Communities of Faith* (Cleveland: Pilgrim Press, 2001), 71.
15. Abraham J. Heschel, *Who Is Man?* (Stanford, CA: Stanford University Press, 1965), 37.

outside the church than in it.[16] In other words, "inside the church" may not be the best place to share in God's work, and if we want to be involved in God's work, we may need to get out more.

> So let's go outside, where Jesus is, where the action is— not trying to be privileged insiders, but taking our share in the abuse of Jesus. This "insider world" is not our home.
>
> —HEBREWS 13:13 IN *THE MESSAGE*[17]

There are two ways to respond to this idea of God being more active outside than inside the church. One is to shame the church for not being more welcoming of God's activity. In other words, we pushed God out, and so God worked where he was accepted—if not *here* in the inn of the church, then *out there* in the stable of the world. This line of response probably has some limited validity.

But it may be even more valid to *celebrate* this idea of God's activity outside the church, because perhaps God's purpose for the church all along has been to equip people to be agents through whom God works in the world. In other words, if we see God at work in the worlds of film and art, in AA meetings and inner cities, in public schools and hospitals, we should say, "Of course! This is where Jesus loved to work—on the hillside, at the wedding feast, along the road, in and out of the boat!" There is a place for the temple, but we never should have thought that God wanted to be confined there. To put it another way, as Paul makes clear, each of us is individually now a temple rather than it being a fixed building on a Jerusalem mount or on every other street corner in Grand Rapids, Michigan.

16. For the best exploration of this idea, see Michael Riddell, *Threshold of the Future: Reforming the Church in the Post-Christian West* (Jacksonville, FL: Capital Books, 1998), and Mike Riddell, Mark Pierson, and Cathy Fitzpatrick, *The Prodigal Project: Journey Into the Emerging Church* (London: SPCK, 2000).

17. Eugene H. Peterson, *The Message: the New Testament in Contemporary Language* (Colorado Springs: NavPress, 1996), 477.

In fact, if we ponder God's majestic identity for very long, we would probably agree that the one thing a creative God wouldn't like at all is to be confined in any way. Jesus worked in the temple and out of it, in the grave and out of it, in the boat and out of it. Confines don't confine God at all.

It may be helpful for us to distinguish between "church work" (i.e., our work inside the church to keep it going) and "the work of the church" (i.e., the church fulfilling its mission in the world). When we get out of the box and out of the boat, we find ourselves less preoccupied with church work and more excited about the work of the church. The old complaint about 20% of the people doing 80% of the church work may in this light be misguided. If the minority (20%) can do church work, then maybe the majority (80%) can focus on serving God outside the box and boat, in the world, in the storm, and maybe even in the neighborhood, where we belonged all along. Can you imagine what this would look like?

P is for PALS (Partnerships, Alliances, Liaisons, Strategic Collaborations)

● What we can't do life without.

An acronym developed by Rosabeth Moss Kanter of Harvard University.

Collaborative enterprises are the postmodern norm. Look at the credits at the end of the movie: Making a movie is impossible without a team effort.

Sad and dying is the insular church/denomination/parachurch organization. Limited gene pools produce woeful results over time, which is why cross-pollination and hybridizing of organizations is on the increase. Therefore, one of the most important questions a church or ministry board can ask is this: Who are our partners? Which alliances, associations, liaisons, and friendships should we cultivate?

It turns out that the junior high kids have been right all along: Your social life is pretty important! Staying at home and not getting out much will stunt your growth and degrade your health.

EPICtivity P: PALS (Partnerships, Alliances, Liaisons, Strategic Collaborations)

Buy a few canisters of Pringles potato chips and some bottles of Sunny Delight and hand them out to your team. Then read the following press release:

> "Coke is it, and so are Pringles and Sunny Delight! Grab a canister of Pringles with that can of Coke or Sunny Delight!"

> So read the headlines in 2001, when Coke and Proctor & Gamble formed a $4 billion joint venture to create a stand-

alone snack and beverage company. The two giants say they will be able to sell more chips and juices more quickly in a smaller, more limber organization than either could do by themselves. Coke is known for its ubiquitous distribution tentacles. P&G, with a full stable of Ph.D.'s, is known for its R&D horsepower.

Ask your group the following questions:

- Offer your evaluation of this partnership.
- Relay stories of other partnerships or alliances you are aware of.
- What do you think might hinder the two companies from forming a successful strategic alliance?
- What creative strategic alliances could our church be making?
- What obstacles would have to be overcome?
- What benefits could come to both organizations, and the community in general, if these partnerships were pursued?
- What opportunities and benefits could be missed if no strategic alliances are pursued among churches in our area?

P is for Paradox

● In the modern world, a puzzle to be solved or problem to be resolved.

● In the postmodern world, a dynamic polarity to be celebrated.

When you aim for the middle, you get middling and sickening. In other words, you get the gray-on-gray spirituality of Laodicea (Rev. 3), about which God says, in effect, "You make me *sick*!" But when you reach for both extremes of a polarity and seek to hold them together in dynamic tension, opposites attract and *electricity* flows.

Too often, churches and ministries of the modern era spent endless hours developing, debating, and defending doctrinal statements that sought to resolve paradoxes into clear, simple, one-dimensional propositions, thereby capturing the truth in black and white. For postmodern churches, paradoxes are full-color renderings of truth in motion. Doctrine is paradoxtrine, the teaching of essential Christian paradoxes.

"Now just a minute!" some readers are thinking. "How can a doctrinal statement reflect paradoxy? That sounds outrageous!" We would respond, "What critical assumption lies behind your question?" After some discussion, eventually we would focus on this: You are assuming that churches need doctrinal statements.

No doubt, they did need doctrinal statements in the modern world (or thought they did). But maybe not so much in the postmodern world. Please understand: We are not saying people do not need to be "devoted ... to the apostles' teaching" (Acts 2:42). But we suspect that the need to design a watertight doctrinal statement will change in the postmodern world. (Did the church in Ephesus or Antioch have a doctrinal statement?) After all, what good are doctrinal statements, really? They are designed to eliminate paradox and exclude—two things you may not want to do, at least not right off the bat.

If your church has a vibrant image statement (or something similar), might it replace your doctrinal statement? Do you really need to sharpen the doctrinal point beyond, say, the Apostles' Creed or the Nicene Creed? What do you gain by doing so? Which paradoxes are you trying to eliminate through your statement? At what cost?

Which element of the following paradoxes would you like to eliminate for the sake of clarity, simplicity, and "good order": God's power or human responsibility? Christ's deity or his humanity? The historical or eternal dimensions of salvation?

The goodness of creation or the brokenness of creation? The inspiration of the Bible or the humanness of the Bible? God's immanence or God's transcendence? Promises or warnings? Forgiveness or accountability?

P is for Participatory

● The anchoring ingredient in all EPIC methodologies. Postmoderns are less "seekers" after meaning in life than participators in experiences that are meaningful.

A participant-observer methodology is one key element of the new New Science.[1] There can be no truly objective "observer." Everyone is both a participant and an observer. What "fact" is uninterpreted? What "data" are without theory?

Leadership is the ability to both observe and participate simultaneously. Worship is both active and reflective, participating and observing. You cannot escape subject-object interaction in any arena of life, especially worship. Walt Whitman described this phenomenon as being "both in and out of the game"[2] at the same time.

In the modern world "critical objectivity" brought every subject into submission and dissection. What's wrong with that, you say? In the words of biologist/ecologist/theologian Wes Jackson, "We have done what the early 17th century philosopher of science René Descartes said we should do, break down a problem to the point at which there is no ambiguity. The

1. For historiographical assessments of this trend, see Leonard Sweet, "Wise as Serpents, Innocent as Doves: The New Evangelical Historiography," *Journal of the American Academy of Religion* 56 (1988), 397–416, and Douglas A. Sweeney, "The Essential Evangelicalism Dialectic: The Historiography of the Early Neo-Evangelical Movement and the Observer-Participant Dilemma," *Church History* 60 (1991), 70–84.

2. As quoted by Ronald A. Heifetz in *Leadership without Easy Answers* (Cambridge, MA: Belknap Press of Harvard, 1994), 252.

paradox is that it is at that precise point where all ambiguity is gone that our object of interest becomes totally irrelevant."[3]

It is clear that this new epistemology challenges our modern approach to theology, which suggests that "God" can be studied "objectively," like any other object of inquiry: broken down, bleached of ambiguity, and subjected to theosection. No, says this new approach: Each object of study makes requirements of its students. If you want to study subatomic particles, you have to submit yourself to the terms under which they "like" to be studied—using the appropriate tools, time frames, measurements, and so on. If you want to study chimpanzees, you need to submit to the necessary disciplines, as Jane Goodall learned in Gombe, Tanzania.[4] If you want to study salmon, another set of disciplines is required, and the same goes for studying meteors, Mars, mosquitoes, money markets, mountains, and metaphors. To be a student, you have to participate in the observation process on terms determined for you by what you are studying.

What terms does God require for those who would understand God? This is a question hardly even imagined by modern theology. That's why we need to ask it, again and again, in the years ahead.

But a primary answer to that question is this: Participation. Canadian theologian Stanley Grenz calls Christian theology "a witness to, as well as participation in, the narrative of the being and acts of the Triune God."[5] Church consultant Reggie McNeal defines faith as an "interactive partnership with God."[6] In fact,

3. Wes Jackson, "Complexity at the Land Institute," *The Land Report* 49 (Spring 1994), 5.

4. Jane Goodall, *Reason for Hope: A Spiritual Journey* (New York: Warner, 1999).

5. Stanley J. Grenz, "Articulating the Christian Belief-Mosaic: Theological Method after the Demise of Foundationalism," in *Evangelical Futures: A Conversation on Theological Method,* ed. John G. Stackhouse Jr. (Grand Rapids: Baker Books, 2001), 131.

6. Reggie McNeal, *A Work of Heart: Understanding How God Shapes Spiritual Leaders* (San Francisco: Jossey-Bass, 2000).

some philosophers are moving toward a definition of religious beliefs as the outgrowth of participation in religious practices.[7] The ongoing participation of Christians in the story of Christ and of his church is at the heart of what we call "revelation."

Postmodern culture is a culture of participation, which is different from teams, from quality circles, from getting everyone involved in everything. In postmodern participation, interactivity either is the content itself or can change the content. That is why Brian Eno says the word "unfinished" is better than "interactive." The real content of phones is not the information, but the interaction. This is the "value" of media—its true content is interaction.

> What matters is not how finished the work looks, but how unfinished it remains.
>
> —Nihonga painter Togyu Okamura[8]

For an experience of reading spiritual tea leaves for your people, take them on a trip of the future. Start with *www.kurzweilcyberart.com*, where you can write poetry in the style of famous poets.[9] Then stop at *www.mixman.com*, which brings interactivity to a new level. After downloading the Mixman software (it's free), you can go to your favorite musical artist and remix their music according to your own creativity. Then end the session with *www.absolutdirector.com*. Like *mixman.com*, the *absolutdj.com* site allows you to remix songs. But in *absolutdirector.com*, which is done in partnership with Spike Lee, you can remix movies as well. Change the dialogue by adding your own; change the background music; add new

---

7. For example, philosopher William Alston's *Perceiving God: The Epistemology of Religious Experience* (Ithaca, NY: Cornell University Press, 1991).

8. As quoted in Makato Fujimura, "Form *and* Content: That Final Dance," in *It Was Good: Making Art to the Glory of God,* ed. Ned Bustard (Baltimore: Square Halo Books, 2000), 59.

9. With thanks to Jeff Chaves for this reference.

cuts. "Everybody is a director, that's the whole thing," says Spike Lee. "On this site, they can see how I did it, but everyone's own film will be about their own vision." (See **Eschaton; Karaokees.**)

Moving in more participatory directions will entail substantial changes and new skills for Christian leaders. For example, worship planners and leaders must descend (metaphorically, at least) from the high stage and bright lights of the broadcast-observer mode reinforced by television. They must rediscover ways for worshipers to participate in the experience of worship, and not just through singing. Chant (another word for reading or reciting aloud in unison), responsive readings, rituals, ceremonies, and the use of parishioner-created multimedia and visual arts and interior design elements all deserve fresh attention.

Where early postmoderns took the "pastoral prayer" and made it interactive through bidding prayers ("Please raise your hand if you are in need, or have someone heavy on your heart"), a recent crop of postmoderns at Greenville College has upped the ante of interactivity. They also ask for prayer requests at college chapel services, but the worship leaders there refuse to move on to the next concern or celebration until someone specifically agrees via an uplifted hand to take up and undergird that particular need.

Beyond worship, leaders may need to function less as problem solvers and answer givers, and more as problem identifiers and question askers. When leaders solve problems and give answers, followers are excluded from participation and are merely observers, audience, and fan club. But when leaders share problems and ask questions, the people participate in seeking solutions and answers together. In this way, pastors, as important as your sermons are, the questions you ask your leaders to grapple with and problems you pose for your congregation may well be your most important leadership contribution.

P is for Persecution

● What is coming and will appear in myriad guises and disguises.

Outside the church: Some of the chief forms of persecution in early postmodern culture are prosecution, silencing, and derogation.[10] Muslims aren't being asked to downplay their beliefs. Buddhists aren't being asked to downplay their beliefs. The Dalai Lama isn't being asked to downplay his beliefs. But Christians are often expected to sit down and shut up.

Our de-Christianized world heightens postmodern sensitivity to the "hegemonic discourse" of a universalizing Christology. (Of course, other religious traditions can be as universalizing as Christians.) Postmoderns who evangelize for Jesus should expect to be mocked, misinterpreted, and hauled into court for every parking-lot expansion. Get prepared: The more Christians put their thoughts online, the more they put their lives on the line.

When a missionary plane was shot down in April 2001, mistaken by the Peruvian Air Force for a drug run, *Politically Incorrect* host Bill Maher mocked all the hoopla and mortification. Even though a missionary and her seven-month-old daughter were killed, the theme of his show on 24 April 2000 was this: What's the big deal? Drug dealers . . . missionaries . . . six of one, a half-dozen of another. Both of them are pushers: one is pushing drugs, the other is pushing religion. Both are in the addiction business.[11]

---

10. See Jim Garlow, "The Church Prepares for a New Day," *Ministries Today* 14 (March/April 1996), 58.

11. See also humorist George Carlin's "Bullets for Believers," written after six worshipers were killed in a Texas church, in *Napalm and Silly Putty* (New York: Hyperion, 2001), 254. Carlin rejoices, "Guns in church! This is a terrific development, isn't it? . . . And finally they're going after the right people: the churchgoers. Let's face it, folks. They're askin' for it. They just want to be with Jesus. Give them a helping hand.

"'Wanna see the Lord?' BANG! 'Off you go!' BANG! 'Are you a Christian?' BANG! 'Say hello to Jesus!'

"Give 'em a Christian helping hand. Don't think they wouldn't do the same for you. They don't call themselves 'Christian soldiers' for nothing."

The handwriting is on the wall for Christians in places around the world like the Sudan and Iran.

Another form of persecution outside the church is the torture of advertising. Ads routinely mock transcendent values and neutralize all narratives by asserting, again and again, that a man's life does indeed consist in the abundance of his possessions. Through advertising, a Christian is told a thousand times a day, "You're an idiot. You are living for the invisible. You are restraining your greed. You are sacrificing instead of consuming and accumulating. You are missing out. What a fool you are!" Persecution by advertising, if translated back into a first-century context, would involve Nero feeding Christians, not to ravenous lions but to clouds of thirsty mosquitoes. This form of persecution appears to be no less effective than the threat of lions, fire, and beheading in convincing people to renounce (or moderate) their faith and to deny (in deed, if not in word) that Jesus is Lord.

Within the church: Persecution comes in many forms, especially from theological death squads on patrol along the well-defined borderlines of modernity eager to snipe at any who dare cross over. Break free to challenge received ideas, and the risks are real . . . from ecclesiocrats to theologians who see themselves as the thought police of theological correctness.

> Indeed, all who want to live a godly life in Christ Jesus will be persecuted.
>
> —2 TIMOTHY 3:12

The persecution climate is heating up for Christians. Surprised? The apostle Paul claimed that persecution is inherent in missionary activity: "In every city the Holy Spirit warns me that prison and hardships are facing me" (Acts 20:23). Postmodern disciples might be well advised to prepare now for increased levels of persecution by sousing our souls in the manual of martyrdom, Philippians.[12]

Of the three kinds of persecution that have killed 40 million Christians since A.D. 33,[13] the most dangerous is the last.

- External: state, religion
- Internal: "angry brothers and sisters" [Mt. 5:22–24] who "bite and devour" and are "consumed by one another" [Gal. 5:15]
- "No persecution at all"[14]

Why the last? Because, as Wolfgang Simson puts it, non-persecution suggests "the church is not worthy of being persecuted; its values and its lifestyle have blended with a godless society, the salt has become saltless and is simply trodden under the feet of society unnoticed."[15]

> If they persecuted me, they will persecute you.
>
> —JESUS (JOHN 15:20)

P is for Possibilities

● The dominant impression we hope you gain from reading this book.

12. Wolfgang Simson defines a "persecution-proof church" as one that "matures under tears, multiplies under pressure, breathes under water, grows under the carpet; it flourishes in the desert, sees in the dark and thrives in the midst of chaos." See his *Houses That Change the World: The Return of the House Churches* (Waynesboro, GA: OM Publishing, 2001), xiii.

13. The statistics come from David B. Barrett, George T. Kurian, and Todd M. Johnson, eds., *World Christian Encyclopedia: A Comparative Survey of Churches and Religions in the Modern World* (New York: Oxford University Press, 2001), 1:11. The 20th century alone has seen 45,400,000 martyrs. The number of martyrs since 1950: 13,300,000, an average of 278,000 annually. Barrett, of the Global Evangelization Movement, predicts that the numbers will rise to 300,000 martyrs each year by 2025.

14. Simson, *Houses That Change the World,* xiii.

15. Ibid., 159.

● The element that is more common than hydrogen in all of creation.

A line from the Cinderella story goes, "Sensible people say it's impossible, but impossible things happen every day." Christians especially believe in "impossibilities."

P is for Postmodernity

● A broad, diverse, and often paradoxical emerging culture defined as having passed through modernity and being ready to move to something better beyond it.

● An umbrella term for an attitude and approach to life, not a single identifiable philosophy or style.

A controversial term with a maddening number of contrary definitions, generally referring to a philosophy that we believe does not yet exist. What does exist is an inchoate urge for a new philosophy or a set of philosophies that provide an alternative to the reductionistic, mechanistic, analytical philosophies grouped under the broad category of "modernism" or "Enlightenment rationalism."[16] The Enlightenment project of reason and progress is over. The modern world was haunted by the fear of an empty universe or an absent God;[17] the postmodern world is hounded by a spiritually charged universe. Postmoderns are "finders" and "experiencers" who are open to new findings and experiences.

What is often referred to as postmodern philosophy is actually, we believe, the earliest attempts at constructing a new path for intellectual discourse. These new paths are being

16. For an early exploration of the philosophical and scientific issues involved in relating faith to a postmodern world, see Diogenes Allen, *Christian Belief in a Postmodern World: The Full Wealth of Conviction* (Louisville: Westminster John Knox Press, 1989).

17. See the poetry of priest R. S. Thomas, for example: "There is no other sound/In the darkness but the sound of a man/Breathing, testing his faith/On emptiness, nailing his questions/One by one to an untenanted cross," "In Church," in his *Collected Poems 1945–1990* (London: Phoenix Giant, 1993), 180.

blazed by people who believe that the Enlightenment rationalism that captured modernity actually led Western (and to a
degree, global) culture down a dead end. These new paths may
themselves lead to dead ends too, but it is uncharitable for
non-pioneers to condemn pioneers for trying and failing at
something that at least needs to be tried. Finding better paths
often involves failing at first attempts.

Many Christians who approach postmodernism as a philosophy misunderstand, oversimplify, and hastily critique it
from their vantage point within modernity, not realizing how
enmeshed with modernity they are and how much they have
made modern culture a cult, and not realizing that their own
modernity may well have modified their Christianity more than
their Christianity has modified their modernity. (See **Categorical
Imperialism.**)

As a result, they tend to make *postmodern* a synonym for relativism, moral anarchy (a gross mischaracterization), and in
general, utter rottenness. This easy dismissal of all things postmodern will serve to firmly entrench many Christians in modernity, and those who choose to stay in the modern bed will have
to sleep there.

Those who take postmodernism as a philosophy a bit more
seriously often emphasize its deconstruction. (See **Deconstruction.**) However, it is wise to remember that every new philosophical movement is deconstructive in its early stages, since
those stages necessarily involve disassembling the reigning
model. For this reason, because we see postmodernism as more
a formative spirit and mentality than a philosophy, we resist trying to define it yet with finality or precision. (Similarly, it would
have been premature to try to define or judge modernity as it
was arising in Copernicus's time, long before Descartes and
others came along to express it in its maturing forms.) The
deconstructing phase of postmodernism is an important early
phase, but cannot last forever.

Postmodern most often goes with the word *philosophy*, although this is its least interesting (yet most confusing) property. There are four variants of postmodernism as a philosophy, each with Anglo-American and Continental varieties (the Anglo-Americans tend to be more constructive than the Europeans):

- Post-structuralism (Jacques Derrida and Michel Foucault)
- The new Marxism or Marxisant (those such as Fredric Jameson, Terry Eagleton, and Edward W. Said who reject Marxism but accept Marxist periodizations, condemnations, and some of its perceptions)
- Neo-pragmatism (Jean-François Lyotard and Richard Rorty)
- Feminism (Donna Haraway)[18]

The more interesting forms of postmodernism are the ones featured in this primer: as intellectual discourse, as style and posture-embodiment, and as culture. In fact, we can observe postmodernity developing as an emerging culture even before postmodernism as a worldview or philosophy is fully formed. This emerging culture can best be understood, we believe, through the lens of the prefix *post-*. "Post-" does not mean anti-, nor does it mean pre- or non-.

This is important. Rather than anti- or pre- or non-, "post-" means "coming through and coming after." For us it makes most sense to try to understand the key themes of modernity and then imagine what a culture does and where it goes after having marinated in these themes for several centuries.

This approach leads us to describe postmodern culture in terms like these:

18. So argues John McGowan in his *Postmodernism and Its Critics* (Ithaca, NY: Cornell University Press, 1991), 89–210.

- Post-conquest = emphasizing conservation and conversation
- Post-mechanistic = emphasizing living social and organic systems rather than mechanical ones
- Post-analytical = emphasizing holism rather than dissection and reductionism
- Post-organizational = emphasizing networks and "chaords" (which combine chaos and order)
- Post-objective = emphasizing communal intersubjectivity rather than individual objectivity or subjectivity
- Post-critical = becoming collaborative and assimilationist rather than polemic
- Post-secular/scientific = becoming spiritual/scientific

For those familiar with Hegelian synthesis, it may be tempting to see modernity as the thesis and postmodernity as the antithesis. We believe a better approach would be to see premodernity as the thesis, modernity as the antithesis, and postmodernity as an attempt at synthesis—an attempt that is still in its earliest stages.[19]

P is for Prayer

To stay on your toes, get on your knees!

---

19. The Anabaptists have given the most thought to the impact of postmodernity on their tribal identity. See, for example, Michael King, *Trackless Wastes and Stars to Steer By: Christian Identity in a Homeless Age* (Scottdale, PA: Herald Press, 1990); J. Denny Weaver, *Anabaptist Theology in the Face of Postmodernity: A Proposal for the Third Millennium* (Telford, PA: Pandora Press, 2000); Susan and Gerald Biesecker-Mast, eds., *Anabaptists and Postmodernity* (Telford, PA: Pandora Press, 2000), which comprises papers given at a conference hosted at Bluffton College in 1998 and contains various perspectives (some pro, some con) on incarnating the gospel in postmodern culture. Especially helpful are Leo Driedger's essay, "Postmodern Experiments: Blips or New Revelation," 385–405, and Marlene Kropf's essay on Anabaptist worship in a postmodern setting, "The Lord Is Still My Shepherd When I Sing: Experiencing God in Postmodern Worship," 244–48.

Prayer is the most powerful force-field in the universe. A byproduct of wonder and awe, prayer is another word for experiencing God and connecting the dots between heaven and earth, the divine and the human. John Calvin captured the essence of prayer as succinctly as anyone before or since: "Prayer is an intimate conversation of the pious with God."[20]

Everybody does some things naturally well. One thing *everyone* does naturally well is pray. You can't pray wrong except by not praying.[21]

Archbishop William Temple once said, "When I pray, miracles occur." A friend traveling with him replied, "Perhaps what you call miracle is nothing more than mere coincidence." The archbishop replied, "Yes, I suppose so, but I have noticed that when I do not pray, the coincidences do not occur."

When combined with the word *prophecy*, the postmodern replacement for "programs." (See **Programs.**)

Artist Makato Fujimura invites the church to "pray with our eyes wide shut." By this he means prayers should "face evil and depravity, but look beneath the surface, to wrestle with the underlying tension of culture at large."[22] Are your "eyes wide shut" in prayer?

P is for Pre-Mortems

Pre-mortems are examinations that look in advance at what can go wrong with our creativity. What would this science be like

---

20. John Calvin, *Institutes of the Christian Religion,* 3.20.16, ed. John T. McNeil, trans. Ford Lewis Battles (Philadelphia: Westminster Press, 1960), 2:872.

21. To visit some online prayer sites, see"30 Second Prayer" and the prayer wall at *www.vurch.com* or *www.christdesert.org* (Monastery of Christ in the Desert, Abiquiu, NM). A monastery (San Damiano Monastery of St. Clare in Fort Myers, FL) will include your prayer in theirs at *www.poorclare.org/fmb/prayer.htm.* My favorite prayer site is *www.new-prayer.com.* It sends your prayer by radio transmitter to "God's last known location," the star system M13 where NASA locates the Big Bang. For more, see Anne Foerst, "MIT Robot Lab Theologian Asks, 'Is Cyber Prayer Just Plain Childish?'" in *Spirituality and Health* 4 (Summer 2001), 24. All websites accessed 16 August 2001.

22. As quoted in Fujimura, "Form *and* Content," 56. Fujimura acknowledges that the phrase "eyes wide shut" comes from the movie *Eyes Wide Shut.*

shorn of its horns? Pre-mortems always ask the question, What's the worst thing that could go wrong here? If we don't have at least one solution to the problem of what happens if the worst happens, we don't go through with the scientific experiment.

A pre-mortem is the attempt to acknowledge the power of sin amid humanity's burst of creativity and innovation, a realization of the divine nemesis that can follow in the wake of human hubris. It is an attempt to keep under check and under inspection what Iris Murdoch calls "the fat, relentless ego." Moderns institute drug checks for athletes. Perhaps postmoderns should institute ego checks for scientists and church leaders, too. (See **Augmentation; NGO.**)

P is for Programs

● What moderns turned everything into.

● What moderns mass produced and thought was "ministry."
The antidote to programs? WIJD (WhatIsJesusDoing) Missions and EPICtivities.

P is for P2P-Driven

● A shorthand way of talking about peer-to-peer-driven ministry, or relationship-driven ministry: ministry that is mutual, self-disclosing, and relational; ministry that shares fears, doubts, anxieties, and weaknesses more than strengths, wisdom, expertise, or skills. True peer ministry sets up self-disclosure and connective distributions.

The more technology becomes invisible and integrated into the body and space, the more human interaction (social relations, rituals, ceremonies) becomes the focus.[23]

23. For the primacy of relationships and the relational nature of being, see Kenneth J. Gergen, *The Saturated Self: Dilemmas of Identity in Contemporary Life* (New York:

Which will it be: individual rationality or loving relatedness?

The church in recent decades has almost had it right with its emphasis on small groups. But predictably, we carried our modern agendas and hierarchies into what should have been an authentically relational, peer-to-peer experience and, as a consequence, frustrated the possibilities of peer ministry in group settings.

What if our groups had one simple mandate: Minister to one another? What if we diverted attention and energy away from formats and studies and structures and homework to this powerfully simple idea: Every Wednesday at 7:30 p.m. I'm going to show up at a living room with a roomful of people who want to minister to one another.

What if we simplified small groups to this level and then trusted people (and the Holy Spirit within them) to do peer-to-peer ministry? Could it be that we have been trying too hard?

How much denominational money could get more mileage if it were invested in sending pastors in groups of three to five for a weeklong semivacation, where they were simply instructed as follows: Relax, have fun, and spend three hours a day in conversation where you seek to minister to one another.

Could seminaries as we know them be replaced by seminaries as P2P-driven enterprises, where (novel thought!) people in church ministry would actually instruct people training for church ministry?

One another: A key term in the New Testament, and the essence of P2P ministry.

Basic Books, 2000), and Colin Gunton, *From the Dust of the Earth* (forthcoming). For a church focus, see Ken Baugh and Rich Hurst, *Getting Real: An Interactive Guide to Relational Ministry* (Colorado Springs: NavPress, 2000).

Q is for Quest-ions

Questions are now quests, not conquests.

If a question can't become a quest (vision quest, grail quest, hope quest), it's not worth asking. A quest implies a question that launches the askers on a journey.

Postmodern quest-ions have slumbered in the church far too long. The three questions most often asked by college-age Xers:

1. What does it mean to have Jesus for a friend?
2. How can I share my faith without sounding like a religious fanatic?
3. How can my faith make a difference when I am tempted?[1]

> There are years that ask questions, and years that answer.
>
> —ZORA NEALE HURSTON

Modern leadership involved answering questions. Authority flowed to the certain, convincing, clear, simple, and firm.

In contrast, postmodern leaders ask at least as many questions as they answer. Authority flows to the stimulating, challenging, provocative, mysterious, and intriguing.

Modern Christians liked the "Christian" bumper sticker that read boldly, I FOUND IT! Modern Christians liked to call non-Christians "seekers," implying that the Christians themselves were the "finders."

Postmodern Christians would rather be called the seekers themselves. The idea of resting satisfied as an insider who has

---

1. Thanks to W. G. Henry for this survey.

> The church should be full of Christians who seek questions rather than answers, mystery instead of solutions, wonder instead of explanations.
>
> —MIKE YACONELLI[2]

found the answer repels them, while the idea of engaging on a lifelong spiritual quest inspires. That is why their leaders are the chief seekers, the lead seekers, rather than resident know-it-alls. They aren't necessarily the ones with the most answers. Instead, they are the ones with the most passion to keep learning, unlearning, relearning, co-learning.

The problem isn't that those outside of Christ are seeking and not finding. Rather, the problem is that too few of them are seeking. That is why postmodern evangelism training will involve practice, not in reciting formulae or drawing diagrams, but asking questions and listening. (See **Ordinary Attempts.**)

Why are questions so important? Why is a passionate quest more important than a complacent rest?

Is your church training Protestants who rest on their "Here I stand!" or post-Protestants who, walking, whisper, "I'm onto something . . . I'm following Christ . . . I've got a lot to learn . . . I'm on a quest in pursuit of God . . . There we go"?

EPICtivity Q: Quest-ions

Purchase the U2 CD *All That You Can't Leave Behind*. Bono, the band's lead lyricist and singer, grew up in Northern Ireland. Death, war, and hate were commonplace. Listen to the song "Peace on Earth" at least twice and provide the song lyrics to all of the team members. Ask them to underline any questions they hear being asked as the song is played.

2. Mike Yaconelli, *Dangerous Wonder* (Colorado Springs: NavPress 1998), 42.

- Describe your thoughts and feelings after hearing the song.
- What underlying questions do you think Bono is asking?
- Do you think asking these kinds of questions shows a lack of faith? Why, or why not?
- What would be a possible shallow or trite religious response to Bono's questions?
- What questions do you have about life, God, or Christianity?
- How would you describe the intensity of your quest for answers to these questions?

If your group responds well to this musical EPICtivity, purchase some of Alanis Morissette's music and discuss both the questions she is asking and the intensity with which she asks them, especially in songs like "You Oughta Know" (rated R), "Forgiven," and "Perfect."

Read the first four chapters of Genesis, only noting the questions that are asked. Do the same with one of the Gospels. What insights do you have, based on these passages, about the importance of questions and quests?

R is for Radical Orthodoxy

● The Continental designation for postmodern theologians operating in a classical Christian framework.

There are three Christian attempts at dealing with faith and culture in contemporary life: the antimodern, the ultramodern (radical modernist), and the postmodern (radical orthodox).[1]

- Antimodernists: thinkers like Alasdair MacIntyre, the new Yale School of postliberal theologies, many evangelical (not fundamentalist) theologies, and Roman Catholic traditional theologies—all of which are repudiating the impact of the Enlightenment and the tyranny of cognitive tools on Christian thought.
- Radical modernists: thinkers like John Shelby Spong, Don Cupitt, the Jesus Seminar in USAmerica, and some advocates of "critical realism" for whom Truth is Reason and thus the game is over for traditional faith. Radical modernists are still fighting Enlightenment battles with Enlightenment weapons and modern (not New Science) scientific assumptions.
- Radical Orthodoxy:[2] thinkers like John Milbank,[3]

1. David Tracy talks about the antimodern and the postmodern responses to modernity in his "Modernity, Antimodernity, and Postmodernity in the American Setting," in *Knowledge and Belief in America: Enlightenment Traditions and Modern Religious Thought*, ed. William M. Shea and Peter A. Huff (Cambridge: Cambridge University Press, 1995), 328–34.

2. John Milbank, Catherine Pickstock, and Graham Ward, eds., *Radical Orthodoxy: A New Theology* (New York: Routledge, 1999).

3. John Milbank: *Theology and Social Theory: Beyond Secular Reason* (Cambridge, MA: Blackwell, 1990).

Graham Ward,[4] Catherine Pickstock,[5] Bruce D. Marshall,[6] Michael Riddell,[7] Stanley Grenz,[8] Nancey Murphy,[9] Peter Ochs (a Jewish scholar),[10] Brian Walsh,[11] and John G. Stackhouse Jr.[12] who refuse to privilege philosophy in the arbitration of what is truth and knowledge, and who resurrect premodern

4. Graham Ward: *The Blackwell Companion to Postmodern Theology* (2001); *Cities of God* (2000); *Theology and Contemporary Critical Theology*, 2d ed. (2000); also, Michel de Certeau, *The Certeau Reader*, ed. Graham Ward (2000); *The Postmodern God: A Theological Reader* (1997); *Barth, Derrida and the Language of Theology* (1995, 1998).

5. Catherine Pickstock: *After Writing: On the Liturgical Consummation of Philosophy* (1998); also, Catherine Pickstock and John Milbank, *Truth in Aquinas* (2001).

6. Bruce D. Marshall, "'We Shall Bear the Image of the Man of Heaven': Theology and the Concept of Truth" in *Rethinking Metaphysics*, ed. L. Gregory Jones and Stephen E. Fowl (1995).

7. Michael Riddell: *Sacred Journey: Spiritual Wisdom for Times of Transition* (2000); *God's Home Page* (1998); *Threshold of the Future: Reforming the Church in the Post-Christian West* (1998); *Alt Spirit@Metro.m3* [Alternative Urban Spirituality for the Third Millennium] (1997); *Godzone: A Traveller's Guide* (1992); also, Cathy Kirkpatrick, Mark Pierson, and Michael Riddell, *The Prodigal Project: Journey into the Emerging Church* (2000). Fiction: *Masks and Shadows* (2000); *Deep Stuff* (1999); *The Insatiable Moon* (1997).

8. Stanley Grenz: *Renewing the Center: Evangelical Theology in a Post-Theological Era* (2000); *Created for Community: Connecting Christian Belief with Christian Living*, 2d ed. (1998); *The Moral Quest: Foundations of Christian Ethics* (1997); *A Primer on Postmodernism* (1996); *Revisioning Evangelical Theology: A Fresh Agenda for the 21st Century* (1993); also, John Franke and Stanley Grenz, *Beyond Foundationalism: Shaping Theology in a Postmodern Context* (2001); Stanley Grenz and Roger E. Olson, *Twentieth-Century Theology: God and the World in a Transitional Age* (1992).

9. Nancey Murphy: *Theology in the Age of Scientific Reasoning* (Ithaca, NY: Cornell University Press, 1990), 201: "Postmodern theologians, then, will be those whose philosophical presuppositions are postmodern rather than modern. We see revisionary philosophical moves in three areas. The first is the change from foundationalism to holism in epistemology. The second is the change from the modern emphasis on reference and representation in philosophy of language to J. L. Austin's and Ludwig Wittgenstein's emphasis on language as action, and meaning as use. Third, we see a major postmodern shift in Alasdair MacIntyre's, Robert Bellah's, and others' renewed sense of the importance and irreducibility of community."

10. Peter Ochs: *Peirce, Pragmatism, and the Logic of Scripture* (1998).

11. Brian Walsh: J. Richard Middleton and Brian J. Walsh, *Truth Is Stranger Than It Used to Be: Biblical Faith in a Postmodern Age* (1995).

12. John G. Stackhouse: *Can God Be Trusted? Faith and the Challenge of Evil* (1998, 2000); also, John G. Stackhouse, ed., *Evangelical Futures: A Conversation on Theological Method* (2001); *No Other Gods before Me: Evangelicals and the Challenge of World Religions* (2001).

insights that modernity squashed, such as the pre-Enlightenment understanding of truth more as participation than representation. This is sometimes called an AncientFuture methodology for moving into the future because it reanimates allegorical, midrashic, and theological modes of interpretation and worship that modernity's "critical project" discredited.[13] For radical orthodoxy, truth is not statements articulated through mere reason; truth is participation in the life of God.

> Truth is the way God does things.
>
> —CALVIN SEERVELD

For Christians thoroughly at home in modernity, the idea of postmodern orthodoxy feels like an oxymoron. But for those who have developed a nose for modern accommodation, the option of remaining in the status quo is increasingly unacceptable. Instead, increasing numbers of us are seeking to uproot ourselves from the confining pot of modernity and to reroot ourselves in the fertile fields of gospel. Postmodern accommodation is not our goal. Radical orthodoxy is.

R is for Receiving (A Theology of)

● What comes before a theology of giving.

In modernity, people who think about spirituality tended to fall into two camps, the activists and the passivists. The activists talked about serving, reaching, sacrificing, achieving, obeying, striving, boldness—good biblical words. The passivists talked

13. Robert E. Webber, *Ancient-Future Faith: Rethinking Evangelicalism for a Postmodern World* (Grand Rapids: Baker Books, 1999).

about waiting, trusting, praying, surrendering, brokenness—also good biblical words.

Postmodern spirituality will seek to rejoin what should never have been dissected. A possible way ahead in this regard will be a spirituality of receptivity. Such a spirituality emphasizes spiritual practices and disciplines—and all the active verbs listed above. Yet they are not ends in themselves or achievements, but rather preparations—ways we make ourselves and our world receptive—to receive the blessing of God, which is the focus of waiting, trusting, praying, surrendering, and brokenness.

Active and passive, serving and waiting, come together in the image of a restaurant waiter, who serves by waiting and waits to serve. Reaching and sacrificing synergize with trusting and praying; achieving, obeying and striving are interwoven with surrendering and brokenness; together they are like a farmer plowing and harrowing his fields, this way and that, preparing them for planting and the miracle of growth—which is always a gift of God.

No action? The seed falls on unreceptive ground and doesn't grow. No waiting? The seed is planted and then trampled by overzealous farmhands, or planted and then dug up so its roots can be checked, thus stunting or destroying its growth.

Seen in this way, receptivity is neither a passive nor an active approach, but a dynamic trust that every farmer embodies and every springtime reveals.

In other words, a theology of receiving comes before a theology of giving. If it doesn't, your soul is in mortal danger.

God's category is "Giver." Our category is "receiver." If giving comes before receiving with God, if we are better givers than receivers, it means we don't like our category and would rather have God's category . . . which means we have a God-complex, which is about the worst thing anyone can have.

It is harder to be a good guest than a good host; it is harder to be a good receiver than a good giver.

Before we learn leadership, we need to learn followership.

> Lord, I am willing
> To receive what You give
> To lack what You withhold
> To relinquish what You take
> To suffer what You inflict
> To be what You require.
> And, Lord, if others are to be
> Your messengers to me,
> I am willing to hear and heed
> What they have to say. Amen.
>
> —A PRAYER WRITTEN DOWN BY CHARLES R. SWINDOLL
> TO HELP HIM BECOME OPEN TO THE COUNSEL OF OTHERS [14]

R is for Relativism

Postmoderns despair that any objective account is possible.

Three umpires are discussing how they do their jobs. The first, who is also the least experienced, says, "I call 'em as they are." The second, who has been in the game a little longer, says, "I call 'em as I see 'em." The third says, "They're nothing till I call 'em." These three could be characterized as objectivism, relativism, and postmodernism.[15]

> A finite point has no meaning unless it has
> an infinite reference point.
>
> —JEAN-PAUL SARTRE

14. As found in Charles R. Swindoll, *Living Above the Level of Mediocrity: A Commitment to Excellence* (Waco, TX: Word Books, 1987).

15. Thanks to Andrew Rawlinson for this story, which originally appeared in Walsh and Middleton, *Truth Is Stranger Than It Used to Be*.

"Everything's relative" is a phrase wrongly assumed to be synonymous with postmodernism. Moderns will box this corner as long as they are left standing. Everything is *not* relative, even though everything is *a* relative (connected, part of us, etc.). What is missing in the former, although not missing in the latter, is the sense that a person's life is morally weighed and relationally judged. Not to be judgmental sometimes betrays a lack of judgment. The admission that all human concepts of rationality and justice are time-bound and immanent does not obviate the belief that there are transcendent, revelatory standards that judge all rationalities and traditions.

● What's behind the redefining of old people as "experientially enhanced," of dead people as "metabolically different," of evil as "morally different."

> Truth is both relativistic—who is to say whose religious truth is right?—and yet dogmatic about the potential power of spirituality.
>
> —LAURA NASH AND WILLIAM (SCOTTY) MCLENNAN[16]

Here, with the nearly universal aversion of Christians to relativism, we Christians find ourselves being *against* something worth being against. Our fight against relativism is really a fight against moral indifference, moral carelessness, pathetic rationalizations and disgusting loophole-finding, rewriting the rules to suit one's drives and tastes, so that rules are rubber and standards are rubber stamps of our desires.

However, in the process, we may find ourselves being *for* something that is not worth defending—namely, an easy answer, or abstracted moral absolutism/legalism that Scripture, far from supporting, actually militates against. For example,

16. Laura Nash and Scotty McLennan, *Church on Sunday, Work on Monday: The Challenge of Fusing Christian Values with Business Life* (San Francisco: Jossey-Bass, 2001).

how would biblically literate people answer the following questions, basing their answers only on the Bible?

Is lifelong monogamy a timeless moral absolute? (What about the Old Testament law requiring that a man with one wife take his widowed sister-in-law as a second? Or Ezra's requirement [chapter 10] that men divorce their wives and send away their children?)

Or how about this question: Is there a moral absolute regarding killing your brother, friend, or neighbor if they rebel against the Lord? (Read Exodus 32.)

Or this one: Is deception always morally prohibited? (Check out Exodus 1.)

Or this one: Should a woman caught in the act of adultery always be stoned, as the law requires? (See John 8.)

Or even this relatively simple one: What is the timeless moral absolute regarding the eating of meat sacrificed to idols? (See Acts 15:29 and Romans 14.)

Wise biblical students will respond to these examples by saying, "These texts need to be put into perspective." In other words, there is a certain kind of perspectival relativism and ethical sensitivity that is found in Scripture, and in fact intensified in the New Testament. In other words, perspective has something to do with the morality of an action, and the morality of an action is in at least some cases relative to perception.

Here, though, is the difference—and a key one. Secular relativism puts the individual, the "I" or the communal "we," in the position of arbiter in situations of moral relativism, whereas Christians always resort to God. Behaviors are moral or immoral relative to what God declares is good, wise, or right in a situation, not relative to our own tastes, urges, drives, or rationalizations.

Against secular relativism—whether modern (tending to emphasize the wishes of the individual "I" in determining morality) or postmodern (tending to emphasize the wishes of the communal "we")—Christians would be wiser to argue not for a kind of wooden, simplistic, legalistic, and thoughtless moral absolutism, but rather for an intense awareness that one's life and choices, and a culture's life and choices, are always morally weighed by God.

A Christian thus lives with a constant and profound sense of accountability, living *coram dei* (in the presence of God). This awareness that a person's life is morally weighed is largely missing in both our dominant modern and emerging postmodern cultures, although it is not entirely missing in the soul, thanks to the realities of conscience and the Holy Spirit.

> He [Jesus] did not make authority his truth, he made truth his authority.
>
> —SOUTH AFRICAN BIBLICAL SCHOLAR DOMINICAN ALBERT NOLAN[17]

Unless postmodern Christians can steer between the Scylla and Charybdis of a facile moral absolutism on the one hand and an autonomous, God-ignoring secular relativism on the other, we will lose our voice in the postmodern world, a world that needs true and transcendent wisdom from God rather than easy answers or baptized human desires.[18] Philosopher Alan G. Padgett puts it like this: "We affirm the reality of Scripture itself apart from interpretation, even as we insist that there is a Reality which is distinct from (but not independent of) human thought and life."[19]

Are we mature enough to handle this?

17. Albert Nolan, *Jesus Before Christianity* (Maryknoll, NY: Orbis Books, 1992), 151.
18. See Stephen Shields essays at *www.faithmaps.org*.
19. Alan G. Padgett, "Profile: David Tracy," *Catalyst* (Contemporary Evangelical Resources for United Methodist Seminaries) 21 (November 1994), 4.

EPICtivity R: Relativism

Peter Unger well expresses the perplexity of relativism:

Some ancient Greeks were exercised by the old problem of the ship of Theseus: This ship, composed of many planks, sails around from port to port. When in each port, some few of its planks are replaced by highly similar planks. After they are replaced, nothing very interesting ever happens with any of the old planks; they might even be allowed to rot. By the end of a year, say, after calling on many ports, all of the original planks have been replaced. ... Even with all new planks and all new matter, it will be the same ship.

It was Hobbes, I think, who proposed a more difficult variation on this old and rather easy problem. On the variation, when a plank is replaced it is saved, perhaps by being put in a certain storehouse. At the end of the year, all of the original planks are in the storehouse. The planks may all have been tagged with numbers. Following the order of the numbers, these planks may be intentionally reassembled into their original arrangement. Then, just as at the beginning of the year, these planks certainly compose a ship. Do they compose the *original* ship? Or, do the planks that replaced them compose the original ship? Or, is neither of these the original ship, that ship having passed out of existence in favor of two intimate descendants, each with its own distinctive route of descent. Or, do none of the previous three questions have determinate answers?

But now suppose we shift our gaze to ourselves. We too are composites: large complex animals with particular combination of abilities, psychological histories, desires and beliefs. As we look to our own pasts and futures, we see how elements of the complex change: I do not have just the same body I

> had ten years ago, nor have I had just the same experiences. But it was still *me*. This feels like a substantial truth, and as we think in first-person terms, we find all the difference in the world between contemplating a situation in which we will be present, from one in which we will not.[20]

R is for Religion

● What postmoderns are temperamentally allergic to. (See **Mainline Church**.)

> Religion is what happens when the Spirit
> has left the building.
>
> U2's BONO[21]

Postmodernity has introduced a new species on the world scene—a "non-affiliated *homo religiosus*."[22] Postmoderns are not made for institutional life. The word *religion* comes from Latin *religare*, which means to be bound to safety, to be tied to an anchor so that you are not carried away into the deep. Postmoderns are natural "lift anchor" types.

Postmoderns think the corrupt world of church politics and "organized religion" is something new or something uniquely Christian. Actually *all religions* have produced good and bad in about equal measure. History offers four great critiques of religion and religious ideology: Marx, Freud, Nietzsche, and Jesus. Postmoderns will read and refer to all four

20. Peter Unger, *Identity, Consciousness and Value* (New York: Cambridge University Press, 1990), 162–63.
21. Anthony DeCurtis, "Bono: The Beliefnet Interview" (20 February 2001); *www.beliefnet.com.* Accessed 20 May 2002.
22. Frederick Franck's self-proclaimed description as played out on every page of *Fingers Pointing toward the Sacred: A Twentieth-Century Pilgrimage on the Eastern and Western Way* (Junction City, OR: Beacon Point Press, 1994) and quoted in James Finn

again and again. (They just don't want to read or watch *The Perfect Storm* while trapped in air turbulence in an airplane.)

> For thousands of years all the bloodiest and most brutal wars have been based on religious hatred. Which, of course, is fine with me; any time "holy" people are killing one another, I'm a happy guy.
>
> —AWARD-WINNING HUMORIST GEORGE CARLIN[23]

R is for Robitis

● What happens to clergy and judges when, comfortable and warm in their robes and status, they start believing what they hear and inhaling their "specialness."

● Also known as "revitis."[24]

The proper psychological condition for church leaders should be one of ragitis, not robitis—a spirit knitted and outfitted in the ragged robes of Jesus' suffering and death.

Carter's review of the book in *Parabola* 20 (August 1995), 98. For a more traditional slant on the compatibility of "religion" and "spirituality," see psychologist Kenneth I. Pargament's study "Religion and Spirituality: Unfuzzying the Fuzzy," *Journal for the Scientific Study of Religion* 36 (1997), 549–64.

23. George Carlin, *Napalm and Silly Putty* (New York: Hyperion, 2001), 226.

24. With thanks to Judge Jesse Caldwell III of Gastonia, North Carolina, for this phrase.

S is for Scenario Thinking

● What has replaced "strategic planning" and "long-range planning" as a strategy for dealing with the future.[1]

Unlike modern approaches to planning, scenario thinking promotes flexibility and preparedness and seeks to keep life more like an adventure than like completing a to-do list.

Cassidy S. Dale, a professional futurist who works with churches and church organizations to realize their God-called futures, distinguishes between "scenario planning" and "scenario thinking" in the following way:

> Scenario planning is easy. It's a matter of finding the trends in motion and speculating how those trends might shape the future.
>
> Scenario thinking is far more difficult. It's more difficult because it requires you to imagine that the future will turn out differently than the way you're *dead-certain* it will.
>
> Scenario planning produces multiple future forecasts based on different ideas of what is going on now.
>
> Scenario thinking requires you to question your own assumptions, biases and preferences—it requires you to challenge what you *believe* is going on now.

The importance of scenario thinking for postmodern leaders is underlined by the doctrine of the Holy Spirit (pneumatology).

---

1. On scenario thinking, see Peter Schwartz, *The Art of the Long View: Planning for the Future in an Uncertain World* (New York: Doubleday/Currency, 1991); Liam Fahey and Robert M. Randall, eds., *Learning from the Future: Competitive Foresight Scenarios* (New York: John Wiley & Sons, 1998); Pamela McCorduck and Nancy Ramsey, *The Futures of Women: Scenarios for the 21st Century* (New York: Addison-Wesley, 1996); Stewart Brand, *The Clock of the Long Now: Time and Responsibility* (New York: Basic Books, 1999).

The Spirit moves in mysterious ways. What scenario thinking does is widen your perspective to see how the Spirit may be in motion. Again in Dale's words,

> Scenario thinking breaks you out of your single view of the present and the future and allows you to re-perceive the present. For example, many people ask themselves very basic questions, "Are things getting better or are they getting worse? Are we dying or being born?" If they decide that things are getting worse, that the world is descending into oblivion, then they will interpret events in their world and their lives to be clear evidence that things are falling apart. If they decide that things are getting better, that a new world is being born, then they will interpret the oddities and chaos of the present as being evidence of the birth pangs. As Paul wrote in Romans, all of creation is involved in one great act of giving birth. How might what is going on now in the world—and in your own life—be a part of that birthing?[2]

The essence of scenario thinking is asking what else could occur? How is the Spirit moving in ways invisible to us because we cannot imagine?

S is for Secularism

● A hoax perpetrated on unsuspecting students by sociologists and other "modern" academics.

There was no such thing. Or if there was, the secularization of the sacred (especially the church)[3] led to the sacralization of the secular. If anything, postmoderns inhabit a world where spirituality has become a kind of fashion accessory. Faith today is like fluoride: It's in the water we drink, and we scarcely know it's there.

2. Email correspondence with Len Sweet (24 June 2001). Cassidy Dale can be reached at Cdale@wnrf.org.
3. Bryan R. Wilson, *Religion in Secular Society: A Sociological Comment* (London: C. A. Watts, 1966).

The church was fighting "secular humanism" when it should have been fighting secular churchism.

For Christians and churches in the emerging culture, we can assume that more and more people not only believe in the existence of the sacred, but are in fact on a quest to rediscover it. This resacralization will require us to reexamine, among other things, the doctrine of creation, seeing God's sacred fingerprint in all of creation, so that we can see, as Isaiah's seraphs did, that "the whole earth is full of his glory" (Isa. 6:3).

This resacralization of creation will have profound effects in our attitudes toward ecology, land use, and resource management. Moreover, the resurgence of interest in the sacred will have implications for the way we talk about sexuality and all of human life (including, but not limited to, unborn human life, aged human life, human life under oppression and damaged by poverty).

S is for Simultaneity

● An advanced form of "intertextuality," where texts are read through the lens of the "other." A function of non-either/or thinking.

In biblical studies and hermeneutics, simultaneity involves listening to multiple and especially marginal voices—unheard readings of the text, along with minority readings, along with women's readings, along with ancient readings, along with contemporary readings, along with children's readings, along with poststructuralist readings.[4] The goal is not to determine which reading is right, but rather to try to see the text simultaneously from many vantage points and, in so doing, to post-critically

4. For an intertextual, simultaneous reading of the Pentecost story, see Michel Serres, "Picaresques and Cybernetics: Pentecost," in his *The Parasite*, trans. Lawrence R. Schehr (Baltimore: Johns Hopkins University Press, 1982), 40–47. For the spirit of intertextuality, hear Michael King's words: "I can never fully escape my context as a white, male, affluent American. But I can learn much about being a better Christian in my context from those who are nonwhite, female, poor, members of other cultures" (King, *Trackless Wastes and Stars to Steer By*, [Scottdale, PA: Herald Press, 1990], 144).

appreciate the text as being multifaceted and multidimensional and therefore wonderful. (See **Double Ring** and **Deconstructionism.**)

Since our thinking is inescapably perspectival, the only way personal subjectivism can be transcended is not through an escape from perspective (whether through a Platonic flight from the body or a Cartesian flight from history) but through a "conversational multiplying of perspectives."[5]

Hence the importance of simultaneity and intertextuality—which is, after all, how the Bible was written. (In 1 and 2 Corinthians alone, there are 27 quotations of the Hebrew Bible and more than 125 allusions and verbal parallels.)[6]

S is for Singularity

● An event horizon beyond which everything becomes unpredictible and unplottable and beyond our ability to grasp it.

Singularities are moments of maximum fuzz because they are both beginning and ending, nothing and everything, alpha and omega.

"Let there be light" was a singularity.

Scientists call "the Big Bang" a singularity. Or was "the Big Bang" more "the Big Bloom?"[7]

Science is thus beginning to acknowledge that our horizons of understanding are limited. This acknowledgment may in turn open the door to further realizations regarding human intellectual limitation, returning us to a world more like the

---

5. See philosopher Art Holmes's works: *Christian Philosophy in the Twentieth Century* (Grand Rapids: Craig Press, 1969); *Faith Seeks Understanding* (Grand Rapids: Eerdmans, 1971); *All Truth Is God's Truth* (Grand Rapids: Eerdmans, 1977, repr. Downers Grove, IL: InterVarsity Press, 1983); *Contours of a World View* (Grand Rapids: Eerdmans, 1983).

6. See *The Greek New Testament*, 4th ed., ed. Barbara Kurt Aland et al. (Stuttgart: Deutsche Bibelgesellschaft, 1994), 887–901.

7. So suggests Ken Wilber, *A Brief History of Everything*, 2d ed. (Boston: Shambala, 2000), 58.

premodern one, a world bounded in mystery. In such a world, humility stands to become a virtue whose value will increase, both outside the church and in it.

S is for Spirituality

The slam of modernity? "That's unscientific."

The slam of postmodernity? "That's unspiritual." Or, "They have no spirituality."

There is a gnawing, growing awareness that the solution to the world's problems does not lie in the realm of politics, or economics, or technology, but in the world of the spirit.

When postmodern people say they are "into spirituality" or "spiritual, but not religious," they probably mean at least two things:

1. They don't believe secular science has all the answers.
2. They don't believe religion does either.

Christians, of course, agree on both counts. (You do believe God is right, not religion, right?)

The best definition of "spirituality" ever penned may be this one by Ewart Cousins:

> Spirituality refers to the experiential dimension of religion in contrast with formal beliefs, external practices, and institutions; it deals with the inner depth of the person that is open to the transcendent; in traditions that affirm the divine, it is concerned with the relation of the person to the divine, the experience of the divine, and the journey of the person to a more intimate relationship with the divine.[8]

8. Ewart Cousins, "Spirituality in Today's World" in *Religion in Today's World: The Religious Situation of the World from 1945 to the Present Day*, ed. Frank Whaling (Edinburgh: T. & T. Clark, 1987), 306. The best Christian look at spirituality is still Francis Schaeffer's *True Spirituality* (Carol Stream, IL: Tyndale House, 1979), reprinted in *The Complete Works of Francis A. Schaeffer: A Christian Worldview* (Westchester, IL: Crossway Books, 1982), 3:193–378. For an excellent look at the history of spirituality and its protean shapes, see

In sum: Spirituality is everything that goes into being in a relationship with God.

S is for Stacking

● The skill of doing many things at once. If postmoderns can only do one thing at a time, or can only climb aboard a one-trick pony, they deem it not worth pursuing. Postmoderns lead highly laminated lives.

Also known as "multitasking," which women are best equipped to implement:

> In 20 years I see myself as a career woman working full-time while juggling a family, kids (maybe!), pets, writing, playing video games, avoiding work, and doing my best to contribute to society.
>
> —HELEN CHENG, 18-YEAR-OLD FROM SAN DIEGO[9]

Add a preference for multitasking to an already busy life, and you will see why church leaders would be wise to find ways for people to stack community building, prayer, Bible study, other spiritual disciplines, Christian service, and committee/planning/board meetings into laminated events. Equally important, imagine how overstacked many people's lives already are, and you willl see why church leaders will also be wise to offer opportunities for people to relax in the luxury of doing one thing—rest, contemplation, celebration, study, prayer, or service.

Joe Holland's essay, "Linking Social Analysis and Theological Reflection: The Place of Root Metaphors in Social and Religious Experience," in *Tracing the Spirit: Communities, Social Action, and Theological Reflection,* ed. James Hug (New York: Paulist Press, 1983), 170–91. Holland views spirituality through three periods: (1) *monastic contemplation,* from the early church fathers through the Middle Ages (seeking God through daily disciplines and routines); (2) *individual privatization,* from the Protestant Reformation through the Industrial Revolution (seeking individual salvation through direct link-ups); and in postmodern culture, a move toward (3) *prophetic transformation,* or praxis.

9. As quoted in Rebecca Gardyn, "Granddaughters of Feminism," *American Demographics* (April 2001), 44.

EPICtivity S: Stacking

Postmoderns are very comfortable doing many things at once: driving while talking on their cell phone, talking with five or six people on AOL's buddy lists, watching MTV's multiple viewing windows. Stacking is becoming a way of life. A great example of stacking can be found in today's bookstores.

Ask your group to meet you at Borders, Joseph Beth's, Barnes and Noble, or a similar bookstore. Tell them that for the first 20 minutes, all should refrain from talking with anyone from the group. Then gather in the coffee shop area and dialogue about the following:

- What makes this bookstore attractive?
- How were bookstores different 15 or 20 years ago?
- What generations does this bookstore attract? Why?
- How many separate businesses exist under this one roof?
- What stories did you see unfolding in this store?
- In what ways is what happens in this store similar to what happens in our church?

Then ask the following:

- Where could we do some stacking in our ministry to better meet the needs of our people?
- Where does some stacking currently exist?
- What dangers should we beware of when it comes to stacking?
- In what ways has this EPICtivity been a stacked experience?

S is for String Theory

● The world as we don't know it, but as it actually may be.

A way of understanding the universe that almost makes you start taking miracles for granted.

String theory (also known as super-string physics) is the mathematical attempt at a TOE (Theory of Everything) that wraps all of physics (gravity, quantum mechanics, subatomic forces) into a simple, sublime formula. String theory is so named because it sees the building blocks of matter as "long, hollow tubes of space and time" roughly a billion trillion times smaller than a proton and a trillionth of a trillionth the size of an atom. Matter is defined as vibrating, 11-dimensional loops of energy. Different vibrational patterns of the "strings" represent different particles in nature.

The new cosmology portrays a cosmos that defies our figuring and confounds every expectation of how things ought to work. The so-called New Science turns out in retrospect to have been even "newer" than we imagined possible. The universe is giving way to a multiverse, an omniverse that boggles the brain.

The implications of this emerging theory, of course, are even harder to predict than the theory is to understand.[10] But it is tempting to speculate that a world where matter is actually an organized form of energy must become a world more open to Spirit, a world where old dichotomies like "natural" and "supernatural" seem rather facile, and a world that is once again vibrant with the voice of God whose "Let there be light" (i.e., "Let there be energy") now invites a new kind of literal interpretation.

10. The best elaboration of string theory is in Brian Greene, *The Elegant Universe: Superstring, Hidden Dimensions, and the Quest for the Ultimate Thing* (New York: W. W. Norton, 1999).

S is for Studio

● The look of a religious leader's office of the future—although features of the earlier "pastor's study" and "pastor's office" will still be present.

The seminary of the future—a reinvented form of the studio system for artists and artisans developed most fully in 13th-century Florence. Postmodern leaders/artists will welcome apprentices into their trial-and-success, shoulder-to-shoulder studio spaces to engage in the "three Cs" of postmodern enlightenment: creativity, collaboration, and communication.

A metaphor for the studio might well be the mixing board or the "mixing chamber." In the new Seattle Public Library, users begin their quest for information at what its architect Rem Koolhaas calls "the mixing chamber." The mixing chamber, Library Director Deborah L. Jacobs explains, "is all about interdisciplinary study and learning."

> Say you want to learn about Aaron Copland. That's not just music. There's a million topics that you could study: music, dance, Brooklyn, homosexuality, Judaism. If you come to the library, you may not know what direction you want to take. So the mixing chamber is the first place you arrive. Our incredibly talented and skilled librarians will be there, and they'll help you look for things in an interdisciplinary way.[11]

Creative experiences require the mixing of difference. The best leaders are the best Mix-Masters.

S is for Surface

● For postmoderns, the doorway into depth.

11. Deborah L. Jacobs, as quoted in Scott Kirsner, "Seattle Reboots Its Future," *Fast Company* (May 2001), 148. See *www.fastcompany.com/online/46/seattle.html.* (Accessed 13 August 2001.) See also Robin Updike, "Downtown Library Space-Age Design Goes Beyond Books," *Seattle Times* (16 December 1999).

Denizens of a world of screens (TV, computer, movie) find meaning in surfaces as well as depths. In fact, the surfaces become the depths where meaning and identity are often found. For postmoderns, there is no Logos without logo.

In a classic case of the way putdowns become pickups, the word *Enlightenment* was first used in the 18th century (1760s to be exact) as a slur and insult, mocking a glib and shallow intellectualizing of the mind as opposed to the full-orbed absorption of content by all the senses. In a postmodern spin on that phenomenon, Mark C. Taylor argues for "the profundity of surface."[12] His books, which attempt to seduce as much as convince, bring together theology, art and architecture, linguistics, literary criticism, and technology in the cause of eliminating distinctions of "style" versus "substance." Get over issues of depth, he argues. Just as you and I are essentially layers of skin ad infinitum, in the "play of surfaces" play can have an "infinite expansion of meanings," and surfaces can have a depth of meaning.

S is for Systems (or Systemic) Theology

● The postmodern equivalent of modernity's systematic theology.

Systematic theology broke down wholes into discrete, disciplinary parts, reducing entities to the properties of their elements. Moderns were trained to think programmatic and systematic. Not systemic, not systems, only systematic.

The systems model or systemic theology is characterized by "integrative thinking" or the ability to see complex organ-

---

12. Mark C. Taylor: *Deconstructing Theology* (New York: Crossroad, 1982); *Erring: A Postmodern A/Theology* (Chicago: University of Chicago Press, 1984); *Altarity* (Chicago: University of Chicago Press, 1987); *Disfiguring: Art, Architecture, Religion* (Chicago: University of Chicago Press, 1992); *Nots* (Chicago: University of Chicago Press, 1993); *Hiding* (Chicago: University of Chicago Press, 1997); *About Religion: Economics of Faith in Virtual Culture* (Chicago: University of Chicago Press, 1999); *The Moment of Complexity: Emerging Network Culture* (Chicago: University of Chicago Press, 2001).

isms like the church as a whole and to make strategic decisions accordingly.[13] When you think in terms of input, output, process, information, boundary, and purposiveness, you are using systems concepts that make the whole primary and the component parts secondary.[14]

Systems thinking provides a framework for seeing interrelationships rather than things, patterns of change rather than snapshots. The science of systems thinking itself was proposed and defined by biologist Ludwig von Bertalanffy in the 1940s.[15] Von Bertalanffy developed the systems theory in reaction to reductionism and in hopes of reviving the unity of science. By focusing on the arrangements of and relations between the parts and the whole, systems theory proposes that "the world is a system of subsystems, all interconnected and interdependent to form a wholistic or holistic system; that within any system is an infrastructure that is analogous across systems, irrespective of physical appearance."[16]

Which approach does your church take?

Systematic/Analytical Approach

1. Starts with today and the current state, issues, and problems

13. Three of the best books on the church as a systems model are Brian D. McLaren, *The Church on the Other Side: Doing Ministry in the Postmodern Matrix* (Grand Rapids: Zondervan, 2000); William M. Easum and Thomas G. Bandy, *Growing Spiritual Redwoods* (Nashville: Abingdon, 1997); and from a sociological standpoint, Bela H. Banathy, *Designing Social Systems in a Changing World* (New York: Plenum Press, 1996).

14. Francis Heylighen and Cliff Joslyn, "Systems Theory," in *The Cambridge Dictionary of Philosophy,* 2d ed., ed. Robert Audi (Cambridge: Cambridge University Press, 1999), 898–99. See their "What Is Systems Theory?" (1992) from the Principia Cybernetica project, *www.pespmcl.vub.ac.be/SYSTHEOR.html.* Accessed 8 August 2001.

15. Ludwig von Bertalanffy, *General System Theory: Foundations, Development, Applications* (New York: George Braziller, 1968), esp. chap. 3, "Some System Concepts on Elementary Mathematical Consideration," 54–88, which relates the introduction of general systems theory in 1945. It was further developed by Ross Ashby in 1956. See Ross Ashby, *Introduction to Cybernetics* (London: Chapman & Hall, 1956).

16. Heylighen and Joslyn, "What Is Systems Theory?" 1.

2. Breaks the issues and/or problems into their smallest components
3. Solves each component separately
4. Has no far-reaching vision or goal beyond the absence of the current problem

Systems/Systemic Thinking Approach

A. Where do we want to be? (That is, what are our ends, outcomes, purposes, goals, holistic vision?)
B. How will we know when we get there? (That is, how can we connect our needs and wants to a quantifiable feedback system?)
C. Where are we now? (How do we view today's issues and problems?)
D. How do we get from here and now to where we want to be? (That is, how do we close the gap between A and C in a completely holistic way?)
E. What will or may change in your environment in the future?[17] (And how will these changes affect your answers to C?)

The dynamics of systems thinking as it has been elaborated in the sciences and leadership arts force the church to return to its original vision as a learning organism of interdependent parts or members that ideally work together in harmony around a common vocation. The New Testament describes the church as an organic system (Rom. 12; 1 Cor. 12). Churches operate as a body and have the requirements of systems.

When the church becomes a "closed system," it exists to serve itself and meet the needs of its members. Entropy takes place. Death follows.

17. The Systems Thinking Approach, Concept #3, *The A-B-C-s of Strategic Management*, www.systemsthinkingpress.com/concept3sta.htm. Accessed 8 August 2001.

When the church becomes a "generative system," it has the capacity to find patterns, make connections, and engender relationships that can precipitate harvests that aren't even conceivable to the present theological establishment.

If von Bertalanffy bemoaned the reductionism of science and the splintering of science into isolated disciplines whose shrinking focus blinded them to larger realities that could only be seen across disciplines, shouldn't wise Christians say, "Enough is enough!" regarding the current state of theology, which has been similarly discipline-ized, professionalized, and modernized?

This new systems approach is reflected in a carefully crafted definition of Christian theology by Stan Grenz and John Franke, a definition that invites phrase by phrase savoring:

> Christian theology is an ongoing, second-order, contextual discipline that engages in critical and constructive reflection on the faith, life, and practices of the Christian community. Its task is the articulation of biblically normed, historically informed, and culturally relevant models of the Christian belief-mosaic for the purpose of assisting the community of Christ's followers in their vocation to live as the people of God in the particular social-historical context in which they are situated.[18]

Perhaps the most fascinating word in the definition is *models*. Models are wholes, systems, integrated metaphors that try to help us get a sense for something that is ultimately beyond our grasp. This model-making, systems-thinking approach invites a comparison of postmodern theology with both science and the arts.

On the one hand, scientists are increasingly aware that they are model makers, designing symbolic systems that help us

---

18. Stanley Grenz and John R. Franke, *Beyond Foundationalism: Shaping Theology in a Postmodern Context* (Louisville: Westminster John Knox Press, 2001), 16.

understand and live and work in the universe. It would be naïve, they would agree, to say that our models are fully and exactly telling us the way things really are when they describe the structure of an atom or the process of photosynthesis. No, they acknowledge that they are many layers removed from what is really happening, using language and metaphor and mathematics to try to capture and simplify and convey realities that are far more mysterious and multifaceted than even the brightest of us can fully comprehend.

And artists can describe their role in similar terms. A novelist creates a fictional world, a model world, a coherent system, if you will, in which characters interact and reveal insights that couldn't be conveyed except through this imaginative, holistic model making. A sculptor similarly creates models, as does a painter, or poet, or dancer, or violinist—each work of art becoming a kind of holistic model of some facet of experience that, when appreciated, helps people feel and understand and even live more fully. No artist ever expects to give the last artistic word on love, or fear, or betrayal, or hope. The models all help, but they never fully render reality—which brings the artist great frustration, perhaps, but also unending challenge and joy.

If artists and scientists accept that they are model makers, if they acknowledge that they will never fully capture their subjects and render them fully comprehensible, doesn't it seem a bit ridiculous (and maybe idolatrous?) for theologians to pose as the full and final explicators of the divine? Doesn't Grenz and Franke's definition, then, feel more humble and therefore ring more true for the next leg of the journey?

So, could theologians present their theologies in a way analogous to a sonata or screenplay or sculpture or poem or scientific model? What would then be lost or gained in comparison with the status quo in the academic discipline of theology?

A certain vision of what is possible in theology flows from Grenz and Franke's definition. Beyond modernity, this vision suggests, theologians can see their work as both exploratory and creative (like science and art): prepared through immersion in the Scriptures and in the life, practices, and mission of the church, they design models, ways of describing the way the universe is and the way God is and the way we are, and the ways they relate.

Then they test their models. They see how they resonate with Scripture, with Christians, with spiritual seekers and skeptics, with experience. They see what problems their models solve and create, what patterns they surface, and what meanings they offer . . . in comparison with other possible models, past and present. They do all this in a spirit of humility and discovery and collaboration, not of partisanship or inquisition.

Finally, they offer these models as their "experimental" findings, their works of art, to the church and to the world, hoping they will, as Grenz and Franke say, "assist the community of Christ's followers in their vocation to live as the people of God in the particular social-historical context in which they are situated." And—we cannot forget—the context in which we are situated is one in need of serious wisdom, vision, and virtue from God to face the challenges of the emerging world.

How different this vision is from a crabbed and contentious guild of isolated academes debating esoterica in the narrow halls of their isolated sub-sub-disciplines, issuing anathemas and launching inquisitions. That guild, perhaps, could earn the kind of vilification Richard Dawkins unleashed: "The achievements of theologians don't do anything, don't affect anything, don't mean anything."[19]

But if the world we live in really is a world God created, and to which God is faithful in spite of our unfaithfulness, a world which God loves with a saving love . . . and if the world we live in really faces the kind of trouble it seems to face . . . then wouldn't we expect God to intend theologians to be a source of hope and meaning and guidance and wisdom for the world

19. Richard Dawkins, "The Emptiness of Theology," *Free Inquiry* (Spring 1998), 6.

once again ... so their work did much, affected much, and meant much?

It is hard to imagine a higher calling than to be a theologian, in this sense of the word, in the kind of world emerging around us, Richard Dawkins notwithstanding. (See **Theologians.**)

T is for Target Marketing

● What postmoderns don't like being sliced and diced into. No one likes having a bulls-eye drawn in red on their foreheads anyway, but postmoderns especially rag and gag at tags (including the tag "postmodern").

Forget "find your target audience." Instead, find your postmodern *neighbor*—everybody, anywhere, anytime who needs Jesus.

T is for Team

● What you can't do postmodern ministry without. Stanley Ott says it best:

> The word "team" comes from Old English meaning the harnessing of two or more animals to pull some vehicle or implement. It's an image that still comes immediately to mind when we think of a team of oxen pulling a plow or a team of horses pulling a wagon. My friend Lewis Christiansen tells of growing up on a farm and learning how to harness as many as five horses to pull the heavy farm wagon. The strength of the horses, their temperaments, and the nature of the load being handled guided how each team was harnessed together. Ministry team life harnesses us together as we join with others to accomplish ministry.[1]

A team should not ordinarily be larger than 14 people or smaller than three. (See **Coaching; Fractals.**)

1. E. Stanley Ott, *The Power of Ministry Teams: Building Community, Fostering Discipleship, Developing Leadership* (San Francisco: Jossey-Bass Pfeiffer, 2001), 5.

> You never start a ministry without a team.
>
> —Wayne Cordeiro, New Hope Christian Fellowship,
> Honolulu, Hawaii

T is for Theologians

● What all Christian are called to be.

Richard Dawkins, high priest of modern scientific fundamentalism, has in his inimitable style smacked theology across the face:

> What has theology ever said that is of the smallest use to anybody? When has theology ever said anything that is demonstrably true and is not obvious? I have listened to theologians, read them, debated against them. I have never heard any of them ever say anything of the smallest use, anything that was not either platitudinously obvious or downright false. If all the achievements of scientists were wiped out tomorrow, there would be no doctors but witch doctors, no transport faster than horses, no computers, no printed books, no agriculture beyond subsistence peasant farming. If all the achievements of theologians were wiped out tomorrow, would anyone notice the slightest difference? Even the bad achievements of scientists, the bombs, and sonar-guided whaling vessels work. The achievements of theologians don't do anything, don't affect anything, don't mean anything.[2]

Whether or not Dawkins wins the Nobel Prize for Overstatement, what if, in the next hundred years, theologians will be the most needed advisors invited to the table of global

2. Richard Dawkins, "The Emptiness of Theology," *Free Inquiry* (Spring 1998), 6.

leadership? What if, just as Joseph's wisdom was needed by Pharaoh, and Daniel's by Nebuchadnezzar, wisdom from our best theologians will be needed by global leaders of the coming centuries?

How could that be, you ask? Consider this: A few years ago, Stephen Hawking—arguably one of the brightest minds of the modern world, perhaps best known for his book A *Brief History of Time*—was invited by President Bill Clinton to give an address at the White House, to offer his conjectures about science in the 21st century.

Among his many stunning predictions was this: In the 21st century, for the first time in the history of our planet (if not the universe), *a species will take control of its own evolution*. Referring to breakthroughs in genetic engineering, Hawking asserted that the development of "designer humans" was not a question of *if*, but rather of *where* and *when* and *by whom*.

Think about the implications of Hawking's prediction, and then try to make a list of the top 10 problems facing the human community in the next century or two. You will probably include overpopulation, famine, disease, ecological destruction, and tribal/racial/ethnic/religious hatred and warfare/terrorism.

Now ask yourself to what degree these problems are, at heart, spiritual issues. And finally, if you are prone to read apocalyptic novels, ask yourself what if Christ does *not* return or rapture you and yours before these potential problems flower into their full intensity? Instead, imagine that you and your children and grandchildren will live in the very world that must deal with these problems. Do you see why the world, not to mention the church, needs Josephs and Daniels again?

Will there be theological sages ready to guide world leaders up the ethical Everests we will need to climb in the new millennium—as Joseph and Daniel did in their time? What kinds of theologies will prepare these kinds of wise men and women in the future?

Probably not our current systematic theologies, which seem pretty maxed out, used up, run down, and boxed in.

Too often, our systematic theologies represent the typically modern attempt to capture all knowable truth in propositions, organized in a master outline, holding for all times and places and people the universal abstractions extracted from the narratives of Scripture. (This extraction, if completed as hoped, would have meant that theology would eventually, in any vital and exploratory sense, be over, completed, finished. What next?) This naïve optimism about theology seems laughable to postmodern ears . . . laughable and either arrogant or quaint, or perhaps quaintly arrogant.

Just as medieval cathedrals in Europe remind us of a bygone Christendom that quaintly (or arrogantly) believed it was actually building the infrastructure of the kingdom of God when it constructed those cathedrals, modern systematic theologies will someday remind us of a bygone modern Christian rationalism that quaintly (or arrogantly) believed it was encoding the absolute and universal truth for all time in its fine print and footnotes.

What new theologies will emerge to replace modern theologies, both liberal and conservative? No one knows. But this is almost certain: If modern theology, cast in the mold of modern analysis, focused its energies on breaking wholes down into parts (dissecting God, as it were, into attributes, and dissecting Scripture into propositions and dispensations, and dissecting ministry into discrete disciplines), postmodern theology will instead seek to restore a sense of the whole.

It will look for integration rather than analysis. It will value holistic systems over systematization of propositions. It will, we believe, follow a course parallel in many ways to a scientific movement called systems theory; it will move from an analytical/systematic to an integrative/systems approach that emphasizes history, narrative, story. And it will be done by a new breed of theologians who work together in a new way. (See **Yes!**)

T is for Tribal

● The boomerang of global.

The world is getting more global and more tribal at the same time. The more global we become, the more tribal we need to be in terms of our identity and pedigree.

Czech President Vaclav Havel, in a commencement address at Harvard in 1995, stated,

> For the first time in the long history of the human race, [our planet has] been covered in the space of a very few decades by a single civilization—one that is essentially technological. The world is now enmeshed in webs of telecommunication networks consisting of millions of tiny threads of capillaries that not only transmit information of all kinds at lightning speed, but also convey integrated models of social, political, and economic behavior.[3]

But "while the world as a whole increasingly accepts the new habits of global civilization, another contradictory process is taking place: Ancient traditions are reviving, different religions and cultures are awakening to new ways of being, seeking new room to exist, and struggling with growing fervor to realize what is unique to them and what makes them different from others."[4]

Consider how television functioned in the industrial as opposed to the informational age. Television started as a medium of shared experience. This was the big fear of TV, that it would turn us all into similar pear-shaped lumps. Now television via cable, satellite, and fiber optics are fragmenting us into niche markets, dividing us by ethnicity (the Jamaican Channel), by interest (the Fly Fishing Channel), by religion (the Christian Channel, the Hindu Channel), and so on. At the same time, television is giving us shared global experiences.

---

3. Vaclav Havel, "The World Can Find Means of Coexistence," *Christian Science Monitor* (9 June 1995), 18.
4. Ibid.

In contrast to the old tribalism (which, in spite of Jesus' story of the Good Samaritan, is still alive and "well" in many places, sowing violence, hatred, and suspicion), the new tribalism kisses rather than kills members of other tribes. The new tribalism eschews the feuds of ecclesiastical feudalisms for fugues and dances. It does not engage in religious apartheid. Postmoderns choose membership in multiple tribes, only some of which are through lineage. And postmodern tribes tend to be acephalous (i.e., headless), less led than fathered/mothered. What other head is needed than Jesus?

> If two or three of you *ever* get together,
> *I'll come to see it Myself!*
> —ONE PASTOR'S TRANSLATION OF MATTHEW 18:20

What tribes are part of your ancestry and identity? Try talking about your denominational affiliation (if any) as your "tribe." How can your church encourage the development of "new tribes" who enrich unity rather than strain it? What are your special tribal rituals (initiation rites, language, colors, songs)?

T is for Transcendent Immanence and Immanent Transcendence

Transcendence refers to the "otherness" of God, God's difference and distance from us, celebrated in biblical language with words like "high" and "holy." Conversely, immanence refers to the nearness of God and is captured in biblical images like a tender shepherd or a nursing mother or a loving father.

Modernity, which had problems with God in general, had serious problems with both immanence and transcendence. Some theologians, by filleting from the gospel records all miracles and "supernatural" elements, eradicated transcendence, tossing away dimensions of the Christian message that were to them an embarrassment in a closed-system, naturalist, reductionist, rationalist universe.[5]

Others cooperated by shrinking the transcendent God into a down-home buddy or a cosmic sugar daddy who gives you his credit card number to "name and claim," always at your disposal like a genie or divine butler.

Others unwittingly bled God of transcendence by making him so well exegeted, so understandable, so explicable, predictable, and principle-bound that his glory was that of a celestial IRS agent.

The "contemporary Christian music" industry also became an accidental accomplice in the banishment of transcendence, filling the airwaves with so many songs about God that the words "God" and "Lord" and "Jesus" began to sound like "Exxon" and "Coca Cola" and "Nabisco," rendering God a product we were promoting day and night. So much for transcendence.

With this abandonment of transcendence, we might at least expect to have enjoyed a high view of God's immanence in modernity. Not so. As science relegated God to "the gaps" (i.e., what we couldn't "explain" by science), and as Christians generally cooperated (even though the gaps kept shrinking), God was generally to be found far, far away if at all:

- As the Creator who cranked up the clock fifteen billion years ago and has since left it to run on its own . . .
- As the Inspirer of Scripture who sent us the Book and leaves us to study it on our own . . .
- As the divine Dispensationalist who was allowed to intervene in other times, but not much in our own . . .
- As the Awaited One who will be active again someday in the future (maybe when revival comes?) but for now seems rather aloof.

5. See, e.g., Gordon D. Kaufman, *In Face of Mystery: A Constructive Theology* (Cambridge, MA: Harvard University Press, 1993).

All of these images tend to downplay God's presence with us in our daily lives here and now, in our knowledge as well as in our mysteries, in our strengths as well as in our weaknesses, in the mundane as well as in the spectacular, during dry times of endurance as well as exciting times of spiritual outpouring.

Is God the Unmoved Mover or the God who moves, especially toward the unmoved? With the waning of modernity, Christian leaders need to reclaim God's immanence and transcendence in the dynamic paradox of Christian orthodoxy—a God who is at once high and holy and near and dear.

T is for Transgressive

● One of the hardest words to say with a postmodern meaning. When you hear postmoderns use this word (as in "transgressive preaching" or "transgressive church"), don't think "sins and transgressions." Think border crossings and boundary burstings.

Postmoderns want to take on the taboos (not that they will call them "taboos") because they are the "outsiders," the "outcasts," the "outlaws." Many postmoderns will be crucified by moderns for exploring the taboos. The danger of "death by friendly fire" will be too great for many.

The greatest taboo subjects in the church today? Money, power, and sexuality. On these topics, the operative principle is "Don't ask. Don't tell."

Will you take on the taboos, whatever they are? For postmoderns "take on" means less "stand against" than "walk alongside." The church is here to destroy fortresses, not build them. A Mighty Fortress is *not* our church. A Mighty Fortress is *our God*.

T is for Trialectics (or Thirding)

The move from binary logic to trinary logic (mind, body, spirit) is trialectics, the recognition that when you bring the ends/edges/extremes together you create a third, or *tertium quid*.

When both affirmation and negation are faced simultaneously, a heretofore unimaginable third position is allowed to emerge.

Perspective is based on having two eyes. Depth perception is based on having three eyes. The third, or inner, eye is symbolized in Hinduism by the red dot in the middle of the forehead.

Ends fray. Think of these two words and their truth. Braiding the two ends together is thirding or trialectics.

The "Rule of Three" tells us that things come in threes. Our heads are wired for three. Two is incomplete; four overmuch; three just right. Some thirdings in Christian history and theology:

Abraham, Isaac, Jacob
Spirit, Water, Blood
Faith, Hope, Love
Righteousness, Peace, Joy
Yesterday, Today, Forever
Was, Is, Is to Come
Outer Court, Inner Court, Holy of Holies
Heart, Soul, Mind
Death, Burial, Resurrection
Acceptable, Good, Perfect
OT, NT, YT (Your Testament)
Now, Tomorrow, Forever
Gold, Frankincense, Myrrh
Mind, Body, Spirit

"Life occurs between people as well as within them."[6] Only in the Third Space or Third Realm—the relational spaces between people—can you create new relationships or improve old ones.

6. These relational concepts are examined in Nathan Schwartz-Salant, *Mystery of Human Relationship: Alchemy and the Transformation of Self* (New York: Routledge, 1998).

T is for Trustee

● The postmodern word for "steward." The only "stewards" still around are serving hundred-dollar bottles of wine at five-star restaurants.

In 1836 Loddige's, the greatest nursery that ever existed, offered for sale 67 species of oak, 29 of birch, 91 of thorns, 180 willow, and 1,549 roses.

That's trusteeship.

Modern cities today, by contrast, can boast a few mass-produced species of trees and flowers and lawn grasses, plus a fauna consisting of one species of squirrel, three species of birds (starlings, sparrows, and pigeons), four of mammals (squirrels, dogs, cats, and rats), no reptiles or amphibians (they were eradicated long ago), and two insects (fruit flies and roaches).

That's trusteeship?

U is for Unknown

● What is often less dangerous than the known, because in the presence of the unknown we are humbled. By contrast, impressed by all we think we know, we become proud.

A sensitivity to the limits of human knowledge is central to the postmodern ethos, just as a sensitivity to the expanse of human knowledge was central to the modern ethos.

Many modern Christians argue with postmoderns about terms like *absolute truth*, and these arguments generally go nowhere—largely because neither side clarifies whether it is talking about absolute *truth* or absolute *knowledge*. Absolute knowledge—which would presumably mean incorrigible knowledge (incapable of being wrong or correctable)—would be, from a Christian perspective, the provenance of God only, since we finite creatures (as 1 Corinthians 13 says) "know only in part" and possess an amazing capacity for self-deception and error. Can you see how ridiculous and arrogant we would seem if we claimed absolute *knowledge*?

Similarly, many modern Christians argue with postmoderns about terms like *objective truth*, and these arguments similarly go nowhere, for the same reason: Do we mean objective *truth*, or objective *knowledge*? Objective knowledge (free from any limiting personal perspective) would similarly be, for Christians, only possible for a knower possessing an unlimited perspective, a position only one Being can claim.

Again, do you want to portray yourself as being a repository of objective *knowledge*? Relax: Releasing know-it-all pretensions to absolute or objective knowledge does not mean that we are laissez-faire know-nothings, spineless relativists, incapable of beliefs, convictions, commitments. No. For us, aware that absolute knowledge is a fruit we are not permitted to taste (does that sound familiar?), we are nevertheless possessed by a God-given hunger and thirst for truth, beauty, and goodness. These we seek, not in the gossamer form of abstract propositions, but rather in a scarred face, a real person, a vital relationship: "Your face, LORD, do I seek."

This is the knowing (*connaitre*) that transcends knowledge (*savoir*), the knowing that takes place in a mysterious world full of unknowns.

EPICtivity U: Unknown

Here is an exercise in the unknown physics of spirit. Find two stones. Push them together. When you push them into each other, why don't you get one twice-as-dense rock? If matter is basically empty space, why not?

Actually, given an intense magnetic field, that is precisely what would happen. Matter is compressed as the empty space is expelled. A gravitational field the force of one neutron star could squeeze planet Earth into an object the size of a marble.

Discuss the "unknowns" in your life.

- Are the greatest "unknowns" where your education and understanding are at their best, or at their least?
- What "unknowns" do you fear most?
- What "unknowns" do you trust most?

Discuss this quote from Mike Leigh:

Was I bored? No I wasn't ... bored. I'm never bored. That's the trouble with everybody, you're all so bored. You've had nature explained to you and you're bored with it; you've had the living body explained to you and you're bored with it; you've had the universe explained to you and you're bored with it. So now you just want cheap thrills and like plenty of them. And it don't matter how tawdry or vacuous as long as it's new, as long as it's new, as long as it flashes and ... bleeps in forty ... colors. Whatever else you can say about me, I'm not ... bored.[1]

With so much unknown out there waiting to be discovered and learned, how could anyone be bored? What is the source of our boredom?

1. As quoted by Richard DeGrandpre in *Ritalin Nation: Rapid-Fire Culture and the Transformation of Human Consciousness* (New York: W.W. Norton, 1999), 172.

V is for Versus
Verses

● A resurrection of older, more authentic readings of Scripture.

One of the odder paradoxes of modernity? While rendering the Bible more ubiquitous than phone books and providing every possible convenience to make it easy to read (complete with designer Bibles for women, men, teens, kids, and vampires), church leaders still needed to resort to constant pressure and guilt to get people to read it.

Even among people who did read it, heard it preached Sunday after Sunday, and listened to sermons ostensibly about it on Christian radio day and night—even among these people, late modernity witnessed an amazing biblical illiteracy. Here are people who are being hounded and pounded and surrounded by the Bible, who still don't seem to get it. Why?

The reasons for this persistent resistance to really "getting" the Bible are many. But two have particular relevance to our primer because they are remediable in the postmodern world.

The first reason is reflected in Martin Luther's once calling the Bible "our enemy." This book is a living text, he argued, and as such it reads us and judges us more than we read and judge it.[1] For the Protestant Reformers like Luther, the Scriptures are something set over us and against us: They are *supposed* to feel exotic, alien, and disorienting.

Poet W. H. Auden once remarked that you should never ask anyone whether they had read any good books lately, only if

---

1. Luther's view of the Bible as a "living text" is somewhat different from what D. C. Parker means by that phrase in his book *The Living Text of the Gospels* (New York: Cambridge University Press, 1997): "The Gospels cannot be properly understood as texts without taking into consideration their physical existence as manuscripts, printed books and electronic text" (i). Of course, Luther's "living text" was calcified into the principle of *sola scriptura*, in which the Bible became an object of exegetical study.

they had been read by any good books lately. Similarly, poet Samuel Taylor Coleridge contended that "I find more in the Bible that finds me, and finds me at deeper levels of my being, than in all secular literature put together." There is a way of Bible reading that involves less our reading it than allowing it to read us.[2]

The second reason is a subtle culprit: *Verses*. When the late singer-songwriter Rich Mullins was asked what his favorite verse in the Bible was, he replied, "The book of Isaiah."[3]

When Jeremiah wrote his prophecies, he didn't write them with 1:1, 1:2, 1:3 notations. Nor did anyone else among the biblical writers guild. The chapter-and-versification of the Bible was a late addition, a convenience for scholars that the Geneva Bible (A.D. 1560) first made available to English-language readers.

What's wrong with versification? Mainly this: It assisted modern preachers, hearers, and readers in focusing on the trees and missing the forest. It facilitated a modern use of the Bible that, sometime in the future, will probably be judged close to abuse.

For modern Bible readers, the Scriptures became like a mountain from which we strip-mine for its modern treasure— abstract propositions or principles. The native stories, poetry, genres, and language were surface distractions—like flowers, trees, elk, and butterflies—that kept us from our real interest that lay beneath all that superficiality. Hence we burn and scrape and cut away the distractions so that we can get to the minerals of abstractions and principles from which we construct our systematic theologies and doctrinal formulations and sermons.

Here is where the versification comes in. Our ever-popular references (John 14:6; Gen. 12:3) become like X's on a map that

---

2. Hans-ruedi Weber, *The Book That Reads Me: A Handbook for Bible Study Encounters* (Geneva: WCC Publications, 1995).

3. As cited in *FaithWorks* (November/December 1999), 20.

tell us where to dig to find the desired minerals or metals. They help us avoid all those distractions of context and dramatic situation, song, narrative and poetic genre, so we can get right to what is *really* valuable to us.

What if the general biblical illiteracy that surrounds us—which we all lament even among the sermoned and radioed and quiet-timed and Bible-studied masses in the church—is the result not of the stupidity or carelessness of the hearers but rather of the denseness and wrongheadedness of us teachers?

What if we are ruining the Bible for parishioners by the modern ways in which we insist on presenting it to them?[4]

What if the reason for postmoderns visiting the mountain is not to extract abstractions and use them back in our cities and suburbs to erect doctrinal scaffolding? What if, instead, postmodern people visit the mountains precisely so they can see the elk and flowers and butterflies and the spruce and the lichen and the rocks covered in glistening snow—not to mention enjoying amazing views from a new perspective and being renewed by the fresh mountain air?

Imagine teaching Bible stories, not so your hearers will remember your points of construction (stone building blocks of doctrinal statements and steel girders of systematic theologies), but so they will simply remember and enjoy the stories themselves (the treasures hidden in the fields)? Can you imagine teaching the Bible so disciples actually get a feel for the big picture, the whole biblical sweep of the expansive story of God's romance with his creatures ... what Stan Grenz and John Franke call the "trajectory"[5] of the biblical story (the megastory in which all the biblical stories are nestled)?

4. For an example of a Bible study for postmoderns, see Michael Riddell, *God's Home Page* (Oxford: Bible Reading Fellowship, 1998).
5. Stanley Grenz and John R. Franke, *Beyond Foundationalism: Shaping Theology in a Postmodern Context* (Louisville: Westminster John Knox Press, 2001), 91.

> Reason as I can, there are passages in the Old and the New Testaments which I am unable to accord with any sensible image, however exalted, of normal authorship, of conception and composition as we seek to grasp them in even the greatest of thinkers and poets. . . . In such biblical instances [e.g., 13–17 in John], the concept of a wholly rational hermeneutic escapes me. I find myself backed up against the harsh radiance of "the scandalous." It is not "theology as grammar" which seems pertinent. It is grammar as theology.
>
> —LITERARY CRITIC GEORGE STEINER[6]

Can you imagine that it would be more helpful for your hearers to show them in 25 or 30 minutes the intense drama of, say, the whole letter to the Ephesians, taken as a personal letter from one man to one church, intervening in the struggles of real-life people grappling with the radical gospel of Jesus in their situation? Can you imagine that this presentation of Ephesians as an episode from an epistolary novel, so to speak, would be more helpful by far than analyzing every word of one verse, down to the Greek prefixes and iota superscripts? And can you see how if you bore them to death with your versified analysis, you will repel them from loving Ephesians or wanting to understand it in more detail?

Conversely, can you see that, by helping postmodern people picture the drama, the story, the situation, the inter-personal action between the writer and the audience, you just may entice them to so love Ephesians that they may someday be interested in really digging into a specific verse, complete with Greek prefixes and suffixes and roots?

6. George Steiner, "The Scandal of Revelation," *Salmagundi* 98/99 (Spring/Summer 1993), 69, 70.

If this impartation of stories and Story is your goal, then the versification of the Bible is at best a somewhat dangerous convenience, and at worst an ugly distraction that spoils the view. (Imagine hiking through the mountains and every eight feet seeing a sign that tells the precise elevation, or your distance from the parking lot where you began.)

In sum, then, the versification of the Bible encourages the kind of abstraction-mining and proof-texting that postmodern readers feel makes the Bible fragmented, frustrating, contradictory, confusing, even dangerous (able to be misused and abused for all kinds of misguided purposes)—and boring. "Just give us the Bible unedited, uncut, and raw!" they say. "Give us the wild stories and passionate poetry and bizarre (to us) cultural settings and foreignness (in geography, culture, and history). Let us get a feel for its grand movements and inspiring landscape. Please, please don't turn our beautiful ecosystem into a strip-mined wasteland."

Versus Children

By the way, this transformation of the biblical landscape into a versified proposition-mine afflicts children, too, not just adults. Sit in a Sunday school class for four-to-seven-year-olds. You will hear Bible stories aplenty, yes, but nine times out of 10, the stories will be "mined" and reduced in the end to morals or arguments, like these:

- The story of Cain and Abel is a story whose point is that siblings should be nice to each other.
- The story of Jesus calming the storm is an argument proving the deity of Christ.
- The story of Jesus as a boy getting lost in Jerusalem tells children to stay close to their parents in supermarkets and other public places so they won't get lost.

Now we are certainly *for* children being safe in the frozen food aisle, and *for* the deity of Christ, and *for* siblings not killing each other. But if you think that is what those stories are "there for," if you think their ultimate purpose is simply to make these kinds of points, then . . . then we hardly know what to say, even though we used to see the Bible the same way. Is it possible that God had good reasons for wanting the Bible to be a story of stories?

Increasing numbers of preachers and teachers with postmodern sensitivities are boycotting chapter-and-versifying their sermons and writings. Instead, they tend to quote longer passages, not just one narrow little "X marks the spot" underneath which one can find the treasured abstraction. Sure, they use the versification system to help their audience find the right place on the right page . . . but having used the numbers to find the passage, they promptly ignore the numbers and try to let the text itself determine what expanse of terrain will occupy them in their explorations.

The post-analytical, post-critical world ahead of us, we believe, is rich in possibilities for rekindling a fervent love for, enthusiastic interest in, and devout following of the Bible, sans a versified, abstraction-mining approach. We can already see this in some recent literature that has "rediscovered" the Bible[7] and in the mushrooming genre of poets and novelists writing chapters on their favorite books of the Bible.[8]

Maybe Americans who lament the Bible's removal from the public schools by its "enemies" in the last century should rather lament the way Bible analysts—ostensibly its friends—inadvertently bored people with the Bible and drove them away from it. Thankfully, if we help people rediscover the Bible as it

---

7. For example, Gregg Easterbrook, *Beside Still Waters: Searching for Meaning in an Age of Doubt* (New York: William Morrow, 1998).

8. Even musicians are getting in on the action. See Elana Zeider, "The Gospel According to Bono," *Rolling Stone,* 2 September 1999: 39, which discusses singer Bono's Introduction to *The Books of the Bible: Selections from the Book of Psalms,* Pocket Canon Series (New York: Grove Press, 1999). See also Cassidy Dale, "A Truth beyond Telling," or *www.faithworks.com.archives/truthbeyond.htm.*

is (Living! Active! Cutting! Wild! Expansive!) rather than as we have presented it (Codified. Nailed down. Analyzed. Dissected. Versified.), it will once again abduct us into its higher views of life, the universe, ourselves, and God. (See **Abductive.**)

V is for Violence

● The brutalities of our drooling desires.[9]

How far we have come in so short a time from the world of Alfred Hitchcock's Psycho, where the famous shower scene conveys horror and terror without the knife ever being seen piercing the flesh.

> I wouldn't mind killing people again, but not in the same teenage genre. It's a hard curve to stay ahead of.
>
> —DIRECTOR WES CRAVEN AT THE PREMIERE OF SCREAM 3[10]

In the century after the century of the Holocaust, a time highly (and rightly) sensitive to torture and violence, Christians would be both wise and innocent (à la Jesus) if they became more discriminating in their "warfare rhetoric." Culture wars, the enemy, spiritual warfare, targeting, ammunition, Christian soldiers, warriors for Christ . . . these terms have their place. But it is time to be more careful in our use of this language, for its effects both on others and on ourselves. (See **Target Marketing.**)

V is for Voice

The authority of an "eye-witness" was boilerplate modernity. The authority of an "ear-witness" is boilerplate postmodernity.

9. For one of the best books on violence, see Rene Girard, I See Satan Falling Like Lightning (Maryknoll, NY: Orbis, 2001).
10. Wes Craven, as quoted in César Soriano, "Lifeline," USA Today (8 February 2000), 1D.

And what postmoderns are listening for is less words than the music of the spheres, especially the heavenly spheres, but sometimes the dances of demons.

> He who possesses in truth the word of Jesus can even hear its silence.
>
> —ST. IGNATIUS OF ANTIOCH

While rhythm is the structuring principle of their lives, postmoderns experience life in terms of sound levels. Some things are too "noisy"; other things have too much "static." Sometimes there is the need for silence; sometimes the silence is deafening.

In the modern world, vision was everything. When moderns thought about sound, they confused voice with volume. Truth was eye-opening. In the postmodern world, where voice has replaced objectivity, truth is ear-opening. Vision is imposing order on chaos. Voice is discovering the intrinsic form through attentive listening through the "auditory imagination" (T. S. Eliot) and "acoustic ideas" (Thomas Mann).

The worst thing a church can do is call a "visionary leader." Any leader who presents a vision without first listening to others and hearing their voices is in danger of becoming a tyrant. Disconnect the ear and eye, and there is danger ahead. Vision is not something you generate. Vision is something you hear into speech and sight.

The primacy of "voice" beckons the church back to a more biblical and more scientific framework. In the Scriptures and throughout Christian history, the primary gateway to the soul was the ear. In a biblical sense, you don't so much "see" a vision as "hear" a vision.

Likewise, in super-string physics the very building blocks of the universe are defined as "vibrating loops of energy." In other words, energized arrangements of matter achieve vibratory resonance. The matter of the universe now appears to be more sound than sight. (See **String Theory.**)

V is for Voice

Martin Heidegger, in his classic essay on Heraclitus, said that this notion of Logos as basically speech and discursive reason is too one-sided, since it suppresses the more intuitive, more experiential sense of "letting-lie-together-before" (or in its verb-form *legein*).[11] In other words, Logos means as much "listening" as "speaking," a "harkening" as much as a "happening," an allowing of things to "come into presence" as much as a controlling and ordering of things into logistics and schematics.

> The [written] Word is the wire along which the voice of God will certainly come to you if the heart is hushed and the attention fixed.
>
> —F. B. MEYER

How does Jesus know us? Our identity shines through variable harmonics. There is tonal resonance between Christ and his sheep: "My sheep hear my voice. I know them, and they follow me" (John 10:27). Postmoderns will develop a sound theology.[12]

In the Celtic tradition there is the image of "listening for the heartbeat of God."[13] According to Celtic legend, at the last supper why did John the Beloved lean against Jesus? To hear the heartbeat of God. After all, Jesus is as "close to the Father's heart" as one can get (John 1:18).

Postmodern leaders are first of all leaners and listeners— people who have trained their beings to lean against life and

11. Martin Heidegger, "Logos (Heraclitas, Fragment B50)," in his *Early Greek Thinking*, trans. David Farrell Krell and Frank A. Capuzzi (New York: Harper, 1950), 59–78.

12. For more on "sound theology" see Leonard Sweet with Denise Marie Suno, *A Cup of Coffee at the Soul Café* (Nashville: Broadman & Holman, 1998), 58–71; *Eleven Genetic Gateways to Spiritual Awakening* (Nashville: Abingdon, 1998), 154–69; and a leadership text, *Forget the Vision Thing: Play It by Ear* (Grand Rapids: Zondervan, forthcoming).

13. J. Philip Newell, *Listening for the Heartbeat of God: A Celtic Spirituality* (New York: Paulist Press, 1997).

their ears to listen to the beat of life. Leadership is being able to hear the "whisper" of God's voice and the "thunder of his power" (Job 26:14) and then to help others sign up and thunder forth what Jesus is already doing in the world (John 14:12).

W is for (The) Way

The first name for followers of Jesus was not "Christian," but "The Way." In fact, "the Way" is the name Jesus gave himself when Thomas asked him, "How can we know the way?" Jesus responded, "I am the way" (John 14:5–6). Yahweh, the Way-maker, sent us The Way himself to set us free to live The Way.

The search for truth is a moral imperative. But Christian "truth" is a person who invites us to join him on "The Way." Christianity is a "way of life." The Christian life is more a journey than jelled beliefs, more pilgrimage and practices than propositions and principles.

> The journey is better than the inn.
>
> —OLD ROMAN SAYING

Most of us have heard of bounded sets as contrasted with centered sets. Bounded sets preoccupy themselves with whether one is in or out, like this diagram, in which A, B, and C are clearly out, and X, Y, and Z are clearly in:

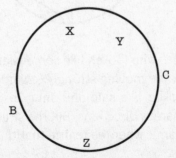

In centered-set thinking, the boundary is de-emphasized and a center point is recognized so that we notice things we didn't notice before, such as the fact that B and C are almost as close to the center as Z.

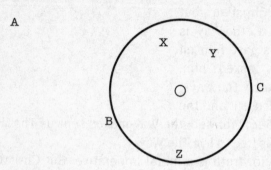

But we can advance our thinking two steps further. First, let's advance beyond static-centered thinking to dynamic-centered thinking, where we realize that all points in our diagram are moving with varying momentum and in varying directions, like this:

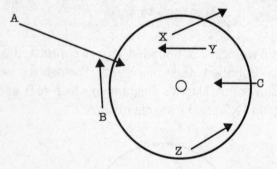

Now A and C, who looked like somewhat distant outsiders before, seem to be moving strongly toward the center, and X and Y, who looked like safe and snug insiders, seem to be drifting in dangerous directions. But the situation can be made even more dynamic when we realize that the center point, if it refers to Christ, the Holy Spirit, or the kingdom of God, is not static either, but dynamic. Consider this:

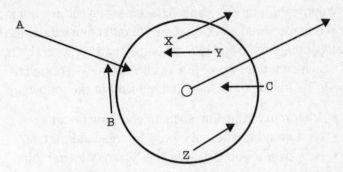

In this diagram it becomes clear that X and Z, who appeared to be in trouble a minute ago, are now the only ones who are really aligned with the dynamic Center, and A and C, who seemed to be closing in on the Center, may actually be in some spiritual danger unless they adjust their course.

This rather facile diagram offers one simple way of picturing Christianity as a truly dynamic way of life as opposed to a static or semi-dynamic position or status. Seeing our faith in this way reconnects us with Jesus' primal words to us: *Follow me.* In-group/out-group thinking and even nearness/farness thinking can bog down discipleship from way to waiting room, from road to inn, from longing to apathy, from journey to arrival. As we deconstruct old boundaries and distrust static status, we hear Jesus saying, "I am the way. Follow me," and we take up our cross and follow . . . often on off-the-beaten-paths. (See **Be-living.**)

> For everyone who thinks he has arrived at his destination has actually hardly begun, and he who continues searching is closer to his destination than he realizes.
>
> —DAVE TOMLINSON[1]

1. Dave Tomlinson, *The Post-Evangelical* (London: Triangle/SPCK, 1995), 62.

EPICtivity W: (The) Way

Way means journey . . . and in the emerging culture, our journey is both personal and collective. No other film expresses the beauty of pilgrimage and journey better than *The Wizard of Oz*.

Watch either the whole film or clips from it—enough to get a fresh feel for the film. Then dialogue about the following:

- What makes this film such an enduring favorite?
- How would you describe Dorothy's leadership style?
- How would you describe the Wizard's leadership style?
- How can these two varying styles represent ministry leaders?
- What changes would take place in your ministry if your team had a "journey" mindset instead of a "destination" mindset? How might evangelism change? Discipleship? Leadership? Worship?
- What makes it hard for churches today to have a "wayfaring" mindset?

If possible, plan a journey for your group: a five-to-eight-mile day hike, or a weekend road trip. While on the journey, tell stories of journeys you have taken in life—funny ones, sad ones, exciting ones.

W is for Wonder

"The way of an eagle in the sky" is nothing short of "wonderfull" (Prov. 30:18–19). But God's greatest gift—the wonder of life itself—is least appreciated. "You knit me together in my mother's womb. I praise you, for I am fearfully and wonderfully made" (Ps. 139:13–14).

W is for Wonder

> It is said children still have a sense of wonder, later one becomes blunted—nonsense. A child takes for granted, and most people get no further. Only an old person, who thinks, is aware of the wondrous.
>
> —Victor Klemperer[2]

"Wonder-fullness" and "awe-fullness" are sources of the most elementary mystical awareness. When transfiguration moments of transparency and wonder take place, it's as if we have been sent kisses from God.[3] Even atheists like Stephen Weinberg, who won a Nobel Prize for his work in physics, admits that "the most powerful point" for people of a religious persuasion is that "the universe is intelligible, governed by extremely simple laws, so that we are left with the wonder."[4]

In the modern world, thaumatology (the study of wonders) became the specialty of Madison Avenue (Wonder Bread) and Wall Street (Wonder Boys). God became less "the cause of our wonder" than "the object of our knowledge."[5] Postmoderns are less interested in object-based, white-bread wonders than subject-based "wonders of it all." Will the church bake the real, the true Wonder Bread for a hungry world?

> I am astonished that people are not astonished.
>
> —G. K. Chesterton

2. Victor Klemperer (1 January 1942), *I Will Bear Witness: A Diary of the Nazi Years, 1942–45*, trans. Martin Chalmers (New York: Random House, 1999), 3.

3. For more on "God's kisses," see Leonard Sweet, *Postmodern Pilgrims* (Nashville: Broadman & Holman, 2000), 18–20.

4. As quoted by Fred Heeren, "Religion Has Nothing to Fear from NASA," *Wall Street Journal* (28 June 2001), A16.

5. This is the reversal of the early church proclamation, "God is not so much the object of our knowledge as the cause of our wonder," as quoted by Cardinal Basil Hume, *The Mystery of the Incarnation* (Brewster, MA: Paraclete Press, 1999), 66.

Wonder was the greatest gift given to Jesus upon his birth, and it was given by the shepherds, the simple people.

The heavens gave a star.

The earth gave a cave.

The Magi gave gold, frankincense, and myrrh.

The angels gave a chorus.

But the smelly shepherds? They gave wonder.

In a world that gives special advantage to the educated and brilliant, the wonderment is that God gives special advantages to special people. Intellectual brainpower and spiritual horsepower aren't necessarily coincident. When the "wise of this world" (and too often, the learned of the church) lose their capacity for wonder, they need to go to the children and the elderly, and perhaps to the mentally handicapped, to be taught the joy of wonder again.

> Concepts create idols. Only wonder understands.
>
> —GREGORY OF NYSSA

W is for World

● First member of the profane trinity (as in "the world, the flesh, and the devil").

● What Jesus came to get into, but what the church is trying to get out of.

We love to love Jesus, but we hate to love the things that Jesus loves.

Question: Would anyone notice if John 3 were rewritten as follows: "For God so loved the church that he gave his one and only son, that whoever believes in him shall not perish but have eternal life. For God did not send his son to condemn the church, but to save the church"? Does this revision make any difference?

X is for Xenophilia

Xenos is Greek for stranger. Xenophilia, often translated *hospitality* in the New Testament, literally means love of strangers. Postmodern Christians will rediscover this primal Christian virtue and turn it from an optional elective to a mandatory requirement for Christian maturity and ministry. (See **Globalization.**)

> *I speak three languages, write in*
> *Two, dream in one....*
> *Why not let me speak in*
> *Any language I like?*
>
> —KAMALA DAS[1]

Mark this: The road is forking. Everyone is being forced to choose between xenophilia and xenophobia. Xenophobia may become the dirty secret passion (a kind of social/ethnic lust) of fundamentalists of all religions who fondle a desire to isolate from and vilify "the other." But for followers of Jesus—for whom loving neighbors constitutes a great commandment and extends to Samaritans and centurions and Syrophoenicians and prostitutes and publicans and Pharisees, too—xenophobia is anti-gospel, anti-Christ, anti-love, anti-heaven, and anti-God.

What is the second most widely spoken language in Britain? Urdu. In England, there are now almost the same number of practicing Muslims as there are practicing Anglicans. In the U.S., Islam grew by 25% from 1990 to 2000, bringing the Muslim population to 4-5 million and growing. Seventy years ago, Islam had no mosques in the U.S.; today there are 1,500, with more than 400 Muslim schools in operation.

---

1. Kamala Das, "An Introduction," as quoted in Steven G. Kellman, *The Translingual Imagination* (Lincoln: University of Nebraska Press, 2000), 13.

Islam's dream is of a theocratic state. This is its voice in the public arena. Will Christianity fight fire with fire and seek to "take back" turf around the world "for Jesus"? Or will it, for Jesus, embody an ethic of love and neighborliness for those who exemplify "the other"—other races, other religions, other economies, other lifestyles, other nations, other languages, other tastes—even "others" who are hostile to and hateful toward us?

Is our gospel simply another interest group vying for dominance? Or is our gospel a higher call?

It is for this call that followers of Jesus may be martyred in the centuries ahead when fundamentalists will demand, "Join us in hating the other, or die," and Christians respond, "I will be hated before I will hate, and I will be killed before I kill." (See **Persecution.**)

Of course, there are more hopeful possibilities too! When you mix things up, they get interesting.[2] Vibrant multiculturalism may open up possibilities that bring to culture and soul the delights that Indian, Mexican, Arabic, and Szechuan restaurants bring to the palate. Asian and Indian music is so the rage among postmoderns that it's easier today to find a good Indian sitar player than a good French horn player. The feel of Indian, Arabic, Balinese, and Asian music is now part of Western culture, thanks partly to tenor sax jazz musician John Coltrane, who shifted our musical consciousness from Western chords to more modal Asian scales.

It is here the church can rush to the curl of the wave. The church represents the most powerful multicultural community on earth, a community commissioned with the words "all nations" first through Abraham ("through you all nations on

2. For the postmodern celebration of diversity and pluralism, see the third chapter, "Listening to Other Voices," in C. David Grant, *Thinking through Our Faith: Theology for 21st-Century Christians* (Nashville: Abingdon, 2001). For a look at how postmodern theologies respond to the issue of religious diversity, see Terence W. Tilley, *Postmodern Theologies: The Challenge of Religious Diversity* (Maryknoll, NY: Orbis Books, 1995).

earth will be blessed") and then through Jesus ("make disciples of all nations").

We have a lot of work to do in this regard. Postmodern folk tend to resent moderns—Christians and non—for their inability to bang differences hard against each other and thus make music instead of war. The National Congregations Study, based on 1998 data, found that 69% of congregations were almost all white and 18% almost all black, while only about 10% of U.S. congregations were multiracial or integrated.[3]

One answer to our scandal of segregation is to get everyone to worship together. More and more of this will take place in the future. Already the emergence of a multicultural church movement is one of the untold stories of our day. But Anglos need to ask themselves: Who stands to gain the most in this scenario, and who stands to lose a lot? For many minorities, the ethnic church is the one place where their cultures of "otherness" are celebrated and preserved. Through integration, dominant culture churches can unwittingly obliterate minority cultures by assimilating them. In this way, white churches can accidentally set back the cause of diversity if they transform minorities into "bananas, oreos, coconuts, and apples" (yellow, black, brown, or red on the outside and white on the inside).

We must begin by recalling John's vision of heaven, where all the nations are gathered before God's throne and worship God in their own languages, tribal identities, and cultural

3. National Congregations Study, 1998. Here are the basic results: If we define "predominantly" to mean at least 80% of one race/ethnic group, then 70% of American congregations are predominantly white and 18% are predominantly black. If we define a "multiracial" congregation as one in which no one group (white, black, Asian, or Latino) composes at least 80% of the congregation, then about 9% of American congregations are interracial in that sense. Michael Emerson of the sociology department at Rice University is engaged in a major research project on interracial congregations. Email from Mark Chaves, chair of the National Congregations Study (4 October 2000): mchaves@u.arizona.edu. For a historical look at cross-cultural diffusion as "the lifeblood of historic Christianity," see Andrew Walls, *The Cross-Cultural Process in Christian History: Studies in the Transmission and Appropriation of Faith* (Maryknoll, NY: Orbis, 2001).

uniquenesses. How can we move beyond isolation without creating a blended gray mush in which each color loses its identity by surrendering to a homogenous, least-common denominator?[4] How can we instead come together, creating a feast that celebrates diversity of color and taste and texture and personality by not melting them together but placing them on the same menu?

Marc Bloch calls history the "science of diversity."[5] Genetics and biology alike teach us what happens when diversity is squelched. The U.S. national motto—E *Pluribus Unum*—captures our challenge. How can the many discover unity without losing their uniqueness?

How diverse is your church? How creative is your church? How exciting is your church?

These are three ways of asking the same question, because creativity comes from the tensions of diversity, difference, disjunction. Staleness comes from sameness.

Gary Hamel and C. K. Prahalad, two business futurists, argue that while restructuring, which says get smaller, and reengineering, which says get better, are good and necessary, there is a third imperative for the future: get different. Better and smaller are not enough; they don't put you out front. Only *different* puts the postmodern organization out front.[6]

Again, modern habits die hard. Think of the modern assembly line, the modern "Pleasantville" subdivision, the modern company man in standard uniform right down to the wingtips and haircut and black plastic glasses. The spirit of modernity was epitomized by former Secretary of the Interior Manual

---

4. For an attack on the notion that Jesus was a Westerner, see Gene Edwards, *The Americanization of Christianity* (Atlanta: Touch of Life, 1994).

5. Marc Bloch, *Apologie Pour L'Histoire ou Métier d'Historien* (Paris: Librairie Armand Colin, 1949), translated into English as *The Historian's Craft*, trans. Peter Putnam (New York: Alfred A. Knopf, 1953).

6. Gary Hamal and C. K. Prahalad, *Competing for the Future* (Boston: Harvard Business School Press, 1994), 267.

Lujan, who asked in May 1989, "Do we really have to save every subspecies? Nobody's told me the difference between a red squirrel, a black one, or a brown one."[7]

Our reply, as postmodern Christians charged to steward the earth for God, must be, "We really do, Mr. Former Secretary Lujan"—even if it means not building telescopes on Mount Graham in Arizona, which would interfere with the "sky island" habitat of the Mount Graham red squirrel. For this reason, postmodern Christians will be green Christians, we believe— or at least we had better be. (See **Creation; Trustee.**)

Diversity is as needed in community as diversity is needed in nature. Creation teaches us that for God, diversity is a good. If a modern Technocrat had created the planet, there would have been one species of insect—the technically correct one, no doubt. But in God's world, a healthy ecosystem is a diverse one. For God, differentness is sacredness. The elimination of difference is killing us in more ways than just environmental. Xenophilia, then, is not only beautiful and delightful and wonderful, but also essential and spiritual.

> If all pulled the same direction, the world would keel over.
>
> —YIDDISH PROVERB

Postmodern ministry demands of us a jubilant celebration of diversity. (See **Other.**) A distinction can be made between difference and diversity that is more than language. Difference in itself is neither negative or positive. It is simply neutral. Diversity, which is more often dealt with than dwelt on, is a positive virtue. "Multiracial," for example, need not mean "color-blind."

For Thomas Aquinas, the "perfection of the universe" resided in its manyness rather than its oneness because the universe is so intricately made that no one thing by itself could

7. As quoted in *HSUS News*, Fall 1990, 35.

encompass the breadth of its perfection. "Hence the whole universe together participates [in] the divine goodness more perfectly, and represents it better than any single creature whatever."[8] Medieval Christians celebrated this concept in an archaic but winsome image known as "the Great Chain of Being," which celebrated the plenitude of God's creation, filling every niche with diversity and wonder.

Business gurus tell us that no one should read only one newspaper anymore. No one should have only one broker any more; you need one broker in a European financial center (London, Zurich), one in an Asian financial center (Hong Kong, Australia/New Zealand), and one in North America too. Similarly, Christians involved in postmodern ministry can't afford to remain cloistered in the impoverished gene pools of their little homogenized denominations. Calvinists can't afford to imbibe only from the pure springs of writers they already agree with, but need a tall foamy drink from Anabaptist kegs. White Iowan Baptists need to attend conferences with Black Georgian Pentecostals, while Koreans and Mexicans and Indians and Minnesotans and Arabs and Jews who love Jesus need to play games and share recipes and tell stories and experience the unity that is only fun because of diversity, as the apostle Paul said again and again.

The recent civil wars over "seeker sensitivity" (which generally involved white middle-class Christians trying to learn to welcome white middle-class non-Christians) and "blended worship" (which generally involves older white middle-class Christians learning to accept the music of younger white middle-class Christians) show us how retarded we are in xenophilia.

Once we begin pursuing xenophilia (which is just one facet of "love"—without which, we are told by an authoritative

8. Thomas Aquinas, *Summa Theologica*, First complete American ed., trans. Fathers of the English Dominican Province [I.Q.47.1](New York: Benziger Brothers, 1947), 1:246. This is one of ecologist Thomas Berry's favorite quotes.

source, we are exactly zero or "nothing"), we can broaden our concerns beyond race and age to other "strangers," such as the disabled and the elderly (a group to which we all will belong if we live long enough). How tolerant will we be of the "alien of age" or the "alien of ability" among us? (How tolerant will we want others to be of us, when such we are?) (See **Disabled.**)

What rich opportunities this moment offers Christians and churches! In this moment the New Testament comes freshly alive as we watch a whole new creation spring into being. The church emerges as a wondrous and historic new kind of community where Jew and Gentile (bridging the most significant religious chasm), male and female (reconciling the protagonists of the primal human power struggle), slave and free (scandalizing economy and class proprieties), and even God and humanity (celebrating "at-one-ment") fuse in unity/diversity ... former strangers experiencing hospitality at God's family table, with Jesus welcoming us in the door.

To be a Christian means becoming a xenophiliac. You love people who think differently; you promote people who don't use your familiar jargon; you hire an outsider to be your pastor; and you throw parties at which many languages are spoken, many flavors tasted, many stories are told, and many colors smile and laugh and learn one another's dances and ways in a foretaste of another party called "heaven."

How true it is that the church is a laboratory for different people living together: "The triumph of our religious history is that it exists only because of the unlikely coalition of diversity that found communion in the leadership of Jesus and thus handed the heritage on to any equally diverse company in every successive generation."[9]

Make no mistake: Diversity isn't always fun, and it is seldom easy. But it is good and right and an outflow of the gospel

9. Sam Portaro and Gary Peluso, *Inquiring and Discerning Hearts: Vocation and Ministry with Young Adults on Campus* (Atlanta: Scholars Press, 1993), 256.

we believe. Xenophilia is a strategic and beautiful investment in the emerging culture.

EPICtivity X: Xenophilia

Creativity comes from diversity. Staleness comes from sameness. So get different! Welcome strangers!

Set up a series of evenings when you invite a homeless person, a homosexual person, an atheist, a Mormon, a Jehovah's Witness, a body piercer, or a representative of some other people group that Jesus would love to have dinner with. Share a full meal or a cup of coffee and dessert. In your invitation, explain exactly what you are doing, with no hidden agendas: We are a group of white, middle-class Christians (or whatever) and we want to get to know some people who are different from ourselves.

Seek to get to know them . . . love them. *Do not give them the Christian pitch*, and do not engage in argument or critique. Simply ask questions and listen, and answer any questions they ask of you.

Here are some possible questions:

- Tell me your story. . . . What was it like growing up? Tell me about your family.
- What is your fondest memory?
- What is your most painful memory?
- What is it like to be you? What is your daily life like?

At your next meeting, share with your team how your life was enriched by spending time with a "stranger," who hopefully became a new friend. Evaluate your success or failure at simply being hospitable, welcoming, non-condemning, and neighborly.

Y is for Yes!

(Warning: This entry may in places exemplify what it is against.)

"The most important difference between churches," a wiser-than-he-realized church consultant once said, "is not their doctrinal statements, liturgies, structures, or architecture. It's in the way they treat people." In postmodern ministry, people are treated with a "yes!" attitude.

In modernity, of course, it was critique before celebration, evaluation before enthusiasm, cool head before warm heart. Critique, cool-headedness, and critical detachment have a value we can't afford to lose in the postmodern world. But in light of a gospel that is God's "yes!" (2 Cor. 1:17–22) to beauty, truth, and goodness, churches must lead with celebration, enthusiasm, and a warm-hearted "yes!" That means placing ardor before order—of which, by the way, you need *more* when you have ardor than when you don't!

No wonder modernity was prone to passionless cynicism, severe skepticism, and blasé moderation. The forces of negation became highly sophisticated and refined their procedures into an art form that can be identified by the following "killer phrases" designed to snuff out creativity and fresh thinking:

> We tried something like that years ago.
> That's ridiculous.
> That's too radical.
> Let's form a committee to consider it.
> That's contrary to policy.
> Has anyone ever tried it?
> It won't work.
> That's too obvious to be considered.
> That's too superficial.

That's interesting, but we don't have the time or the
manpower.
Tell me right now—what's the potential profit in it?
That's not the kind of idea we expect from you.[1]

In modernity's seeking to tame verve and vision, spirit was
exorcised by naturalism, leaving a bland "nothing-but" world
of mere mechanics and matter. Nothing to get excited about.

In the emerging culture, the "nothing but-ery"of mechanistic reductionism is being left behind. And with it go the cynicism, skepticism, and mediocrity of modernity. If "doubt
endless doubt" has been "the motor of modern thought,"[2] faith
(even passionate belief) has been the driver of postmodernity.
It is little wonder that intense involvement in religion has not
declined; only lukewarm church membership has.[3] And we
might say, "Good riddance."

Trade in your modern sterile water for the Spirit's living water,
and your old whine will become new wine, transforming lukewarm modern churchgoers from bores and boors who mumble
"no, no, no, I don't think so, we can't do that, no, no" into water-
walking boosters who seem to believe that anything is possible,
humming "yes, yes, yes, through Christ I can do all things."

Late-modern seriousness was cautious about "yes" and
ambivalent about "maybe." Wild hilarity was cooled to mild
interest; risky enthusiasm was moderated to careful correctness; dangerous wonder and outrageous hope were tamed to
tepid and respectable sobriety. Revelation 3:14–22 became
sadly fitting for the late-modern church in both its conservative
and liberal incarnations: "Because you are lukewarm—neither

1. As quoted in Thomas L. Martin Jr., *Malice in Blunderland* (New York: McGraw-Hill,
1973), 101.
2. Catherine Gallagher and Stephen Greenblatt, *Practicing the New Historicism*
(Chicago: University of Chicago Press, 2000), 166.
3. Robert D. Putnam, *Bowling Alone: The Collapse and Revival of American Community* (New York: Simon & Schuster, 2000), 65-79.

hot nor cold—I am about to spit you out of my mouth." The RSV uses the word "spew," which is graphic enough but really means "vomit." God's judgment on a Laodicean version of Christianity that moderates from passionate "yes!" to passionless "maybe" can be paraphrased like this:

> Dear Church:
> "You make me sick!"
> God

In modernity, we were pretty concerned about your doctrinal correctness, but we cared little about your attitudinal correctness (even though Paul urged the Philippians to have the attitude of Christ). We were concerned about the orthodoxy of your faith, but not about the orthodoxy of your face. All modern churches need to tape the following sign to the back of each pew (or chair), so the parishioners will see these words of Tony Campolo each Sunday: "If you believe the good news in your heart, please notify your face." Think about yourself: Do you wear a yes-face or a no-face?

No-faces obsess exclusively on what's wrong rather than what's right. How many Christian churches and organizations fish for amens and contributions by screwing their face into a witch-hunt for wickedness "out there"? (One wonders if some of us in the church are so miserable that the only way we can survive is to convince ourselves that those outside are even more miserable, hence our penchant for focusing on "the bad stuff" out there, as if God had abandoned the world rather than entered it!)

This Isaac Asimov story illustrates the effect of a "no-no life":

> A Jewish seminary student died, went to heaven, and found himself before God's great judgment seat.
> The ineffable voice of the Lord made itself heard beautifully to the student's ears. "My son, what was it you did on earth?"

"O Holy One," said the student, "I studied the Law."

"Well done, my son. Expound, then, a point of the Law to Me for My pleasure."

Thus confronted with the request of the Lord, the student felt his mind go blank. For an agitated moment or two, he could find no point he could make.

And then he cried out, "At the moment, O Holy One, I can think of nothing adequate for Your hearing, but I tell You what. If *You* expound a point of the Law, I will show You how to refute it."[4]

To say amen was an omen of weakness to moderns, who privileged critique over celebration and participation. The word *critical* operated as an almost metronomic tic whereby moderns patted themselves on their "BMW" backs.[5] Even modern professional schools taught more what you couldn't do than what was possible.

While some admitted the modern "bind"—"to admire is to lack critical edge, to criticize is to lack respect"[6]—by and large Thomas Jefferson spoke for most when he admitted, "I find the pain of a little censure, even when it is unfounded, is more acute than the pleasure of much praise."[7] As the bumper-sticker says (in paraphrase), UNDESIRABLE STUFF HAPPENS. The fact is, life doesn't need help discouraging us.

That is why postmodern Christians love to counteract the "undesirable stuff" with the word *yes* and, as a result, wish to declare an annual celebration of a new season of LENT (Let's

4. *Isaac Asimov's Treasury of Humor: A Lifetime Collection of Favorite Jokes, Anecdotes, and Limericks with Copious Notes on How to Tell Them and Why* (Boston: Houghton Mifflin, 1971), 315–16.

5. The "BMW mode" is a phrase invented by two Harvard researchers to describe the prevalent state of many organizations—bellyaching, "moaning," and "whining." See Robert Kegan and Lisa Laskow, *How the Way We Talk Can Change the Way We Work: Seven Languages for Transformation* (San Francisco: Jossey-Bass, 2000), 18.

6. T. M. Luhrmann, "The Touch of the Real," *TLS: Times Literary Supplement* (12 January 2001), 3.

7. Douglas L. Wilson, "Jefferson and the Republic of Letters," in *Jeffersonian Legacies*, ed. Peter S. Onuf (Charlottesville: University Press of Virginia, 1993), 54.

Eliminate Negative Thinking).Becoming more "yes-ive" will help us become less worldly, because the negativity of modernity was by no means restricted to the church.

Those academics who celebrated someone else's scholarship rarely heard the sound of even one hand clapping among their colleagues. Negative voices were listened to as "smarter" and more "discerning" than positive voices. When one wasn't knee-deep in the aftermath of academic warfare, with opponents smitten hip-and-thigh, the very enterprise itself was called into question. To take but one example from the world of cognitive science: One reviewer complained of some of the new studies of the young-turk cognitive scientists like Francisco Varela who are taking on the old-guard cognitive scientists for whom the mind is just another computer. What's wrong with these guys? he says. They're just too nice!

> Do these authors despise no one? The book is remarkable for the openmindedness and generosity of its interpretations; the authors have clearly paid as much good attention to those they are criticizing as to their favorites. They thus set a good example—much needed in cognitive science—but if you are like me, you will find yourself wondering if it is too good. . . . Does the move from traditional academic fisticuffs (good, clean Marquis of Queensbury stuff) to a Rortian "conversation" not inevitably devalue both the support a good argument can provide, and the clarification a good sharp disagreement can yield? This kinder, gentler vision of cognitive science runs the risk of diluting its revolutionary impact.[8]

Academics had such trouble saying "yes," whether to a book or to each other, that even "critics" who gave their work

8. Dominic W. Massaro, review of *The Embodied Mind: Cognitive Science and Human Experience* in *American Journal of Psychology* 106 (Spring 1993), 124.

enthusiastic reviews would get lambasted if they didn't get all of the facts right.[9] That's why modern churches opposed "praise music" so much: It was too much affirmation, too little discrimination.

> Yes Lord, Yes Lord, Yes, Yes Lord
> Yes Lord, Yes Lord, Yes, Yes Lord
> Yes Lord, Yes Lord, Yes, Yes Lord
> Amen.
>
> —DARRYL EVANS, "TRADING MY SORROWS"

To be sure, much critique in the academy has been accurate, deadly accurate. But no less dangerous for its accuracy. Like the magic rings of Tolkein's *Lord of the Rings* trilogy, criticism becomes more dangerous the more you use it—and for largely the same reason. The more we criticize others, the more we tend to feel that we are invisible and thus exempt from deserving critique ourselves. In other words, it is dangerous to judge others, because in so doing we forget that we ourselves will be judged in like kind and in like measure. We can no more stop negatives from being dangerous than we can stop nitro from being explosive.

> I've never found a "Church Critic" want ad in the newspaper, although I have looked.
>
> —WORSHIP LEADER/AUTHOR KIM MILLER

Theologian Leander E. Keck argues that we need a "hermeneutics of affirmation" to replace the "hermeneutics

9. See Hilary Mantel's response to Amanda Craig's positive review of her novel *A Change of Climate* in *Literary Review* (London), April 1994, 34. Thanks to David Himrod for researching this.

of alienation" that developed from the "hermeneutics of "suspicion."[10] Certain sectors of the Christian community seem to have venerated the hermeneutics of suspicion and alienation to the status of spiritual practice. Meanwhile, back in the New Testament, Barnabas was known as the "Son of Encouragement"? Whatever happened to his gene pool?

Ask yourself: What affirmers surround you? How many of your Christian friends truly and consistently encourage you? Then ask yourself how many of your friends, if asking the same questions, would have you on their list.

Perhaps the most positive initiative many readers could embark upon, having read this complaint against complaining, would be to spend a year asking and re-asking these simple questions of our church boards and members:

1. In what ways are we a negative people?
2. What would change if we said no less and yes more?
3. How can we become more affirmative in our faith and life?
4. If we can quickly list five things we are against, how can we preoccupy ourselves with 25 things we are for?
5. How can we preoccupy ourselves with these 25 things for the next five years?

Robert Hughes's *Culture of Complaint* is a 300-page complaint about complaining.[11]

And now we had better wrap up this entry quickly, or we will add to the background noise of groaning and moaning that has become as ubiquitous as the white noise of traffic.

---

10. Keck argues that "the hermeneutic of suspicion and the hermeneutic of affirmation belong together." The hermeneutic of suspicion taught us not to "accept without murmur everything handed to us from the past." The hermeneutic of affirmation "will reclaim, renew, and release critically the classical Christian tradition into the life of the churches." See Leander E. Keck, *The Church Confident* (Nashville: Abingdon Press, 1993), 64, 59–67.

11. Robert Hughes, *Culture of Complaint: A Passionate Look into the Ailing Heart of America* (New York: Warner Books, 1994).

> It's easy to criticize others and
> make them feel unwanted.
> Anyone can do it.
> What takes effort and skill is
> picking them up and
> making them feel good.
>
> —REBBE NACHMAN OF BRESLOV[12]

EPICtivity Y: Yes!

Just before he died in 1996, Henri Nouwen told a story about an experience he had while leading a small chapel service for mentally handicapped adults. During the service a lady named Mary stood up and said, "Henri, I need a blessing." Thinking quickly on his feet, Henri waved the sign of the cross with his hand, hoping that would suffice. After the spiritual wave, Mary responded, "Henri, that did nothing for me!" It then dawned on Henri what Mary was needing. Henri laid his hands on Mary's shoulders and shared how much he appreciated her and loved her and how much God must love her as well. She sat down, deeply touched by the experience. Henri was deeply moved by his own longing to be blessed by someone. That day a line formed, as other people were wanting a blessing from Henri.

During one of your regular team meetings, allow at least 30 minutes for blessing one member of the group. Ask each member:

- What do you appreciate or admire about _____?
- What strengths, virtues, and skills does this person have?

12. As quoted in Moshe Mykoff, *The Empty Chair: Finding Hope and Joy: Timeless Wisdom from a Hasidic Master Rebbe Nachman of Breslau* (New York: Jewish Lights Publishing, 1994), 31.

> - What has this person done for you, and for our group?
> - What would we lose if this person were not part of our group?
> - What good memories do you have of specific episodes or experiences shared with this person?
>
> Instruct the person being affirmed that he or she can only say one thing in response to what is being said: "Thank you." At the end of the session, lay hands on the blessed person and have someone pray for him or her.

Y is for Y-Chromosome

To the question, "What do most people do on a date?" Martin, 10 years old, responded, "On the first date, they just tell each other lies, and that usually gets them interested enough to go for a second date." Lynnette, eight, answered, "Dates are for having fun, and people should use them to get to know each other. Even boys have something to say if you listen long enough."[13]

Modern culture was largely a man's world. Postmodern culture promises to be a . . . human's world, where men and women learn a level of respect perhaps unknown in human culture. Late modernity flirted with a gender-blended unisex blandness. But indicators suggest that postmodern sensitivities will reassert "vive la différence" regarding gender identities.

For modern Christians who felt that faithfulness to Scripture required perpetuation of the patriarchal culture of biblical times, this change is as threatening as it is to radical modern feminists who wished to cast the sexes in perpetual war rather than perpetual companionship.

13. As cited by Doug Jackson in "On Second Thought," *www.aslan@2bc.org*.

There are challenges yet to be faced. How do we acknowl-edge the damage done to women in modern and pre-modern times without trashing the biblical revelation and the progress of the gospel that coexisted with cultures that failed to give women the respect due them as co-image bearers of God? Some suggest that all vestiges of those cultures must be removed, giving us a sterile lab for the future free from the threat of chauvinist contamination.

This approach underestimates the threat of oppressive infection by failing to fix the locus of oppression where it actually resides: not merely in cultural artifacts of yesterday, but in human hearts today. A postmodern reading of ancient texts requires us to take the text at face value rather than reprocess it by pressing it through the grid of our current prej-udices. As novelist/critic P. D. James has said, "It is a central tenet of the Christian faith that God was incarnate as a human male at a particular moment in history. Some feminist Chris-tians may feel that God would have been better advised to have waited for a more enlightened century and a less patriarchal society, but that would hardly seem a justification for refusing to use the words 'Our Father' or for parading 'Christa' on a cross in Manchester Cathedral."[14]

Late-modern victimology and victim-chic have had their day, but a maturing postmodern ethos will likely move beyond these disempowering approaches, as evidenced by Naomi Wolf's *Fire with Fire*,[15] which articulates a "power-feminism" in contrast to the angry "victim-feminism" that has dominated the women's movement for too long. We women already have the power, she argues, so now let's use it in a positive way and with a cheerful spirit.

14. P. D. James, "Litany of Discontent," *TLS: Times Literary Supplement* (11 Novem-ber 1994), 27.
15. Naomi Wolf, *Fire with Fire: The New Female Power and How It Will Change the 21st Century* (New York: Random House, 1993).

About that power: According to the Small Business Admin-istration, USAmerican women "own more than 40% of busi-nesses and are starting new businesses at twice the rate for men."[16] A Rubicon was crossed in 2000 when the number of women online surpassed the number of men. The younger you are on the generation scale, the more preference there is for a female boss rather than a "Yes, sir!" Gen-Xers actually prefer by 41 to 21% to work for a woman rather than a man.[17]

One of the top management consultants in North America, Nancy H. Bancroft, has written a book in which she tackles the gender question head-on. She devotes a portion of chapter 3 to exploring how women and men are different, using the work of Anne Wilson Schaef, Carol Gilligan, and Deborah Tannen as guides. She then devotes a portion of the chapter to exploring how women and men are the same. She asks: "So Which Is It—Same or Different?"

She concludes with the double ring: "Ultimately, men and women are both similar and different. Certainly women are as motivated to succeed as men, and certainly women and men can have similar personalities. . . . However, that there are similarities in behavior and performance does not negate the fact that there are essential differences between the genders. Regardless of cause, they exist."[18]

So which is it—same, different, or double ring?

Either way, modern chauvinists beware: Although many postmodern women may have tired of the feminist label, they are no more willing to become the church's silent, cookie-baking, baby-sitting, coffee-serving, seen-but-not-heard brigade than their late-modern mothers and aunts.

16. Roger Lewin and Birute Regine, *The Soul at Work: Listen, Respond, Let Go: Embracing Complexity Science for Business Success* (New York: Simon & Schuster, 2000), 319.

17. The Gallup Poll Monthly, as reported in "Who's the Boss?" *The Boomer Report* (15 February 1994), 6.

18. Nancy H. Bancroft, *The Feminine Quest for Success: How to Prosper in Business and Be True to Yourself* (San Francisco: Berrett-Koehler, 1995), 48–49.

> When Israel was a child, I loved him,
> and out of Egypt I called my son. . . .
> It was I who taught [them] to walk,
> I took them up in my arms; . . .
> I led them with cords of human kindness,
> with bands of love.
> I was to them like those
> who lift infants to their cheeks.
> I bent down to them and fed them.
>
> —THE PROPHET HOSEA, 11:1–4

Emerging church leaders will be wise to look back at Western European and American bungling of race and ethnicity during the 15th through 20th centuries: What should we learn from past mistakes that can help us get ahead of the curve now—or at least to get back into the curve that has already passed us by?

Churches that have dealt decisively and affirmatively with "the women's issue" universally agree: They could never go back, nor would they want to. The future church will be molded by women. Women owned the houses in which the early Christians met. The more postmoderns rediscover and explore the house-church model of being the body of Christ, the more important women's leadership becomes. The handwriting is on the wall for Roman Catholics: There are only two dioceses left in USAmerica that do not yet permit altar girls.

One thinks of the late-modern classic *The Wizard of Oz*. The film adroitly contrasts the late-modern male model of leadership exemplified by the Wizard with the new model of leadership exemplified by Dorothy. Dorothy is young and naïve, but her youth casts her in the role of a quester. Similarly, today postmodern leaders present themselves, not as the know-it-all or answer-man, but rather as questers themselves, who inspire others (tin men in search of a heart, scarecrows in search of wisdom, cowardly lions in search of courage) to join in the search.

As "lead seeker," Dorothy inspires her companions through friendship rather than command/control authority, and through earnestness (a.k.a. passion) rather than knowledge, and through hope rather than a clearly defined plan or thought-out strategy. In regard to this characteristic of hope rather than strategy, Dorothy, after all, is on a journey into the unknown, and she follows a yellow-brick road she has never trod before. (Sound familiar, postmodern pilgrims?)

How will churches that have sanctioned the exclusion of women from leadership on biblical grounds escape from the corner they have painted themselves into?[19] How can they discover fresh biblical grounds to welcome women into partnership in ministry, as God so clearly did through Christ, from the Mary who gave him birth to the Mary who sat at his feet to the Mary who first touched the Risen Christ?[20] How can our belief in the priesthood of all believers rise above the priesthood of all *male* believers?

EPICtivity Y: Y-Chromosome

Do a Bible study comparing God as Warrior (Exod. 15:3), Husband (Hos. 2:16), King (Ps. 98:6), and Father (Ps. 103:13) with God as Birth-giver (Isa. 66:9), Midwife (Ps. 22:9), Mistress of a Household (Ps. 123:2), and Mother (Isa. 66:13).

---

19. Of course, there is what scholars call the "gender paradox," whereby the tribes most resistant to women's ministry actually engage in practices that liberate women for ministry. See, for example, Elaine M. Mcduff, "The Gender Paradox in Work Satisfaction and the Protestant Clergy," *Sociology of Religion* 62 (Spring 2001), 1–22.

20. For an example of one church's grappling with this issue, see Cedar Ridge Community Church's website, *www.crcc.org,* and click on their "policies" link.

If your group is all male or all female, invite a group of the opposite sex to join you for an evening to answer (without interruption, critique, or controversy) this question: What does it feel like to be a [man/woman] in our church, and in the - Christian faith in general?

If your group is mixed, allow the women a whole session to explore this question. During this entire session, do not allow the men present to speak, ask any question, or make any comment.

At your next meeting, allow the men a short time to share what it felt like to not be allowed to speak at the previous meeting, and ask them what they could learn from that experience that would help them understand how women feel about church life in many churches today.

Z is for Zending[1]

Zen chic rules postmodern culture. It is filled with Zenistas who love all things Zen. Mention a famous Zen aphorism, and all ears perk up. Mention a famous Christian aphorism, and all ears close up. In fact, some sayings of Jesus are being passed off as Zen koans.[2]

> In Zen "sitting," I found a way back to Christian prayer.
>
> —POET/NOVELIST DAN WAKEFIELD[3]

Christians are now the "outsiders." What reigns is the faith-of-any-flavor mentality. The slogan of belief.net says it all: "We all believe in something." But that "something" is likely laced with "Zen," the closest thing to an "established religion" of postmodernity.

1. The word *zending* was invented by Faith Popcorn to describe the dominance of Zen styles in U.S. culture. See Faith Popcorn and Lys Marigold, *Clicking: 16 Trends to Future Fit Your Life, Your Work, and Your Business* (New York: HarperCollins, 1996), 117.

2. In his handbook on "zentrepreneurism" as a floor trader in the Standard & Poor futures pit, Edward Allen Toppel quotes as a Zen saying Jesus' claim that "to find your self, you must lose your self first." See Toppel's *Zen in the Markets: Confessions of a Samurai Trader* (New York: Time Warner, 1992), 23. Paul Park's novel *The Gospel of Corax* (New York: Soho Press, 1996), called by some "a masterpiece of spiritual fiction," speculates on whether Jesus was a Buddhist and whether or not he discovered his true identity on the way to Tibet.

3. Dan Wakefield, "New Age, New Opportunities," *Theology Today* 51 (April 1994), 145. Frederick Buechner recalls his days of teaching religion at an Exeter boarding school in his autobiographical *Now and Then* (San Francisco: HarperSanFrancisco, 1983), 51. "What made Buddhism such a valuable subject to study along with Christianity was that it was both so like it in some ways and so different in others that to study the two side by side was, both by comparison and by contrast, to discover something new about each. Christian ideas that students thought of as stale and obvious through having been overexposed to them since childhood took on new life when they, or ideas very close to them, appeared with exotic Pali or Sanskrit names and a whole new set of images, myths, and parables to illustrate them."

The culture of Christianity exerts a less powerful gravitational pull than at any time in modern history. The postmodern world, disillusioned with both Christianity and Marxism, is making Zen Buddhism the belief system of choice. It is the religion that fits most snugly into postmodern culture.

In the modern world there was a reservoir of good will toward Christianity. Postmoderns often find just the opposite. Alisdair Gray, in his introduction to the books of Jonah, Micah, and Nahum, describes the patriarchs Abraham and Isaac as "polygamous nomads who get cattle or revenge by prostituting their wives or cheating foreigners or relatives."[4] When mystery writer John Grisham attempts to introduce Christianity to a wider audience, he is attacked for having written "a prudish morality tale, self-righteously proclaiming a set of distinctly Victorian values."[5] Utne Reader printed a "Guess Who's Coming to Dinner?" picture of the Last Supper in which the disciples and Jesus were insects. The magazine would never have done an Insect Buddha or a Termite Moses. It's cool now to make fun of Christian faith.

But we don't recommend whining about our nonprivileged status or fighting to get back to the favored place at the table. (See **Persecution.**) If Jesus is right, there are advantages to having the lowest place at the table. For starters, we are more likely to ask what we can learn from this humbler perspective, including what we can learn from Zen.

Possibly *the* "fastest growing subarea of sacred/spiritual/religious publishing in America today" is the "positive mushrooming of interest in Buddhism."[6] Since there are only 600,000 practicing

4. Alisdair Gray, *The Books of the Bible: Jonah, Micah and Nahum*, Pocket Canons series (New York: Grove Press, 1999).

5. Phyllis A. Tickle, *Re-Discovering the Sacred: Spirituality in America* (New York: Crossroad, 1995), 44, 45. On top of exclusively Buddhist outlets like Snow Lion or Parallax Publishing, established publishers such as Beacon, HarperSanFrancisco, Shambhala, Charles Tuttle, and the like expanded their Buddhism publishing in the late 20th and early 21st centuries (44–45).

6. Heather O'Donoghue, "The Law of the Jungle" (Review of John Grisham's *The Testament*), *TLS: Times Literary Supplement* (29 October 1999), 23.

Buddhists in the U.S. and Canada, its influence on USAmerican culture is far beyond its numbers. Consider this current crop of Buddhist boosters—from Steven Segal to Richard Gere, from Natalie Merchant to Tina Turner, from Martin Scorsese to Oliver Stone, from Adam Yauch to Lou Rawls, from Harrison Ford to the cultural elite and philanthropic families like the Luces and Rockefellers.[7] When postmoderns want to compliment the Amish, for example, they say, "There is something . . . akin to Zen in their anachronistic lifestyle."[8]

> I'm religious. . . . Probably, to a lot of people's thought, I'm extremely religious. My practice is Buddhism, but I believe in God. . . . I've really given up my life to God and I know that's why I'm OK and at peace.
>
> —ACTRESS SHARON STONE[9]

NBA coach Phil Jackson, the son of Pentecostal preachers, has been a practicing Zen Buddhist since the 1970s (although sometimes he calls himself a "Zen Christian"). His book *Sacred Hoops* credits Zen with his success with the Chicago Bulls and the Los Angeles Lakers.[10]

> I have a Jewish background, Jesus inside—he is still there—and Zen. I feel bilingual. But you have got to decide which language you are going to dream in. The language I dream in is Zen.
>
> —SALES EXECUTIVE JANE SHUMAN[11]

7. Sallie Dinkel, "In with the Om Crowd," *New York* (6 June 1994), 30–34.

8. Amanda Jones in *Eco Traveler* (May/June 1994).

9. Sharon Stone, as quoted in "Sharon Stone: Balancing Religion and Acting, Buddhism and God," in *The Living Dharma*, Website of West Covina Buddist Temple, *www.livingdharma.org/Real.World.Buddhism/S.Stone-BuddhismPractice.html*. Accessed 25 April 2001.

10. Phil Jackson, *Sacred Hoops: Spiritual Lessons of a Hardwood Warrior* (New York: Hyperion, 1995), 51.

11. As quoted in Katherine Kurs, "Voices of a New America," *Spirituality & Health* (Spring 2001), 29.

Observe the dialogue about God and faith between economist Michael Novak and his 26-year-old daughter Jana Novak
that they co-authored together as *Tell Me Why*. Jana admits that
her peers are on a spiritual quest, but they mix and match
"whatever religion they have been brought up in combined with
this sort of Zen Buddhist mentality."[12] Many people in our
churches see themselves as both Christian and something else
like Zen. Becca Barnett, an ordained parishioner at St. Gregory's
Episcopal Church in San Francisco, sees herself as both a
Christian priest and a Zen Buddhist practitioner.[13]

Postmodern Christians are not threatened by other belief
systems. In fact, encounters with other religious traditions—
even encounters that enter their rituals on their own terms—
do not threaten one's own Christian witness, but enhance it.
The issue is not that we need to understand another religious
tradition; it's that we need other religious traditions to understand our own. So what if Christians have to learn to say, "*Min
taka oyasin*" (all things are related). If E. Stanley Jones could
conduct Christian *ashrams*, maybe it's time for Christians to go
on *sesshins* (week-long intensive retreats).

This sort of suggestion almost inevitably (and perhaps
properly) arouses suspicions of "syncretism," the mixing of
Christianity with other religions or philosophies. Unfortunately,
the most vigilant anti-syncretists tend to be oblivious to the
complexities of the relationship between Christianity and
culture. They often seem to believe that their version of the

12. Michael Novak and Jana Novak, *Tell Me Why: A Father Answers His Daughter's
Questions about God* (New York: Pocket Books, 1998). Jana's statement was made in
response to comments from her peers about the book and is quoted in Michael Rust,
"Youth and Faith," *Insight on the News* (28 December 1998), 10.

13. Andrea Young Ward, "Treasures Old and New," *Common Boundary* 13
(May/June 1995), 53. This priest needs the "external motion of spirit" she finds in Christian worship at St. Gregory's; but she finds a more "internal movement and being present
with God" in Zen practice. See the book of dialogue by "the unofficial American dean of
Zen," Robert Aitken, and the most respected Christian contemplative today, Benedictine
monk David Steindl-Rast, *The Ground We Share: Everyday Practice, Buddhist and Christian,* ed. Nelson Foster (New York: Triumph Books, 1994; repr. Boston: Shambhala, 1996).

faith, unlike those they critique, is culture-free and purely biblical. But this belief is naïve. (See **Culture.**)

Christians have covered the spectrum in their understanding of the relationship between the gospel and the cultures of the world. In the second century, Justin Martyr sought to articulate the gospel into the educated Greco-Roman culture of his day, asserting that Christianity is the "true philosophy." Clement of Alexandria, in the third century, went so far as to pronounce Socrates a "Christian before Christ." Meanwhile, Tertullian, also in the third century, asked, "What has Athens to do with Jerusalem?"—suggesting his discomfort with the accommodations his fellow church leaders were making to the prevailing Greek-inspired culture of the Roman Empire.

It is certainly easy to cast the current interest in all things Zen as a dangerous syncretizing force, a potent threat to Christian faith. But there is another way of seeing the current postmodern Zenization of the West. A medieval analogy may be useful.

In the Middle Ages, Thomas Aquinas felt that the influence of Plato was playing too heavily in the thinking of the church. He sought to correct this imbalance by bringing Aristotle to the table.[14]

What if the church in late modernity has been overly westernized? What if the cultural assumptions of modern western Europe have created a syncretism that we in the West are as unaware of as are trout of their stream-water? Could it be that a dose of Zen—a dose, not an overdose—could help us get back on course and actually correct an unconscious syncretism?

We tend to forget, as innovative church-planter/mentor Chris Seay says, that Christianity began as an Eastern religion, or at the very least, a Middle Eastern religion.

---

14. Of course, Aquinas's success could later be seen as creating an over-accommodation to Aristotle in the succeeding centuries, but intellectual history seems to progress like inexperienced canoeists, veering this way, then overcorrecting, and so on.

If modern western Christianity has become overly dualistic, might a measured dose of Zenlike monism help correct our hyperdualism? If we are overstimulated with activism and overburdened with messiah complexes, might a Zenish practice of mindfulness and contemplation help snap us out of our hyperactive hysteria? If we are stricken with a modern Western phobia regarding pain and a corresponding allergy to bearing pain, might not a Zen-influenced reappraisal of the role of pain in the enlightened life help us see our own Scriptures in a new light—revealing a far more nuanced and profound theology of pain than either modern Western Christianity or pop Zenism seems to have done?

> Made this "joke" up after trying to access my favorite Buddhist site inundated with "Christian" scoundrels.
> Q: How do you find the nearest Buddhist Temple?
> A: Follow the line of Christians with rocks to throw.
>
> —"SPIRITOUS"[15]

If our modern Western steering wheel always pulls to the right side of the road, threatening to steer us onto the off-ramp of judgmentalism, couldn't a Zen-realignment toward compassion actually help us stay on the narrow road? If modern Western Christianity has so adopted a reductionist view of our humanity that we have become ghosts in machines, with selves so bifurcated between body/flesh and soul/spirit that our sexuality and emotionality and physicality are for us more curse than blessing, might a few minutes of slowing down to become mindful of our breathing actually do us some good, helping us

15. Sidebar "What Do You Think of What Bono Says," entry for March 10, 2001, 1:15 p.m., in Anthony DeCurtis, "Bono: The Beliefnet Interview," 20 February 1921. www.beliefnet.com.

remember that when God created us as bodies inspired with his own breath of life, he said the package was *very good*?

There are dangers here, of course. But there is an equal or greater danger in maintaining our present course, if that course has for five hundred years been altered, say five degrees (and that's probably conservative), by modern Western culture, an influence we are almost totally unaware of. At least when we take a drink of Zen tonic, it tastes strange enough that we are aware of it. Meanwhile, our own modern Western water is tasteless to us, even though it contains all kinds of unknown chemicals that are affecting us.

The goal, in the end, can never be to be trendy and Zendy. The goal is trying to rediscover the path of the gospel, the path of Jesus—who, in reality, was among us less as a modern Western professor or broadcaster or politician or bureaucrat, and more in the mode of the middle-Eastern sage, wise man, rabbi, guru. It is no accident that popular evangelical author Philip Yancey has written *The Jesus I Never Knew*.[16] We modern Western Christians are well poised to rediscover Jesus and the whole glorious story that surrounds him as if for the first time. Rather than entrenching ourselves in our modern Western interpretation of the faith on the one hand, and rather than leaving it for a Zenista tossed salad of do-it-yourself spirituality on the other, we have in this transitional moment the breathtaking opportunity to rediscover how good the Good News really is—how it is wide, deep, high, and expansive beyond all we have discovered so far—eclipsing the light we have seen so far with brightness we have not yet imagined, reminding us that the Alpha and Omega begins before our beginnings and beyond our endings, always beginning anew.

16. Philip Yancey, *The Jesus I Never Knew* (Grand Rapids: Zondervan, 1999).

EPICtivity Z: Zending

Go to a bookstore and buy several copies of *Tricycle* magazine, the equivalent of *Christianity Today* for many American Buddhists.

Leaf through the magazines during your gathering, and make observations about the articles, graphics, and tone of the publication. Feel free to take 10 or 15 minutes to allow participants to read an article silently and then summarize for the group what they have read.

Note: For the first 45 minutes, no critical comments are allowed—only observations that are offered without judgment.

Dialogue about these questions:

- What good things in Buddhism are attractive to the readers of this magazine?
- How do these strengths of Buddhism contrast with weaknesses in our Christian practice?

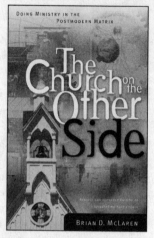

More Ready Than You Realize

Evangelism as Dance in the Postmodern Matrix

Brian D. McLaren

The words "evangelizing" and "post-moderns" and "matrix" are all buzzwords and are heard in the same sentence quite a bit these days. Now that evangelicals are alerted to the presence of change in our culture and discovering ways to adjust to that change, the next step is to take the initiative and meet the new society head-on. We are talking about emerging-culture evangelism.

Brian McLaren is particularly gifted to show us how it can be done. His ministry at Cedar Ridge Community Church has an evangelistic emphasis and is growing. He is practicing what he preaches.

This book draws on his experiences in a striking way. To those other three words we could add the word "Internet." Or Email. The context for this book is a series of real email conversations between Brian and a cyberseeker. Brian uses these conversations to elicit insights into the changing nature of evangelism in these postmodern times. In fact, he shows why the most profound synonym for the word "evangelism" is the term "disciple making."

There are two appendices that can be used one-on-one or in small groups. One offers a Bible study on disciple making, the other a Scripture guide to some important concepts. These resources are effective with postmoderns because they take the approach that preachers are using more and more—the principle of "try it for a while and see if it works."

The range of readers for this book includes college students in para-church groups (such as InterVarsity and Campus Crusade), but it's really as wide as the Internet. Moreover, while the book is effective for individuals, it also appeals to church small groups, not to mention the pastors and church leaders themselves.

Softcover   0-310-23964-8

ZONDERVAN™

GRAND RAPIDS, MICHIGAN 49530 USA

WWW.ZONDERVAN.COM

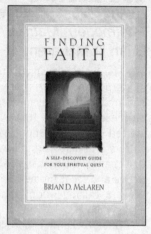

Wake up and dance!

SoulSalsa

17 Surprising Steps for Godly Living in the 21st Century
Leonard Sweet

Leonard Sweet wants to show you the ins and outs of living an old-fashioned faith in these newfangled times. In his engaging, wonderful, thought-bytes style, Sweet invites you to

- Mezuzah your universe
- Do dirt and do the dishes
- Cycle to church
- Give history a shove
- Cheer rivals from the bench
- Dance the salsa

SoulSalsa unpacks it all in ways that can change how you live if you let them. You can be a man or woman who walks the ancient path of a disciple in the world of the future. Because the future is now—and now is the time to practice the "17 Lifestyle Requirements for Membership in the Postmodern Body of Christ." Time to enter the dance of a culture that desperately needs to see your moves.

Check out the *SoulSalsa* song, playing on a Christian music station near you—or download the mp3 from www.SoulSalsa.com.

Softcover 0-310-24280-0
Abridged Audio Pages® Cassette 0-310-23482-4
www.Soulsalsa.com
www.pm4j.com

Pick up a copy today at your favorite bookstore!

ZONDERVAN™

GRAND RAPIDS, MICHIGAN 49530 USA

WWW.ZONDERVAN.COM

The Emerging Church

Vintage Christianity for New Generations
Dan Kimball

Around twenty-five years ago the evangelical church underwent a shift with the arrival of seeker-style churches. A whole generation of baby-boomers resonated with that approach, and the movement was used greatly by God. But now there are rumblings around the country that the generations of teens, twenties, and thirties have changing perceptions and preferences. Some of the very "spiritual" things that were removed from church are the very things that post-Christian generations are connecting with and finding attractive in a church.

The Emerging Church addresses this change and provides practical ideas on how churches can adjust and be more effective to reach emerging generations. Dan Kimball, founding pastor of Graceland, does not present his church as "the" new model, but offers a road map to help open the eyes of churches to some changes that are occurring in various places around the country.

Kimball explains the postmodern shifts and what practical implications they hold for worship, preaching, evangelism, discipleship, and leadership. He provides an encouraging cross-generational bridge between a new breed of young church leaders and those who have been in ministry for some time.

Softcover   0-310-24564-8

Pick up a copy today at your favorite bookstore!

ZONDERVAN™

GRAND RAPIDS, MICHIGAN 49530 USA

WWW.ZONDERVAN.COM

Youth Specialties

Postmodern Youth Ministry

*Exploring Cultural Shift,
Creating Holistic
Connections, Cultivating
Authentic Community*
Tony Jones

Opens the door for youth workers, pastors, and the church at large to contemplate the church today and how post modernism is affecting their youth ministry.

The rules have changed. Everything you believe is suspect. The world is up for grabs. Welcome to the emerging postmodern culture. A "free zone" of rapid change that places high value on community, authenticity, and even God—but has little interest in modern, Western-tinged Christianity. *Postmodern Youth Ministry* addresses these enormous philosophical shifts and shows how they're affecting teenagers.

Softcover   0-310-23817-X

Pick up a copy today at your favorite bookstore!

Telling the Truth

Evangelizing Postmoderns
D. A. Carson, General Editor

This thoughtful cultural analysis probes important turning points of biblical theology, describes successful contemporary evangelism, and exposes readers to the strategy and practice of Christian thinkers who are reaching the postmodern world.

Softcover   0-310-24334-3

Worship Evangelism

Inviting Unbelievers into the Presence of God
Sally Morgenthaler

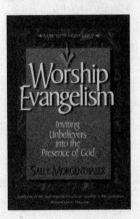

In Worship Evangelism, Sally Morgenthaler calls the church to consider the remarkable, untapped potential of worship as an opportunity for those who aren't yet followers of Jesus Christ as well as those who are to encounter the presence of God. Combining the best of traditional and contemporary worship music and practices, Morgenthaler shows how to achieve worship that is both culturally relevant and authentic. She helps pastors, worship leaders, and musicians

- Understand worship and its attraction for non-Christians
- Tear down walls that keep unbelievers from meeting God in church worship
- Make worship evangelism happen in any culture.

Morgenthaler draws on sound research and extensive experience as a worship leader to offer an energetic, hands-on approach. Now with a study guide that encourages group discussion and personal action, this timely book offers fresh vision for worship evangelism and provides the strategies to implement it.

Softcover   0-310-22649-X

Pick up a copy today at your favorite bookstore!

ZONDERVAN™

GRAND RAPIDS, MICHIGAN 49530 USA

WWW.ZONDERVAN.COM

We want to hear from you. Please send your comments about this
book to us in care of the address below. Thank you.

GRAND RAPIDS, MICHIGAN 49530 USA

WWW.ZONDERVAN.COM